ADORNO ON
POPULAR CULTURE

In the decades since his death, Adorno's thinking has lost none of its capacity to unsettle the settled, and has proved hugely influential in social and cultural thought. To most people, the entertainment provided by television, radio, film, newspapers, astrology charts and CD players seems harmless enough. For Adorno, however, the culture industry that produces them is ultimately toxic in its effect on the social process. He argues that modern mass entertainment is manufactured under conditions that reflect the interests of producers and the market, both of which demand the domination and manipulation of mass consciousness.

Here Robert W. Witkin unpacks Adorno's notoriously difficult critique of popular culture in an engaging and accessible style. Looking first at its grounding in a wider theory of the totalitarian tendencies of late capitalist society, he then goes on to examine, in some detail, Adorno's writing on specific aspects of popular culture such as astrology, radio, film, television, popular music and jazz. He concludes with his own critical reflections on Adorno's cultural theory.

This book will be essential reading for students of the sociology of culture, of cultural studies, and of critical theory more generally.

Robert W. Witkin is Professor of Sociology at the University of Exeter and is the author of *Adorno on Music* (1998) and *Art and Social Structure* (1995).

ADORNO ON POPULAR CULTURE

Robert W. Witkin

Routledge
Taylor & Francis Group

LONDON AND NEW YORK

First published 2003
by Routledge
11 New Fetter Lane, London EC4P 4EE

Simultaneously published in the USA and Canada
by Routledge
29 West 35th Street, New York, NY 10001

Routledge is an imprint of the Taylor & Francis Group

© 2003 Robert W. Witkin

Typeset in Garamond by Exe Valley Dataset Ltd, Exeter
Printed and bound in Great Britain by MPG Books Ltd, Bodmin

British Library Cataloguing in Publication Data
A catalogue record for this book is available from the British Library

Library of Congress Cataloging in Publication Data
Witkin, Robert W. (Robert Winston)
Adorno on popular culture / Robert W. Witkin.
p. cm. – (International library of sociology)
Includes bibliographical references and index.
1. Adorno, Theodor W., 1903–1969. 2. Popular culture.
I. Title. II. Series.

B3199.A34 W58 2002
306´.092–dc21   2002069895

ISBN 0-415-26824-9 (hbk)
ISBN 0-415-26825-7 (pbk)

CONTENTS

PREFACE

Adorno on Popular Culture completes a critical review of Adorno's writings on culture that began with the publication of my earlier book *Adorno on Music*. I would like to express my thanks to my good friend, Chris Rojek for his encouragement to me personally and his enthusiasm for the writings of Adorno. I am grateful to Mari Shullaw, the senior sociology editor at Routledge who agreed to take the project on and to find a space for the new volume in the ILS. Finally, I wish to express my thanks to the Leverhulme Trust for the award of a Major Research Fellowship (2001–3) which has provided me with a period of sustained research and writing time.

Most of the chapters of the present text centre themselves around a reading of an article – sometimes more than one – or a chapter of a book by Adorno. This was also the method of *Adorno on Music*. In both volumes, I opted to undertake a close reading of primary texts and to preserve, for the reader, so far as is possible, the sustained theoretical tension of Adorno's argumentation in the specific writings chosen for discussion. There is inevitably a certain degree of thematic overlap among topics but that, too, is a feature of Adorno's own writings which, like the music he admires, develop a great many variations from a very few basic themes.

It would be wrong, however, to see this book as a straightforward exposition of Adorno's ideas. Notwithstanding the care I have taken to capture his line of argumentation, I have always had an agenda of my own that drives my interest in his writings. It will be apparent to the reader at key points in the text; for example, where I juxtapose Adorno's ideas with those of others – none of them, with the exception of Benjamin, is selected from the pantheon of theorists with whom he is usually associated. Some of these juxtapositions reveal the wider associations of Adorno's cultural critique with the work of American critics, for example, David Riesman. Adorno is also confronted with himself in other guises as in the chapter in which a connection is drawn between the *Dialectic of Enlightenment* and Wagner's *Ring* cycle. In the chapter on Popular Music Adorno's arguments are brought up against the very different and in many ways opposed views of Winthrop

Sargeant, the jazz critic that Adorno himself repeatedly cited in support of his ideas. Adorno is also confronted with the very different ideas of Benjamin concerning the work of art in the modern age, ideas that open the way to a critique of Adorno's theory of popular culture. It is in the last two chapters, however, that I have taken the most theoretical licence, developing a critical approach to Adorno's thesis concerning popular culture through pursuing my own agenda in the sociology of art. In Chapter 10 I have brought Adorno's work on radio and film into relationship with two 'movies' that deal with popular culture of the period in which Adorno was writing, Woody Allen's *Radio Days* and *The Purple Rose of Cairo*. In the final chapter, I have drawn even more directly on my own theorizing in order to put Adorno's ideas under a degree of critical pressure and to complete the process of 'walking a critical line' that I began in the final chapter of the previous volume.

There are other secondary works, many of them excellent, that discuss Adorno's ideas on popular culture and music. There are books, too, that locate his ideas in the discourse universes of Marxism and Critical Theory to which he clearly belongs. If I have chosen a different approach to his work, it is largely because my method has been to narrow my focus in the exposition to a fresh reading of primary texts. Nevertheless, the secondary literature on Adorno has most certainly helped to shape my understanding of his work. In this regard, no-one will be surprised to see me name the following as those whose books have personally influenced me the most: Rose Subotnik (1990, 1996), Max Halle Paddison (1993), Martin Jay (1973), Susan Buck-Morss (1977), Gillian Rose (1978), Jay Bernstein (1993). There are other excellent secondary sources in addition to these (see Deborah Cook 1996).

Notwithstanding the critical agenda that is carried both implicitly through-out and explicitly in the latter part of this book – and the disagreements I have with Adorno, which are significant, perhaps fundamental – it will not escape the reader that this book, like its predecessor, is a critical appreciation of Adorno's ideas with the accent on 'appreciation'. I have learned too much from him for it to be otherwise.

Robert Witkin
Exeter, January 2002

1

CULTURAL NEMESIS

In the decades since his death, Adorno's thinking has lost none of its capacity to unsettle the settled, to discomfort those who believe, implicitly or explicitly, that the world can be mastered, or even that they have a secure home in it. Adorno struck out against modern popular culture in all its forms. He spared nothing in his relentless critique. To most people, the comforts at the heart of modern living, the entertainment provided by television, radio, film, newspapers, astrology charts and CD players seem harmless enough. The 'media' give pleasure, put people in touch with the wider world, provide amusement, excitement and entertainment, improve the access of all social classes to what were hitherto the cultural goods of the rich, relieve the boredom and loneliness of living alone and so forth. The best of their contents are genuinely 'popular'. For Adorno, however, this popularity becomes part of the object of criticism. He challenges the notion that the elements of popular culture are harmless. He insists on treating popular culture as a deadly serious business, as something that is ultimately toxic in its effects on the social process. If the defenders of popular culture have not been persuaded by Adorno, they have often been discomforted by him, and his thesis, like a bone in the throat, still commands their attention.

To appreciate the force of Adorno's critique of popular culture, however, it is necessary to set on one side all those easy judgements to the effect that his is a snobbish reaction to the vulgarity of popular art advanced by a devotee of so-called high art. What Adorno offers is not a judgement of taste but a theory concerning the moral and political projects inhering in both 'serious' and 'popular' art. It is not even true to say that he was incapable of appreciating any popular culture. He was certainly responsive to the films of Chaplin and to the anarchistic humour of the Marx Brothers. And it is clear from his writings that he kept abreast of developments in the major media – films, radio, television and advertising. The odd comment betrays certain implicit preferences – for the screen personality of Greta Garbo, for example. Nor did Adorno fail to recognize that there were highly skilled and talented

1

artists and musicians working in the culture industries. However, it was not skill or talent that mattered to him, here, but the interests it served and the uses to which it was put.

Adorno took all art – and that includes the art produced by the culture industries – very seriously. Many of his critics regard them less seriously than he does and, to them, his judgements are more likely to seem extreme or unwarranted. He preferred the term 'culture industry' and even 'mass culture' to that of 'popular art' or 'popular culture'. The latter terms carried a connotation of 'coming from the people'. The products of the culture industry, in Adorno's view, did not come from the people, were not an expression of the life-process of individuals or communities but were manufactured and disseminated under conditions that reflected the interests of the producers and the exigencies of the market, both of which demanded the domination and manipulation of mass consciousness. The disparity in power between the individual and the rational-technical monolith of modern capitalism that dominated every waking and sleeping moment was at the heart of his preoccupations. The machinery of this administered world operated to disempower those whom it organized. This was true for the individual at work, where the advances of the micro-division of labour were making each individual into a more or less de-skilled and disempowered cog in the machine; it was true, too, for the individual in his leisure time, where the Hollywood dream machine, radio and television, Tin Pan Alley and the music industry, were disempowering him further, rendering him even more conformist and dependent. The entertainment industry directed its appeal to the more regressive features of a collective narcissism. Adorno did not deny that people desired the products of the culture industry. He simply saw that desire as an index of the pathology of modern society, as capitulation to the domination of a total machinery. For the individual to resist this process is difficult. It requires both an appreciation of the fact that it is actually happening and some understanding of how it all works. Today, as Martin Jay has argued, we should perhaps view Adorno's writings on popular culture as prototypical deconstructions (Jay 1984).

The theoretical roots of Adorno's thesis concerning popular culture are as wide as they are deep. He was a sophisticated philosopher, steeped in German idealist philosophy, writing critically about the philosophies of Hegel, Heidegger, Kierkegaard , Husserl, etc. He was a serious musician and composer, a pupil of Alban Berg and a member of the circle of composers and musicians surrounding Arnold Schoenberg. He was a Marxist sociologist (albeit an unorthodox one) and together with Horkheimer and other members of the Frankfurt Institute, developed the critical theory of modern culture along Marxist lines. He was also a student of psychology and a Freudian thinker (again, an unorthodox one) who developed a Freudian analysis of modern character. The strength of his theoretical contribution owes a great deal to the originality with which he traced pathways between the central themes of German idealist philosophy, Marxist sociology and Freudian psychopathology.

Those persistent themes of Adorno's critique of modern culture – the commodification, fetishization and standardization of its products, together with the authoritarian submissiveness, irrationality, conformity, ego-weakness and dependency behaviour of its recipients – are developed by him in ways that forge tacit links among diverse theoretical sources, making, for example, the theory of 'commodity fetishism' from a Marxist point of view continuous with ideas about authoritarianism in a Freudian context. Adorno does not attempt to unify theories, to create some kind of master system that subsumes them all. That would be a betrayal of his version of dialectical method. If we liken theoretical systems to an archipelago, then Adorno's links are the pathways traced by the movement of his thinking as it charts its own course between the separate islands. Nevertheless, his restless theoretical work in charting this course effectively develops, albeit tacitly, a unified theory of art and social formation; one that maps the ground between the structuration of social, political and economic relations and their psychic correlates in the consciousness of individuals.

Alienation

In so-called simple societies, where goods are produced by families and communities in the process of providing for known local needs and for realizing and sustaining a traditional way of life, an individual could see the life-process of his or her community reflected in the goods produced. A pot or a spear in such a society would not appear to consciousness as a thing detached from the social relations involved in its production; those relations – aesthetic, political and religious as well as instrumental – would fill out such objects as their spiritual core.

In Marx's analysis of capitalism, the objects 'manufactured' are *commodities*. They are not the outcome of any such 'organic' social process; they are not the expression or realization of the life-process of genuine 'communities' nor of the life-process of the individual labourers whose labour power is utilized for their manufacture (Marx 1986: 31–78). The development of capitalism demands, in the interests of a relentless pursuit of economic efficiency, a progressive de-sociation and de-skilling of labour. The process of production comes to be initiated, ordered and controlled not by the direct producers but by the production system that keeps them employed. Workers become 'appendages' to this system, estranged from the product of their labour. They do not choose it, nor does it express their social being. Work is progressively de-skilled and each individual performs routinized, atomized and meaningless tasks at a pace and under conditions s/he does not control. These atomized performances become the elementary particles of a system of production, external to the subject that has garnered to itself all power of initiative, design and control. Finally, workers are estranged from their fellow workers. The organic ties that should bind workers in a genuine process of social co-operation have been destroyed and with them the basis of mutual respect and a spirit of 'community'.

Fetish-consciousness

It is this radical disjunction between the subject and the objects that are made through him but not by him that is the key factor in the alienation of man from the world of commodities. Marx' s depiction of alienated consciousness can be referred to Vico's epistemological principle advanced a century earlier, which proclaimed that the only things of which one can be said to have true knowledge or understanding are those things which one has made oneself. Capitalism is portrayed by Marx as a system that progressively destroys the individual's sense of himself as participating in ordering, shaping and making his world. To that extent, the world is opaque to the subject. What stands apart from us in our consciousness – what is 'alien' – appears self-possessed and sui generis and ceases, as a consequence, to be 'historical'; it becomes a fetish-object. Its qualities and powers are projected onto it by individuals who then submit to them as though they truly were powers originating outside themselves. The desire of the individual registers as the power of the object over him, his dependency upon it. From here it is easy to move into the Freudian realm of psychopathology and to see, from Adorno's perspective, that psychoses and even illnesses such as schizophrenia can be assimilated to a discourse of capitalist economic relations and alienation.

The system of consumption is no less authoritarian than the system of production. It, too, is not answerable to the subjects whose lives it shapes. Submissiveness and dependency is demanded of individuals both at work and in leisure. The appeal of the (desociated) fetish-object is always to the de-sociated consumer. It reinforces the narcissism of the individual whose ego-weakness and dependency is a manifestation of the loss of any formative or constructive power in relation to commodities. The consumer submits to the 'appeal' of commodities, to the effects they can work upon him as a de-sociated body, but lacks power over them; lacks the power, that is, to express or realize his life-process in them. The object's gain in power here is the subject's loss. The subject responds rigidly to fetish-objects (stimulus–response fashion) and every response becomes a more or less reliable and predictable reflex.

The psychological correlates of fetish-consciousness are the counterpart of the socio-economic form of capitalist social relations. Products are standardized; the response of the consumer to the product is presupposed in the design of the product. It could not be otherwise unless the recipients were to be freely involved in the creation of the product and they are not. Marketization does not encourage self-expression but is its antithesis; it maximizes predictability and repeatability. The system of production thus manipulates and controls the psyches of those who must make it work both as producers and as consumers; as a consequence, the individual ends up disempowered in both domains.

In the modern world, the entertainment industry, radio, television, jazz and popular music as well as film, variety, etc., had become central to everyday life. Adorno believed that all these media helped to reinforce the regressive and dependent personality. Show business was taken seriously by the masses and its stars fetishized and 'hero-worshipped'. The repetitive and formulaic character of cultural goods, their utter standardization, makes them more 'cosy' and predictable and capable of answering to the individual's need for security and for meeting the producer's need for predicatability in the market.

Domination

While Adorno subscribed to Marxist ideas about the economy and about the exploitative relations of capitalism, exploitation in the more limited economic sense is less a key concept for Adorno than is the broader notion of 'domination'. In his major writings, and especially (with Horkheimer) in *The Dialectic of Enlightenment* (Adorno and Horkheimer 1979), he subsumes the exploitation of nature and the exploitation of man by man in the concept of *domination*. The latter is not restricted in its application to descriptions of modern capitalist societies but is used to categorize social relationships in societies that are neither modern nor capitalist. The formula Adorno resorts to is simple enough. Nature is experienced as overwhelmingly powerful and humankind as weak. In an effort to turn the tables and to dominate nature, society organizes itself as an instrument of domination. It achieves this by taking the principle of domination into its internal relations – man's domination of man. These antagonistic relations manifest at an ideological level in mythology and in art. Domination takes root in the psyche as fetishized authority; it is built into the psychology – the intra-psychic constitution – of the individual. In its efforts to free itself from the domination of nature, mankind ends up as the victim of its own pursuit of self-mastery.

With the development of science and technology and the disenchantment of the world, the principle of domination becomes more or less total. It becomes possible to dream of a purely rational and technical organization of society purged of all non-rational factors. Even subjective desires and needs can be gratified, but only when assimilated to a means–end rationality and brought within a totally instrumental order. At the extreme, conformity is demanded of all and each individual is rendered maximally dependent and submissive. Intelligence, skill, initiative and control drain from the life-process of the subject and reappear, transmuted, in the sterile operations of the vast administrative machinery that commands both the working day and the leisured night.

Adorno's Marxism was unorthodox, even heretical. Antagonistic relations were seen as characteristic of all societies; they were not restricted to capitalist societies but embraced state-socialist and communist societies. Like Weber, Adorno places the emphasis on the development of administrative machineries through which societies seek to exercise their wills. In the age of communist revolutions he had no faith in the view that 'communist' societies were anything other than tyrannies; nor did he believe that a working-class revolution was even likely, let alone inevitable, nor that such a revolution, if it occurred, would liberate the world from the totalitarian threat. The development of the so-called free world led, in his view, in the very opposite direction to that indicated by its ideology. In reality, liberal democracies were subject to an inherent totalizing tendency that was antithetical to the ideal of a social order driven from below; an order that is susceptible to its constitutive members who, in turn, are susceptible to each other and to the social whole which they, together, are in the process of forming.

Adorno's structuration model

At the heart of Adorno's critique of radio, film, jazz, variety theatre and popular culture of all kinds is what he and so many modernist writers and artists of his generation perceived as a crisis of the 'subject' and of 'subjectivity' in the modern world; the sense, widespread among contemporary intellectuals, of a subjectivity increasingly overwhelmed and absorbed by the all-powerful machinery of the 'totally administered' society. Anxiety and doubt about the spiritual well-being of the subject extended to all modern societies, no matter how politically benign they might appear to be. That spark of personal initiative, of spontaneity and expressivity in social life and relations, was being crushed, in the view of these critics, by a monolithic capitalism rushing headlong towards a totalitarian future. In the totally administered society, the system is master and each individual member is a manipulated cog; every response is programmed by the machine, all is calculated and prefigured, including pleasure. The direction of determination and force in such a system is from above, from the totality or collectivity and not from below, from the free movement of the elements or individuals themselves. Huxley, Orwell and others had already imaginatively explored variants of such a future in their famous dystopias. The stark choice confronting those individuals who were still considered to have a choice in late capitalist society was either to resist being assimilated (thereby securing, through critical force, the continued existence of the subject), or to throw in one's lot with the collective 'machine', thereby sacrificing one's life as an expressive subject in the delusion that identification with the machine would permit one both to escape the threat to oneself that it posed and, vicariously, to share in its power.

6

Adorno takes it for granted that the arts, both 'serious' and popular, are constitutive elements in the formation of mind and spirit. Such a claim had been a pillar of the German Romantic reaction to the French Enlightenment from the late eighteenth century through to the early twentieth. It was a pivotal element in Adorno's intellectual heritage and it is key to both his aesthetic theory and his critique of popular culture. The equating of art with knowledge is not meant to suggest that art provides a propositional knowledge of the world. The implication is, rather, that works of art inscribe the condition and experience of the human subject; they constitute an understanding that is at once sensuous, affective and spiritual. To know, in this sense, is to 'form' a 'being', to become, and is thus is equivalent to the self-understanding and self-development of the subject. His theory effectively polarizes art works, indeed cultural forms generally, by dividing them between two categories, those that speak to the self-formation of the subject and those that undermine any such process. The latter displace the social process of self-formation with a 'sensationism' that impacts upon and 'manipulates' the consciousness of the subject, thereby reinforcing egoism and narcissism in modern society.

Notwithstanding his style of writing, his dialectical thinking and his sometimes surprising turns of argument, Adorno was profoundly structured and 'structural' in his thinking. There is a basic formulation of part–whole relations, a set of fundamental conditions, that recurs in all his discussions of forms and structures, from social systems to musical structures such as the sonata-allegro or the rondo. The state of part–whole relations that Adorno viewed as healthy, was one in which the whole structure – for example, a society or a work of art – develops out of the interactions among its elements. The elements in such a structuration are all open and responsive to each other, changing each other and being changed by each other, thereby giving rise to the totality that is the outcome of these relations and which remains responsive to them. While Adorno's ideal of freedom rests upon the free and spontaneous movement of the parts – the individuals in a social system or the musical motives in a sonata – it also rests on the responsiveness of the parts or elements to each other, their mutual susceptibility.

These two aspects are inseparable in his approach to structuration. Freedom, in Adorno's theoretic, is grounded in the sociation of individuals. It is in and through relations with others that the individual develops a substance, a solidity or plenitude. The individual in the sense of an isolated and de-sociated monad lacks all substance, all power of self-determination and self-understanding, and can only be conceived of as a kind of emptiness. A genuine sociality (this is something differing from and opposed to certain forms of what might be called false sociality or even pseudo-sociality such as 'joining-in', 'fashion-following' or 'social conformity') is the defining characteristic of Adorno's 'individual'.

7

Because Adorno's ideal individual is formed in and through social relations in which s/he changes others as others change her, the idea of individuation is inseparable from the notion of the historical. At any given point in time, the individual is the precipitate of all the social relations in the past that have gone into its making. Each individual or element carries within – in its very constitution – a congealed history that is undergoing further development in the present; that is through answering to problems in the present. Congealed history – as an inner 'suspense' within each individual – has its own kinetic force, lending direction and tendency, a reflexive project, to the movements and actions of the individual. However, that very same social and historical development may itself bring about new social conditions which effectively undermine the liberty of the individual to develop freely in relations with others and which thus make it impossible for him to express his historically constituted subjectivity. It is this latter impediment, conceived of as central to modernity, to which Adorno's critical theory is addressed.

Adorno therefore has a structural standard or ideal by which to measure the truth-value and moral integrity of social structures and of cultural forms. We can define his ideal as that of a social system constituted from below by the mutual susceptibility of individuals to one another in interactional relations from which a social whole is continuously emergent and in which there is a mutual and reflexive susceptibility between this emergent whole and the individuals who constitute it. All such relations are *historical* in character and carry within them the precipitates of past relations that make their claim on the present. To the extent that these conditions are met, the consciousness of the world to which they give rise has truth-value and is not distorted because all the constitutive relations of the system as a whole enter into the formation of that consciousness and mediate all knowledge and all cultural forms. This ideal (utopian) social system has integrity. Its relations are non-antagonistic and non-dominating, a product of autonomy. (Domination and antagonism, in Adorno's philosophy, are the product of heteronomy, of the imposition of an external force that is not susceptible to those subject to it.)

Taylorism

The anthithesis of Adorno's utopian structuration is the model of productive relations offered by Taylor's principles of scientific management (Taylor 1947). The ideal here is that of a system that imposes order on its constituent members from above. Individual workers are de-skilled and the labour process atomized to the point where individuals are no longer connected through meaningful interactions with others in producing goods but are, in the extreme, co-actional units performing operations that are mechanically sequenced and ordered from above. Mutual susceptibility of the individuals who make up the discrete units is minimized. They are not involved in an interactional project through which each changes and is changed by others. Nor is the organization as a whole the outcome of the actions and interactions of its constituent members. Authority is hetero-nomous, imposed from above. Skill and intelligence of the individual worker has been carefully designed out of this ideal system together with all autonomy, organic interaction and the historical element that such inter-action carries within it. To the extent that Taylor's principles of scientific management are actually met in practice, they give rise to a consciousness, which, in Adorno's terms, lacks truth-value. Consciousness is distorted to the extent that the constitutive relations of the system as a whole do not enter into its formation and thus do not mediate experience of the system. The system lacks moral integrity, in Adorno's terms, for the same reasons. Its relations are the product of heteronomy, of the imposition of an external force that is not susceptible to being changed from below.

Works of art and culture are the products of social praxis. Insofar as such forms provide a medium of reflection on social praxis and on the human condition, they do so only to the extent that they incorporate the principles of structuration governing social action generally, in their formation. This will always be the case whether such cultural developments are progressive or reactionary. What is of critical importance to Adorno is the matter of how the principles of structuration governing the social order are inscribed in cultural artifacts. Depending upon the orientation of the artist, their inscription may serve either to reinforce the lack of moral integrity and truth-value that inheres in the social order or they may, on the contrary, provide a true understanding of both social praxis and the human condition. In the age of administration and scientific management, the only art that could possess truth-value would be one that took this atomizing process into itself and used it as a coded language of suffering; as a vehicle for expressing the life-process that had been mutilated by it.

Music and society

It is hardly possible to understand Adorno's critique of modern culture and of popular culture, especially, without taking into account the extent of his commitment to this formal model of structuration. When he attacks jazz or films or variety entertainment he is always deploying it, albeit sometimes in a tacit rather than explicitly formulated way. Adorno's commitment in his writing and rhetoric to an anti-system philosophy, to a 'musique informelle' ought not to deceive the reader into believing that structuration and formation, in the sense of an ideal systematics, is not central to his thinking and analyses of culture. On the contrary, it is from this structural under-pinning that he generates the model of freedom and spontaneity on which his anti-system philosophy is built. There is some real value, therefore, in making the structuration model that Adorno privileged, throughout four decades of academic writing, our point of entry into his texts, not simply because it allows us to set aside, for the present, the labyrinthine complexities of the originating discourses, but because it is Adorno's way of thinking structural relations that is the key to all his work. It provides a link between his papers on the theory of pseudo-culture, the culture industry, popular culture and jazz as well as his papers on television, radio, film, comedy and music in the classical tradition. Through exploring the homology that he establishes between part–whole relations in society, on the one hand, and part–whole relations in musical structures, on the other, we can gain an understanding of Adorno's treatment of culture generally.

The central antinomy of a bourgeois society, in Adorno's philosophy, is the conflict between individual freedom and societal constraint. Corresponding to individuals, in his musicology are the basic elements of a composition, the musical 'motives' or, at the extreme, the individual tones that make up a composition; corresponding to the society is the developed composition, the musical totality which is formed by relations among these elements. Just as individuals, as social subjects in relations with others, undergo development (biography) and in their mutual relations bring about the development of society (history), so, too, in a nineteenth-century classical musical composition such as a Beethoven symphony, the basic elements – the musical 'motives' – undergo development through being repeated, varied and juxtaposed, and contribute to the development of the composition as a whole. In both society and music (considered *ideally*), the process described is a fully temporal and historical one. In each case there is a dialectical unfolding of relations in which consequents and antecedents are *necessarily* connected – develop out of one another, push one another – and are not merely co-incidentals.

The parallel between music and society should not be seen as an unmediated one, however. Music is not of a different order but is part of social praxis. Its material has been socially formed. Social relations and social organization are congealed in it. When Adorno attacks Jazz (Witkin 2000), for example, or the music of Stravinsky (Adorno 1980, 1992), he is not merely making a judgement of taste; he is condemning these musics because, in their inner cells, in their motivic elements and notes, the principle of a dialectical working out of relations in which consequents develop out of antecedents (that is, of a fully historical or temporal process), has been replaced by one in which relations among elements are co-incidental, their co-presence reflecting only their instrumental value, the effects they bring about in the body of the recipient. An art that aims to transform itself into an instrument for the construction of *effects* has turned its back on history, on the living process of life. Such an art no longer serves the self-development of the subject. It is an art that has lost all distance and autonomy in relation to collective forces; it has become their instrument. It does not bring its order out of itself but orders itself in complete conformity with the effects it is 'impelled ' to bring about, extinguishing everything within itself that is not in conformity with these effects.

For Adorno, art is not a moral good simply because people are entertained or diverted by it or because they obtain excitement or pleasure from it, but because it sustains the subject and, therefore, the spiritual element in life. Conversely, in his view, an art that extinguishes the subject, and with it the spiritual, is a moral evil. Adorno draws the contrast as starkly as that. The transmuting of the living process of life into an instrument for the construction of 'effects' that are produced within individuals through working upon them is equivalent to the perfection of a machinery of domination, of exploitation. An agency that aims at the total domination of its objects only achieves its aims through dominating itself, through extinguishing everything within itself that does not serve an instrumental purpose. It thus becomes its own victim; the would-be liberator ends up enslaving itself. It is the living subject that is overcome, annihilated in the securing of a totalitarian command of the world. This theme runs throughout Adorno's work like an iron seam.

This ideal of a structuration from below informs all of Adorno's music studies. At an ideological level its exemplification is classical sonata-form as perfected in the music of Beethoven. The musical motives and themes that constitute the elements of the sonata-allegro, as a form, are introduced, at the outset of the composition, like the characters in a play. They undergo variation in the development section and finally return in the recapitulation that reflects the development undergone, restoring the equilibrium disturbed by that development. The thrust of Adorno's critique of music and of popular culture is directed towards finding, in the very structuration of art works as texts, analogues of both the process of becoming, that is, of (social) self-formation, and of its antithesis. The use of sonata-form in classical music then becomes an object of special theoretical attention, for example, as does the use of rondo-form in jazz. The structural relations among elements – part–part and part–whole relations – become charged, in Adorno's theory with epistemological and semiotic significance and are integrated into a theory of social formation. The sonata-allegro thus models an historical process in which the elements, themselves historically grounded, developing through their mutual relations, give rise to the larger whole with which each is identified. It, too, is a form of bourgeois ideology.

Adorno never relinquished the concept of identity at an ideological level. The longing for identity between part and whole was something he held onto as a driving force in the development of his negative dialectics (Adorno 1973: 149). The longing for such an identity was to be distinguished altogether from the presumption or claim that such an identity exists. Adorno rejected as false and ideological the claims of an identity or reconciliation between individual and society, while preserving the ideal of identity as a principle governing the sociality of individuals; in the same way, he

11

rejected as false and ideological the claims of the sonata-allegro to bring about a reconciliation between parts and whole, while preserving the ideal of such a reconciliatory process. This is fundamental in Adorno's thinking; the longing for a reconciliation between part and whole, subject and object, individual and society, concept and thing – the longing, that is, for identity – is brought to confront the reality of the world and the experience of the pain of non-identity. The pain of non-identity is the truth about identity as surely as dissonance is the truth about harmony.

The draining of dialectical relations

The cultural commodities of modern times, be they films, radio or television programmes or pop songs are governed by a model of formation that is the antithesis of Adorno's ideal of dialectical structuration. Whether he was analysing popular music (most noticeably, jazz) or Hollywood movies, radio, television or astrology columns, he applied the same structural logic. All of them were instances of the draining of dialectical relations from cultural forms. They corresponded to the draining of dialectical relations in the increasingly mechanized work process and in the totally administered society generally. The elements of pop songs or jazz or the Hollywood movie did not form a coherent developmental movement; they did not follow from each other as antecedents and consequents; as co-incidentals they were brought together to engender and maximize *effects* upon the psyche of the individual. The force ordering and controlling these effects was the capitalist market; it secured its own operations through disempowering both producers and consumers. Whatever aspect Adorno chooses as his point of entry in his analysis of a cultural form, you can discern his structuration model working away beneath it. Thus in his discussion of varieté, he remarks on the fact that an apparent preparedness for something, an apparent suspense (e.g. in the act of a juggler or trapeze artist) that leaves an audience waiting for something, ends up cheating the audience of all but the waiting, the anticipation, which finally turns out to be the real object of the performance. In effect, he argues varieté stills time and he equates it with an industrial model of production emphasizing sameness, standardization and repetition. The first audiences to attend Beckett's play *Waiting for Godot* may have experienced something of this. The model that he is drawing upon to make sense of this is the structuration model concerning part–whole and part–part relations described above. When Adorno argues, in his paper 'The Radio Symphony' (see Chapter 8), that the playing of a classical symphony on the radio, effectively degrades it into a series of 'quotations' from the symphony (e.g. the tunes that the individual commits to memory and whistles) and that the symphony as such is progressively lost through this process of decay, he is again appealing to the same structuration model concerning part–whole relations and asking us to see how the culture industry inevitably destroys the

12

structural richness of cultural forms and replaces structural integrity with an emphasis on isolated details and sensuous features and highlights.

Late Romantic art

There were developments in so-called serious art that Adorno saw in the same terms, and it is useful to observe the parallel. From the middle of the nineteenth century, European literature, music, theatre and art underwent a formal revolution that culminated in the varieties of avant-garde and modernist art. However, there were many creative artists, from every branch of the different arts, who did not take this direction but continued to use traditional formal means or classical 'languages' in making and composing works of art. In music, for example, there were composers who continued composing 'tonal' music that observed the strictures of the key system. In general, these artists have been a great deal more popular with the public than were avant-garde artists. Their art, music and writings appeared to be comprehensible and to *communicate*. There was a sensuous and emotional warmth to be had from art of this kind that was withheld from the typical work of avant-garde art. This was particularly true of neo-Romantic music such as that of Tchaikovsky, Elgar, or Rachmaninov. Adorno, always critical of neo-Romantic art in any of its forms, rejected as false any music that was not structurally equal to the demands made by modern times. If tonal or diatonic music had some relevance to the heroic phase of nineteenth-century entrepreneurial capitalism, it was because it could speak in a relevant way to the social ideals and conditions of that time. The principle governing the ideal construction of social relations was reproduced in the inner cells of the work of art. That same model, however, could not speak to the conditions of twentieth-century monopoly capitalism and the totalitarian tendencies of the administered society. Modern composers who composed in these earlier styles dealt in untruths. To Adorno, art that had truth-value had to reflect the social conditions of its time and to do so in its inner cells, in its structural relations.

Neo-Romantic art, which formally subscribes to traditional means of aesthetic construction is, in fact, significantly different from its classical forebears. Adorno argued that the differences are not superficial; they were fundamental. The structural perfection that Adorno reads into the great sonatas and symphonies of Beethoven's second-period compositions does not really have any equivalent in the music of Tchaikovsky who, nevertheless, continued to write symphonies in the grand manner and in diatonic form. Adorno argues that such music is structurally degraded. At the same time, what neo-Romantic music loses at the level of structural relations and development it seeks to compensate for at the level of distinctive features and details. It is music that, in Adorno's perspective, is structure-poor and feature-rich. Formerly the themes in music were unimportant in and of themselves; they derived their value from the contribution they made to the development of the work as a whole. In neo-Romantic music, by contrast, there is an extreme assertion of the themes themselves for which structural relations exist merely to set them off and to set them up as well as to ornament them. This change is much more than stylistic. The emotional import of the classical Beethovian symphony derives from the total movement of the elements and what Adorno calls the 'nothingness of the parts'. The classical experience of Romantic feeling, therefore, is produced by the dialectical and historical process that constitutes the work as a whole and not by the impression of any of its isolated moments. In the transition to neo-Romantic art, the assertion of the detail, the feature or part, leads to the latter taking upon itself the affective import that formerly belonged to the total structure. In the music of such different composers as Wagner and Rachmaninov, distinctive features and details are asserted ever more loudly, forcefully, with more posturing and acclamation and ornamentation as though the detail had not only become indistinguishable from the whole but had actually replaced it. In Adorno's analysis, an art that is devoted to the production of sensuous *effects* reduces the romantic element to pure sentimentality or sensationism. It becomes manipulative. (Films are said to be 'tear-jerkers' when they manipulate sentiment in this way.)

Adorno viewed late Romantic art as a decaying of the classical tradition and as a way-station to the culture industry. It was itself part of the culture industry. Popular art had much in common with it. It was manufactured, gift-wrapped with a hard sheen to it; its contents consisted of the sentimental residues of a defunct romanticism. The power of the culture industry to manipulate affect and subjectivity was something to be truly feared. Adorno was not claiming that it had some crude propagandist end in mind. Rather, the threat lay in the very exercise of this manipulative power and the associated dependency and conformity of the masses. It is the power of capitalism to transform the population into dependent and conformist consumers that undermines all responsibility and autonomy, and with it any formative role the subject might have in the shaping of the social world. Instead, that world increasingly approximates to a machinery and all its citizens to trained operators, prevented from ever becoming innovators. What is done to subjectivity through the medium of popular culture is seen by Adorno as an index of what is done to subjects within modern society. The decay of the organic work of art to the level of its details and features had its counterpart in the de-sociation of the individual to the level of the isolated ego. Both processes were inextricably bound up with the development of late capitalism in which the machineries of modern production, administration and consumption annihilated the expressive subject, replacing it with an existence altogether more docile, conformist and 'fit for business'.

14

Concentration versus distraction

The decay of serious art and the rise of the culture industry are also associated with changes in the mode of reception. Consumers relate to cultural goods in a way that contrasts with the mode of appreciation characteristic, for example, of the devotee of classical music. The ideal-typical work of serious art can be appreciated only though entering imaginatively into the work, into the formation of its internal relations. To bring off such an entry into the formative process of a work demands concentration and absorption, whether in the reading of a novel, the watching of a play or in the concentrative listening of an audience at a philharmonic concert. This type of concentrative awareness was an attitude that Adorno identified with serious art or art that had truth-value. Popular art, on the other hand, was attended to in a deconcentrative (distractive) way – Adorno termed the listening habits associated with popular music 'regressive listening' (see Chapter 4) – and he viewed it as the mark of the shallowness and banality of the goods produced by the culture industry that they stimulated and reinforced a distractive absorption that made attention itself the victim of the authoritarian stimulus.

Ultimately, Adorno takes his place among the major theorists who have interpreted modernity as the expropriation of the subject – of freedom, autonomy, community and spirit – by the very 'machineries' that have been developed to master nature and to maximize control over material resources. As a Marxist, he believed that the economic machinery of capitalism was fundamental in this expropriation of the subject. The culture industry was part of that. In all of the texts that are discussed in this book, Adorno seeks repeatedly to analyse the ways in which the subject, and subjectivity itself, is undermined by the rising tide of popular culture and popular entertainment. To those key questions, How shall we live? What shall we do next? Adorno's answer was to resist, to refuse identity with oppressive totalitarian forces. However, Adorno was not an activist in the crude sense. His revolutionary drive was centered on the readying of the spirit, on a strengthening of the subject, of its self-development and self-understanding, through realizing its non-identity with an antagonistic world. It was to a critical deconstruction of culture rather than an attack on economic or political institutions *per se* that he turned in his personal 'revolution'. Adorno mistrusted action that was not in itself an expression of the life-process of the subject, a manifestation of freedom and autonomy; revolutions could also be tyrannies. Adorno's refusal to identify with the student activists in the 1968 troubles at Frankfurt University led, shortly before his death, to the mounting of a personal and humiliating 'demonstration' against him, during his last lecture course, by a group of student activists.

2

THE THEORY OF
PSEUDO-CULTURE

The abiding image of Adorno's sojourn in the US is of a man ill at ease in his host culture, a man who became a citizen without ever overcoming his condition of being an exile. On meeting him for the first time, Paul Lazarsfeld described Adorno as the most foreign man he had ever met. The mismatch between Adorno's rootedness in High German Culture and the brashness of American society was by no means unique to him. Many European émigrés to the US – artists, writers and scholars – lived uneasily with the mass culture of America. Nevertheless, when subjected to closer examination, these conclusions require a degree of qualification. Adorno does affirm, in his own memoir of his American years, that the culture shock he endured on arrival in America was very great. He also acknowledges that he remained unrelentingly European; he saw the refusal to adapt and assimilate as essential to being an 'individual', to experiencing freedom and autonomy in a relationship of non-identity with and difference from the host culture. Nevertheless, Adorno was profoundly affected by his American experience. He learned a great deal from American culture and even expressed admiration for certain aspects of it that he felt to be superior to his own. In particular, he experienced the democratic spirit of American culture as something real and profound and he reflected on the deficiencies of his own culture of origin by comparison:

> More important and more gratifying was my experience of the substantiality of democratic forms: that in America they have seeped into life itself, whereas, at least in Germany, they were, and I feel still are, nothing more than formal rules of the game. Over there I became acquainted with a potential for real humanitarianism that is hardly to be found in old Europe. The political form of democracy is infinitely closer to the people. American everyday life, despite the oft' lamented hustle and bustle has an inherent element of peacableness, good-naturedness and generosity, in sharpest contrast to the pent-up malice and envy that exploded in Germany between 1933 and 1945.
>
> (Adorno 1998: 231)

Peter Hohendahl, in his paper 'The Displaced Intellectual: Adorno's American Years Revisited', acknowledges the difficulties of Adorno's American sojourn but points to the important and largely unacknowledged effects of the US experience on the directions taken in the thinking of Adorno and Horkheimer as the leading intellectuals of the Frankfurt School. The evolution of the School's thinking away from earlier commitments to the unity of theory and praxis and the anticipation of a working-class revolution together with the turn to an intense cultural critique were not uninfluenced by, or unrelated to, perspectives developed in an American cultural context. Hohendahl argued (citing Lipset) that domestic US politics, in the period immediately after the Great Depression, could no longer serve as an arena for serious critical activity on the left, and many American intellectuals at this time turned from a basic concern with political and economic systems to criticism of the culture of American society.

> In the writings of Macdonald, Daniel Boorstin, Mary McCarthy and David Riesman, the focus of criticism shifted from the political to the social and cultural. For the affluent society with its new suburban middle class, the traditional tools of liberal and Marxist theory appeared to be less effective. In particular the impact of the new media (radio, film, and television) resisted traditional analysis. Radical left cultural criticism of the 1950's, articulated in the writings of Macdonald, Bell, Greenberg, and Paul Goodman, parallels the work of Adorno, particularly in its concern about traditional high culture and literature.
>
> (Hohendahl 1992)

Notwithstanding the fact that there were important differences between these cultural critics and the critical theorists of the Frankfurt School, the parallels Hohendahl speaks of were real enough and mutual influence and reinforcement clearly did take place. It is interesting to note that Clement Greenberg's article 'Avant-garde and kitsch', which preceded the publication of Adorno's analysis of the culture industry by eight years, contained many arguments and judgements that are echoed in Adorno and Horkheimer's study (Greenberg 1992). Among the American critics, David Riesman is repeatedly cited by Adorno for his development of a polar contrast between two cultural orientations, the 'inner-directed' and the 'other-directed' man or woman. Adorno was very familiar with Riesman's work and the theoretical parallels between the American and the European thinker, both of them trained in different fields, have so far received insufficient attention.

The importance of this link to Riesman's work is nowhere more in evidence than in the theory of modern culture that Adorno developed during his American years. However, it is not at all a case of one thinker taking his ideas from the other. When Adorno cites Riesman he is recognizing that the latter has developed a structuration model of the transition from traditional to modern culture that resonates with his own, even though the intellectual contexts and implications for the two models may have been very different. Riesman's structural model is presented in a pragmatic and less intellectually encumbered form than Adorno's and it can therefore be used as a key to understanding one of Adorno's most important contributions to the critique of modernity, namely his paper 'The Theory of Pseudo-Culture' (Adorno 1993)

The social origins of character formation were topical during the decades in which Adorno was writing. The work on cultural character and on national character became fashionable in the post-war situation (Gorer 1948; Gorer and Rickman 1949; Kluckhohn and Murray 1953). The notion of character or personality as an organized and coherent dispositional system mediating the subject's relations and actions in the world was more or less taken for granted. What was of interest was to account for the development and persistence of certain character types by studying the systems of social relationships in which they developed and the social factors that reinforced them. Thus, in his study of Russian national character, Gorer invoked such child-rearing practices as the swaddling of infants to account for features of the Russian adult character (Gorer and Rickman 1949). History provides many examples of character types that are idealized in a specific cultural context – the English gentleman, the Prussian officer, etc., each with its own litany of personal qualities and attributes and its roots in class and property. A given character type may hold centre-stage for a time but only insofar as social conditions favour its persistence; it then gives way to 'types' with very different characteristics.

Riesman

I immediately think of Rudyard Kipling's poem 'If', which I had to learn by heart at school, in connection with Riesman's inner-directed individualism. And yet, even when that poem was written it served to mark an ideal-type already passing into history, the so-called 'man of principle', a type of human being whose every action was said to be guided by a set of internalized values. To those with a nostalgia for so-called Victorian values of self-reliance and independence of judgement, Kipling's 'If' captures the moral essence of a 'free' and self-possessed individualism. Whatever basis such an ideal-type may once have had in the formation of a capitalist society, its time is now past even if some residues continue to persist in the claims that are made in respect of the rights and freedoms of individuals in a democratic society. The modern world makes its own very different demands upon individuals and sets very different challenges at the level of action and choice. It has therefore called forth its own type of social being, a type of individual that contrasts in every way with its predecessor. To some critics, the appearance of this new type on the stage of history heralds a disaster in the making, while to others it marks a positive and liberating development.

David Riesman contributed in a significant way to theorizing the historical transition between character types and especially the emergence of the modern type. His typology actually distinguished between three character types, the 'traditional', the 'inner-directed' and the 'other-directed'. It is the polarization of the latter two types that was widely taken up in the literature. Riesman's inner-directed individual corresponds to the type of autonomous man of principle celebrated by Kipling. The metaphor upon which Riesman drew to describe the guidance system for such an individual was that of the gyroscope:

> . . . a new psychological mechanism appropriate to the more open society is invented: it is what I like to describe as a psychological gyroscope. This instrument, once it is set by the parents and other authorities, keeps the inner-directed person, as we shall see, 'on course' even when tradition, as responded to by his character, no longer dictates his moves. The inner-directed person becomes capable of maintaining a delicate balance between the demands upon him of his goal in life and the buffetings of his external environment.
>
> (Riesman 1961: 16)

Riesman's 'inner-directed' individual is able to maintain a certain degree of distance from his social milieu that enables him to be and to act in a context-independent way. It is the possession of a system of 'internalized values, operating like a servo-mechanism' and mediating the individual's every encounter in the world, that makes this possible. Both Riesman and Adorno saw the internalization of values, as had Durkheim and Tonnies, in terms of the pressure of one generation upon the next. Freud had provided a psychological mechanism for such an internalization process with his theory of identification. Children were said to model themselves on parents through internalizing the 'ego-ideals' of parent figures. These ego-ideals, in Freudian theory, are installed in the personality as an internalized agency, a superego or moral conscience. What the child internalizes, as Bronfenbrenner points out, is not so much a set of specific prescriptions for action but a system of moral principles for generating moral judgements and for acting morally (Bronfenbrenner 1960). Riesman's internal gyroscope conveys a similar idea. The inner-directed man or woman's actions are mediated by an internalized system of principles that ensures some degree of freedom from identification with the existent. Such an individual can stand back from the crowd, can choose not to conform or to follow the line of least resistance.

The type that Riesman identified as modern (other-directed) has the opposite tendency in that s/he is governed by a heightened sensitivity to the opinions and attitudes of others. S/he is acutely responsive to social signals and takes her cues as to appropriate action from peers. The metaphor on which Riesman drew to describe his contrasting type – the modern 'other-directed' individual – was that of the 'radar':

. . . the other-directed person learns to respond to signals from a far wider circle than is constituted by his parents. The family is no longer a closely knit unit to which he belongs but merely part of a wider social environment to which he early becomes attentive . . . The other-directed person is cosmopolitan . . . While the inner-directed person could be 'at home abroad' by virtue of his relative insensitivity to others, the other-directed person is, in a sense, at home everywhere and nowhere, capable of a rapid if sometimes superficial intimacy with and response to everyone. The tradition-directed person takes his signals from others, but these come in a cultural monotone; he needs no complex receiving equipment to pick them up. The other-directed person must be able to receive signals from far and near; the sources are many, the changes rapid. What can be internalized, then, is not a code of behavior but the elaborate equipment needed to attend to such messages and occasionally to participate in their circulation. As against guilt-and-shame controls, though of course these survive, one prime psychological lever of the other-directed person is a diffuse *anxiety*. This control equipment, instead of being like a gyroscope, is like radar.

(Riesman 1961: 25)

Riesman identifies this transition between character types with a socio-economic change in society that he expressed not in Marxist terms but demographically, as entry into a period of 'incipient population decline'. The society in this period becomes increasingly bureaucratized and such a heightened administrative apparatus in production involves the development of extended chains of interdependence:

As the birth rate begins to follow the death rate downward, societies move toward the epoch of incipient decline of population. Fewer and fewer people work on the land or in the extractive industries or even in manufacturing. Hours are short. People may have material abundance and leisure besides. They pay for these changes however – here, as always, the solution of old problems gives rise to new ones – by finding themselves in a centralized and bureaucratized society and a world shrunken and agitated by the contact – accelerated by industrialization – of races, nations, and cultures.

(Riesman 1961: 18)

Riesman also drew attention to the shift in the balance between production and consumption in favour of the latter. In these societies of incipient population decline, he argues, there are increasing numbers of unproductive consumers – old people and also the young, the latter in extended periods of education. The society becomes oriented around a high level of consumption.

Riesman saw the rise of consumerism as undermining individuality. Consumption behaviour is constrained, directed and guided not by goals but by the 'others' with whom one compares oneself. One should not consume so much so as to incur the envy of others; nor should one consume so little that it provokes envy in oneself. Sensitivity to the signals given off by others becomes a key controlling factor. Children and adults consume in essentially similar ways even though the commodities they consume may differ. Both are controlled by what Riesman calls 'the consumer's union of the peer group' and for the children, training in the use of the radar of 'other-direction' begins very early in life.

> The inner-directed child was supposed to be job-minded even if the job itself was not clear in his mind. Today the future occupation of all moppets is to be skilled consumers.
>
> (Riesman 1961: 79)

Riesman identified the psychology of the inner-directed person – the man or woman of principle – with the psychological disposition that Weber attributed to the beginnings of modern capitalism. Above all, he argued, the scarcity economy, with its concern for production, developed ascetic attitudes towards consumption. Such an ascetic individualism is hardly appropriate under modern conditions. The conditions of production have also changed and they, too, favour the new other-directed type over the inner-directed individual of the earlier period. In place of the latter there develops what is essentially a de-centred subjectivity, that is, an inter-subjectivity, to cope with the problems individuals face both as producers and as consumers in the modern world.

The functional claims for the superiority of this new character type over its predecessor are made on the basis of its supposed flexibility in the face of demands for a rapid sociation of response. The extended chains of interdependence in modern organizations and production systems favour individuals being 'other-directed'. Both as producers and consumers, men and women come to be increasingly dependent on the peer group, for what Festinger called 'consensual validation' (Festinger 1954), in order to know whether they are performing adequately or whether the evaluations and choices they are making are the ones that identify them as people who belong, who have some assurance of being acceptable to others. This dependence on others to validate even one's own personal experiences is something that has been investigated in other contexts. It is interesting to reflect on Becker's roughly contemporary study of the marijuana user (Becker 1963), which argues that individuals have to learn from others how to read and interpret what they are experiencing when they use the drug. At the same time, the psychologists Schachter and Singer made similar claims concerning the effects of epinephrine on subjects in laboratory experiments

(Schachter and Singer 1962). All of these studies in their different ways could be seen as registering the extent to which individuals are dependent in their construction of reality upon signals from others; the extent, that is, to which they are other-directed.

Riesman's other-directed man or woman is the model of adaptation that Adorno criticized in his 'theory of pseudo-culture'. The central anxiety of the adaptive type springs from the need to fit in, to be assimilated, to identify with the collective order which, in Adorno's philosophy, is oppressing the individual. The very existence of the individual, in any meaningful sense, is dependent upon her maintaining that non-identity between subject and world that is the antithesis of the culture of adaptation. The concepts of both 'difference' and 'distance' are key to Adorno's treatment of the crisis of individuation in the modern world. Only through continuously realizing a difference from and resistance to, society, is the subject able to preserve itself as a moral centre and it is only as a moral centre that the subject is capable of summoning better times.

The polar contrast in Adorno's writings on culture, therefore, lies in the opposition he draws between an autonomous subjectivity that keeps its distance, that struggles with the world, and a subjectivity that has been assimilated by the world, that has become society's (manipulated) object. Empirically, the difference between Culture and pseudo-culture is not immediately obvious or self-evident. A symphony by Brahms or a performance of Shakespeare can be instances of pseudo-culture. If either performance takes place on the radio or on television or in the cinema, it is, in Adorno's perspective, very likely to be the case. Adorno believed that so-called serious Culture had, in the modern world, undergone a kind of internal decomposition and that modern mass media were instrumental in bringing about this decomposition. Instead of a work of art being a vital 'organism' made up of elements that are dynamically interdependent – elements that change and develop each other and that orient themselves to the development of the larger whole – the work becomes an aggregate of discrete contents, each of them appreciated for the effect it brings about. The reduction of the symphony to highlights, themes and climaxes – to quotations from the symphony, that is – or the reduction of a philosophy or a scientific discipline to a 'digest' of its key ideas, are instances of what Adorno means by *pseudo-culture* (Adorno 1993).

The decomposition of serious Culture reduced it to the condition of all culture produced by the culture industry; to the 'bits' of information or manufactured 'effects' that are the elements of modern mass culture – appropriated, exchanged and communicated. The elements of the emerging pseudo-culture lost any relationship they may formerly have had to an integral and developing totality. They became a machinery for generating 'effects' upon the psyche of the individual. All so-called high art was being swallowed up by this 'effect-culture'; a culture closer in every way to the model of advertising than to the system of Culture proper. It was this degradation of culture to the level of atomized effects and to the business of 'communication' that was the focus of Adorno's critique. The atomized contents of pseudo-culture answer to the lives of atomized individuals; those who are no longer capable of self-formation and who have already surrendered to the overwhelming power of the collective.

> In the concept of pseudo-culture the commodified, reified content of culture survives at the expense of its truth content and its vital relation to living subjects. This roughly accords with its definition . . . in a society which has lost virtually all of its qualities as a result of the domination of the exchange principle, the individual gains neither form nor structure, the elements which enable him to cultivate himself in the most literal sense of the term. But on the other hand the power of totality over the individual has reached such proportions that he must himself reflect the formlessness without.
>
> (Adorno 1993: 23)

If the subject has no means, within itself, of going beyond immediate empirical reality; if his or her experience is co-extensive with the empirical entanglements of the present, then there is no way for the subject to gain a foothold outside of those entanglements. Such a subject has fallen into the midst of the world and been assimilated by it. To hold distance from the world, the subject must be able to call upon experience that extends beyond the boundaries of the empirical present. This implies that the subject's wider experience of situations and events – those that are not present, that are historical – has been conserved in its very constitution. The possession of a Culture, with a capital 'C', is key to the conservation of human experience from which the subject can derive a sense of itself in its 'otherness' from society. Culture in this larger sense secures, for the subject, a footing on ground that extends in breadth and depth beyond the status quo; that is, beyond the existent social reality with which s/he must contend:

> Culture needed protection from the onslaughts of the external world, it needed a certain regard for the individual subject, perhaps even the fragmentation of socialization. Holderlin wrote: 'I have understood the language of the gods; never have I understood the language of men.' One hundred and fifty years later a young man thinking the same way would be ridiculed or handed over to the benevolent care of a psychiatrist on account of his autism. However, if the distinction between the language of the gods – the idea of a true language, one having to do with substantive matters – and the practical language of communication is no longer perceived, then culture is lost.
>
> (Adorno 1993: 25–6)

Throughout this 'difficult' paper, Adorno refers to culture in both the senses outlined above; Culture in the 'traditional' sense is for him identified with the intellectual and aesthetic systems that developed in the eighteenth century; those grand systems of Enlightenment ideas and of speculative metaphysics that constituted, for example, the Culture of German Idealism, together with the aesthetic ideals embodied in the literature and music with which it was closely associated. Culture in the modern sense is what he refers to in the title of the paper as 'pseudo-culture'. His purpose is to set off the characteristics of pseudo-culture, which he sees as ubiquitous and all-pervasive in the modern world, against the character of Culture proper. Culture 'proper' is a version of the organic structuration model that guides all Adorno's thinking; it suggests a coherent system of reflection, a body of interrelated ideas and values that mediates the individual's response to empirical reality. What is presupposed here is that the possession of Culture in this larger sense secures for the individual some degree of autonomy and integrity at the level of agency; it ensures that the individual remains his or her own person (an inner-directed individual) and is not absorbed or subsumed by society and its dominating institutions. Like the ego, with which it is inextricably linked, Culture is a structured and structuring agency, an internalized formation, a precipitate of social relations. This idea of Culture fits with Adorno's reasoning about the structuration of part–whole relations in music. The elements that make up the Culture are integral and interdependent; they go out to and into one another and form an integral totality.

To make clear which concept is being referred to in the text, I shall capitalize the word 'Culture' when using it in Adorno's first sense and give it a lower-case 'c' when referring to 'culture' in any other sense (including that of pseudo-culture). There are two important theoretical implications of his reasoning concerning the development of pseudo-culture. While pseudo-culture might be more prevalent among certain middle-class groups, it is in the ascendancy in all social groups. The so-called modern intelligentsia does not equate, therefore, to the intellectual classes of yesterday. Its culture, too, is rapidly becoming pseudo-culture and the relationship of its members to grand opera or the classical concert repertoire, is that of being consumers of the cultural 'goods' on offer. The second implication concerns the role of education. Those who see modern culture as somehow degrading the Culture of the past may attribute the failure to education and imagine that the solution to the problem of this growing Philistinism can be addressed through educational reforms. Adorno explicitly rejects such an argument. Education is merely one of society's institutions and like the others it is not immune to the transformations in culture that are taking place.

> The symptoms of the decline of culture, which are recognizable
> everywhere, even among the highly educated, cannot be explained

entirely by the inadequacies of educational systems and teaching methods, which have been blamed for generations.

(Adorno 1993: 15)

What has to be addressed here is the ubiquitous spread of pseudo-culture as the dominant form of contemporary consciousness. Not only is it fed from the world outside of formal education but it actually comes to pervade formal education itself, and the changes and so-called reforms that do take place in schools bear the unmistakable marks of pseudo-culture. How vindicated Adorno might have felt had he lived to see existing university degree courses that are made up of 'modules'; organized in terms of aims and objectives; listing the contents or bits of knowledge and information together with discrete skills that are to be acquired; and making clear that the delivery of the 'packaged' description is to form the basis of the contractual agreements between university, teacher and student. As for the actual contents of intellectual works, Adorno accuses modern educators of 'marketing' elements of culture that are unassimilated and unassimilable in any coherent intellectual formation. They thus became reified contents:

> For someone who comes across Spinoza's Ethics unprepared to understand them in terms of the Cartesian doctrine of substance and the difficulties of mediating between res cogitans and res extensa, the definitions with which the book begins assume the character of something dogmatically opaque and abstrusely arbitrary. Only when the concept and the dynamic of rationalism are understood in relation to the role of definitions does this character disappear. Anyone unprepared will neither know what these definitions should be nor what inherently justifies them. He will either reject them as gibberish and thereby easily adopt a superior attitude toward philosophy as a whole or, by resorting to the authority of the famous name, swallow them all and thus become authoritarian, just as citations of so-called great thinkers wandering like ghosts in ideological manuscripts reinforce the trivial opinions of dilettantes.
>
> (Adorno 1993: 30)

Adorno's remarks here have all the appearance of the complaint of an intellectual mandarin about the decline of standards but it is much more than that. It is, above all, a warning about what he perceives as the menace deriving from the formation of a blind relation to cultural products that are improperly understood. Far from adding anything to life, he saw such knowledge as ultimately toxic and as crippling the spirit that could no longer find expression in it.

Autarchy and adaptation

The sharp distinction that is frequently drawn between Culture and praxis stresses both the intellectual aspect of Culture and its autarchy, its self-sufficiency. Adorno argues that at the high point of the development of bourgeois society, the link between ideas and their practical realization in the world was not only occluded but the linkage itself was made into a taboo. Culture became something to be valued in itself, as something divorced from ordinary practical life, in that it could be seen as perfect in and of itself, because, in the Kantian sense, it was purposeful purposelessness. The formation of the great speculative systems of metaphysics, and of the great aesthetic movements in art and in music, owe their existence, argues Adorno, to the autarchy of Culture, to its growing self-sufficiency and internal consistency and its distance from the world of practical and mundane experience. This did not occur all at once of course. The types of cultural and characterological ideals – the gentleman, the officer and so forth – were gradually emancipated from their real-world functions, purposes and traditional contexts and became more or less self-sufficient, to be pursued as ideals for their own sake:

> Culture was supposed to benefit the free individual – an individual grounded in his own consciousness but developing within society, sublimating his instincts purely as his own spirit.
>
> (Adorno 1993: 19)

However, Adorno remains ambivalent with respect to the autarchy of Culture and this is a key element in all his analyses of Culture. On the one hand, it was this very claim to self-sufficiency, and to the distance and independence of Culture from empirical reality, which ensured that Culture's relationship to society was one of resistance and criticism. On the other hand, the self-sufficiency of Culture meant that it was, in effect, exiled from the praxis of everyday life and made no real contribution, in the positive sense, to shaping that life. Thus modernist art had attained an autonomy status that meant it was free to be critical but the very attainment of this freedom coincided with the loss of any consequential relationship to the praxis of everyday life. The same point is made by Peter Burger (Burger 1984).

Furthermore, Adorno argued, this dream of Culture as freedom from the dictatorship of means, from sterile utility, served as an apology for a world in which the domination of means and slavish conformity was established as fundamental. Adorno's defence of the autarchy of Culture has thus to be seen in dialectical terms. There is a tension between the claims of Culture to be free and independent, to be a value in itself, and the claims upon culture to be adaptive and thus to negotiate the demands of an empirical world and its entanglements. Culture that fits the model of the 'adaptive type' is what Adorno refers to throughout as 'pseudo-culture'. As usual, Adorno holds on to the dialectical tension between these two poles and opposes any attempt to dispose of one or other of them or to seek some middle way. He dismisses as false the notion of autarchy as a guarantee of the goodness of Culture, citing the case of certain individuals in Nazi Germany who could cultivate an exquisite sensitivity to aesthetic Culture while at the same time being prepared to engage in acts of barbarous cruelty towards human beings singled out for persecution. The isolation of culture from life is dangerous. Not only does such isolation culminate in a divided consciousness but it belies the very content of consciousness, the claims of Culture to be about humanity and spirit. The latter become, in a divided consciousness, merely cultural goods. Tradition, too, is an essential ingredient in Culture with a capital 'C'. Tradition, established through practice and association, ensures the continuity and development of consciousness in which everything not actually present survives and plays its part in shaping events. The traditional is the antipode of the instrumentalization of culture; that is, of pseudo-culture:

> the loss of tradition through the disenchantment of the world ultimately leads to a condition of culturelessness (Bilderlosigkeit), to a sclerosis of the spirit through its instrumentalization – which is incompatible with culture from the start. Nothing keeps the spirit in a vital relation to ideas any longer.
>
> (Adorno 1993: 25)

On the other hand, to conceive of culture as moulding real life is to stress the anti-tradition element of adaptation. It is a function of pseudo-culture to keep people in line, to keep them conforming slavishly to the demands of empirical life; those who are swallowed up by the world, cease to be subjects and become objects of manipulation, even of self-manipulation. Adaptation means more than the repression of animal instincts. It is, according to Adorno, the schema of progressive domination. Only by making itself equal to nature, by disciplining and organizing itself to master the facticity of empirical events, does the subject become capable of controlling what exists. Socially, this control presents itself as a means of controlling human instincts in order to master nature; ultimately, claims Adorno; it is a means of controlling the life-process of society as a whole, of degrading humanity to the level of de-spiritualized automata. Adorno was again ambivalent concerning this second 'pole' of the relationship between culture and 'life'. The engagement with the world is both necessary and desirable. However, it is also the case that a concern with adaptation to the demands of an existent reality fostered both conformism and repression:

> It did so to fortify the precarious continuity of socialization and to contain those chaotic outbreaks which occur periodically precisely

where a tradition of autonomous intellectual culture is established. At best the philosophical idea of culture (Bildungsidee) sought to protectively shape natural existence. It meant both the repression of animal instincts by making people conform to each other and the redemption of the natural in the face of the pressure from the frail man-made order.

(Adorno 1993: 17)

This dualism constituted by the autarchy of Culture, on the one hand, and the adaptive conformity of culture to empirical reality, on the other, derived from the unresolved antagonistic relations between mankind and nature. Domination is always at the heart of all Adorno's conceptions of pathology. The attempt to establish dominion over nature, which in turn brings about a separation of intellectual and spiritual from manual labour, gives rise also to the development of cultures of adaptation. In modern times adaptive conformist culture has been raised to a new level as pseudo-culture. However, adaptation to society can never resolve the antagonistic social relations that gave rise to the dichotomy of autonomous Culture and adaptive pseudo-culture:

But adaptation is immediately the schema of progressive domination. Only by making itself equal to nature, by restricting itself to what exists, did the subject become capable of controlling what exists . . . But the price for this is that nature triumphs because it always tames the animal tamer, who vainly approximates it, first through magic and ultimately through rigorous scientific objectivity. In the process of such approximation – the elimination of the subject in the interest of its own self-preservation – in a society which now simply exists and blindly develops . . .

(Adorno 1993: 18)

Class and pseudo-culture

Adorno points out that the situation of the rising bourgeoisie that developed Culture, at the time of the Enlightenement, contrasted greatly with the cultural situation of the proletariat that it brought into existence. Even in a society that was formally governed by relations of equality, the dominant social classes retained a monopoly over culture. Marx had developed the model of the superstructure to account for the cultural ascendancy of the ideas developed by the economically dominant class in society. The lower classes were denied the leisure necessary to develop Culture. Their historical role was deduced by socialists from their real economic situation and not from their spiritual condition, which was subjectively much less advanced than that of the bourgeois classes. In theorizing the cultural situation of the working classes in the twentieth century, Adorno was dealing with a changed situation in which the growth of leisure and of mass culture had reached the point where the lower classes were inundated with cultural goods and were provided with ready access to what had formerly been the cultural monopoly of the rich. He set himself sharply against the ideological conclusions that were drawn from this expanding access to cultural goods, that it was in some sense an enrichment of cultural life; that it was liberating people. He insisted that the growth of leisure in a capitalistic society does not provide working people with the freedom to develop Culture; it opens a space that is almost entirely colonized by the very commercial forces that disseminate pseudo-culture, weakening and undermining resistance in all those who are subject to its 'toxic' effects.

If urban society has experienced a descent from the high bourgeois Culture that celebrated freedom and autonomy in the individual to the depths of pseudo-culture and the culture industry, rural society has made the journey to the same place from a different beginning, from a pre-bourgeois conception of the world, essentially that of a traditionally religious outlook. Autonomy had not had time to lay down roots and therefore rural and peasant societies passed quickly, with the aid of the mass media, from one heteronomy to another. 'The authority of the Bible was replaced by the 'authority of the stadium, television and "true stories" which claim to be literal, actual, on this side of the productive imagination.' Echoing Weber, Adorno insists that the loss of tradition through the disenchantment of the world ultimately leads to the condition of culturelessness (*Bilderlosigkeit*), to the atrophy of spirit through its instrumentalization. All such instrumentalization is incompatible with any idea of Culture proper:

> In an age of spiritual disenchantment, the individual experiences the need for substitute images of the 'divine'. It obtains these through pseudo-culture. Hollywood idols, soaps, novels, pop tunes, lyrics and film genres such as the Wild West or the Mafia movie, fashion substitute mythologies for the masses.
>
> (Adorno 1993: 27)

Whereas some saw the democratization of culture and the ubiquity of cultural goods in modern society as heralding the advent of a classless society that would be some kind of golden age, Adorno saw the matter quite differently. He certainly agreed that the spread of mass culture had a levelling effect upon consciousness; it erased differences. *Subjectively*, the boundaries between class groups were becoming blurred at the level of consciousness; however, this was attributable to the mass dissemination of pseudo-culture, which induced conformity, and kept people in line everywhere. The consciousness of different classes was converging and becoming standardized even though differences between them in their objective situation may have been moving in the opposite direction. People who were formerly unacquainted with cultural goods were now being inundated with them and were unprepared to deal with them psychologically. Adorno saw the stratum of middle-class white-collar workers and their consciousness as the model for pseudo-culture. Again, his view here converged with that of Riesman.

While committed to Culture with a capital 'C', Adorno never did believe that Culture had actually succeeded in realizing the freedom of the individual; nor had it brought about a reconciliation of individual and society. Given the antagonistic nature of modern society, it could never have achieved either of these objectives no matter how much it was described as Enlightenment. However, the pursuit of reconciliation between individual and society still remained the truth-moment of ideology for Adorno. The fact that they are not reconciled does not mean that one abandons them. On the contrary, it is this truth-moment which must be held onto. Culture, as ideology, is still the prerequisite of an autonomous society. It is necessary to hold fast to Culture even after socio-historical developments have deprived it of any foundation. For Adorno, the only way that the spirit can survive is through critical reflection on pseudo-culture and, for that, Culture is essential.

High Culture into mass culture

And yet, he saw participation in Culture proper as dwindling fast. Only those isolated individuals who have not been completely absorbed into the melting pot, or those professional groups that celebrate themselves as elites, still participated in Culture (Adorno 1993: 23). (The further erosion and subversion of these latter groups has continued apace in the years since Adorno's death.) The mass media and the culture industry exploit this situation. They have a voracious appetite for reproducing the cultural goods that were formerly restricted to elites and disseminating them to the masses that never previously enjoyed access to Culture proper. Nor do the masses have access to Culture now, argued Adorno, other than in a corrupt and degraded form. If Culture, proper was once a means of change and of self-development, the spirit of the culture industry – what Adorno means by pseudo-culture – as the product of the capitalist market mechanism, is there to keep people in line, in slavish conformity, neutralized. Pseudo-culture also brings the element of 'worship' into its treatment of all those elements of Culture proper that it appropriates. In the transmutation of serious art, literature or music into the cultural goods produced by the culture industry, all genuine spiritual content attaching to the original is lost while pseudo-cultural piety towards these appropriations is heightened. This too is an instance of 'authoritarian submission' in the face of the unassimilable. The very response of audiences, which is designed into the production and dissemination of cultural goods, is one of dependency and fetishization.

The idea of Culture proper does not, however, lose its hold on those in the grip of pseudo-culture. On the contrary, the latter celebrate its prestige even though, as Culture proper, they can no longer genuinely experience it. Adorno treats the relationship of the pseudo-cultured individual to Culture, his or her abortive identification with elements of traditional Culture, as a form of collective narcissism. By this he means that people compensate for their social powerlessness and for their failure to live up to their ego ideals by turning themselves, either in fact or in imagination, into members of something higher and more encompassing to which they attribute the qualities that they themselves lack but from which they seek to benefit by vicarious participation. Adorno's use of the term collective narcissism here embraces the whole fetishized relationship to cultural goods including the pseudo-cultural worship of high art and culture by middle-class-taste publics. 'The pseudo-cultured person practices self-preservation without a self' (Adorno 1993: 33). He or she can no longer realize subjectivity in the sense of coherent experience and ideas. Tradition, which is the product of practice and association, has been replaced by the 'selective, disconnected interchangeable and ephemeral state of being informed' (Adorno 1993: 33). The succession of gobbets of information that displace one another in the 'information society' provides no coherent or cohesive life, no life that can support temporal development or history. Pseudo-culture destroys memory and memory is needed for that synthesis of experience essential to freedom, imagination and judgement.

The appropriation of so-called high Culture by the culture industry is a theme that preoccupied Adorno in different ways in many of his writings. Reverence may be accorded such cultural icons, he notes, but the works themselves are never truly and genuinely experienced under these conditions despite the 'endless prattle and sales talk' that surrounds them. Pursuing a line of argument that was to be later developed by Bourdieu, Adorno argues that the consumer relates to such cultural goods as status markers. One needs only to know how to deal with cultural goods, including works of art, in order to justify one's claim to be a cultivated person. The performance of so-called classic works or the concerts of great jazz performers has less to do with genuinely experiencing art and more to do with convincing oneself of the importance of the occasion, the greatness of the performer and so forth. Adorno comments on the practice of musical commentators on the radio and in the media who prefer to talk about the history of a work's conception rather than to tell us about the specific nature of its construction. What we are learning about, suggests Adorno, is mass culture itself. The publicity for a film such as *Titanic* seeks first and foremost to persuade us of the awesome expense that has gone into its making and the tremendous feats involved in reconstructing the ship and so forth. All this should command our attention and make us aware that the product is superior to any of a number of earlier versions on that account alone. 'All genuine experience of art is devalued into a matter of evaluation.'

Even the solemn transmission of Beethoven's Ninth Symphony, much publicized and impressively mounted as it is and never missing an opportunity to present itself as a truly historic event, is more concerned with instructing the listener about the event he is about to witness and the powers that have staged it than about encouraging him to participate in the work itself.

(Adorno and Horkheimer 1991: 70)

3

THE DIALECTIC OF ENLIGHTENMENT AND THE RING OF THE NIBELUNGEN

It is somewhat ironic that the most famous ideas with which Adorno was associated, namely the theory of popular culture and of the culture industry, should have been promulgated as a central part of a text that is as difficult, complex and unusual as *The Dialectic of Enlightenment*, written with Horkheimer (Adorno and Horkheimer 1979). The birth of the theory of the culture industry thus emerges in the midst of a 'grand narrative' about man's 'original' separation from and domination of nature, the rise of myth and the mythic consciousness, of mankind's enslavement of itself in the quest to become as strong as the forces of nature, and of the part played by science as a new and totalistic mythology in the development of this self-enslavement, this reduction of men and women to the status of manipulated things, of objects, even to themselves. The culture industry serves the aims of this manipulative life; it undermines all genuine sociality and spontaneity, all expressivity in the subject, and imposes, upon the psyches of individuals, the calculated 'effects' of manufactured cultural goods.

The rootedness of this work in German idealist themes that these exiled thinkers had inherited has been insufficiently acknowledged. In part, perhaps, this is occluded by the fact that the most important resonances and parallels are to thinkers of whom Adorno was critical. He is disparaging in his infrequent 'asides' about Schopenhauer. Nevertheless, the Schopenhaurian resonances in this work are very clear. Where Schopenhauer speaks of the primacy of the 'will', Adorno speaks of 'domination'. Both see 'art' and the 'aesthetic' as liberating and seek a praxis that is non-antagonistic, non-dominating; both eschew any response to domination and to the imposition of will that is in itself a process of domination (Adorno suffered from the wrath of German students in the 1968 protests and demonstrations because they had clearly not understood him on this point and thought that the famous critic of modern oppression ought to join them in active rebellion against authority); both may be seen by their critics as ultimately being philosophies of quietism or renunciation that paralyse political action; both thinkers have been accused of fostering a pessimistic outlook. None of these parallels imply that the two were not also opposed in their thinking. Equally, however, there is no denying 'the turn to Schopenhauer' that critical theory took in the writing of this particular book.

The Dialectic of Enlightenment and The Ring of the Nibelungen

Schopenhauer had been an important influence on the thinking of Richard Wagner and of Nietzche, too. Schopenhaurian themes and thought enter into Wagner's most important musical dramas, especially the cycle of operas known as *The Ring of the Nibelungen*. Adorno had already published a critique of Wagner's work before the publication of the *Dialectic of Enlightenment* (Adorno 1991b). His rejection of what he saw as the regressive features of Wagner's project did not prevent him from acknowledging the major contribution made by Wagner to the development of modern music. In my view, he and Horkheimer were indebted to Wagner for the very form and structural tension at the heart of their own critique of the Enlightenment.

Andreas Huyssen has argued, in his 'Reading of Adorno, in Reverse' (Huyssen 1983: 8–38), that Adorno's pre-war essays on Richard Wagner's music anticipate the theory of the culture industry that was developed later in Adorno and Horkheimer's *Dialectic of Enlightenment*. In Adorno's essays on Wagner, the key categories of 'fetishism' and 'reification', 'ego-weakness', 'regression', and 'myth' are already fully developed, 'waiting, as it were, to be articulated in terms of the American culture industry' (Huyssen 1983). However, while the framework for Adorno's theory of the culture industry was certainly in place *before* his exile in America, it does not predate his encounters with American mass culture. Those encounters were antecedent to the Wagner essays and are reflected in the papers on popular music, especially in the most important of Adorno's jazz papers, 'Uber Jazz', originally published in 1936 (Adorno 1989: 45–69). While Huyssens is right to identify a key connection between the earlier critique of Wagner and the later *Dialectic of Enlightenment*, there is an altogether different way of perceiving this link, a different way, perhaps, to read Adorno in reverse. It is to ask, what was the relationship of Adorno and Horkheimer's project, in the *Dialectic of Enlightenment*, to Wagner's own project? Specifically, what was the relationship of the *Dialectic of Enlightenment* to Wagner's cycle of operas known as the *Ring of the Nibelungen?* If it is true that Adorno's later analyses of the culture industry are foreshadowed in his critique of Wagner, it is also the case that Wagner's own project as realized in the *Ring* and also in his writings about his work (Wagner 1993, 1995) is a key element in the very construction of the Adorno–Horkheimer critique of the Enlightenment; the *Ring* cycle is an immanent presence in the cells of the latter work.

Wagner himself described the *Ring* as 'an understandable image of the whole history of mankind from the beginnings of society to the requisite collapse of the state' (Wagner 1995). The structural resonances of the *Dialectic of Enlightenment* with the story told by Wagner in his giant music drama is clear. An act of theft from nature takes place when the ring of the Nibelungs, which gives, to whoever possesses it, power over the world and access to the Nibelung treasure, is stolen by Albrech and then taken from him by Wotan, the chief of the Gods. The evil that spreads from this crime cannot be expunged before the Gods have fallen and the ring has been returned to nature. Wotan seeks with every means possible to extend his power and, by subjecting others to his will through calculative reasoning and the making of alliances and treaties, to impose an everlasting order on the world. His project is damned and mired in the sin he cannot expiate and he ultimately resigns himself to his doom.

The *Dialectic of Enlightenment* provides a clear parallel. It develops, from the beginning, its thesis that the rigid forms of the 'mythic' consciousness inscribe the alienated antagonistic power of nature which ultimately manifests as the power exerted by man over himself and his fellows in the effort to master the world and exploit nature. In their critique of the mythic element in consciousness, Adorno and Horkheimer incorporate an analysis of Homeric myths. The emergence of science and of Enlightenment thinking sweeps away the old myths claiming to replace them with a true knowledge of the world and its workings. But science and the Enlightenment are the inheritors of the power of domination, the successor myth. The power of nature so feared by 'primitives' manifests in the inner cells of the Enlightenment, in the mythic powers of science through which men and women degrade their lives to the level of objects.

The more complete is this control over nature, the more total is the system of social domination by which this control is achieved. Science and technology are integral to the rational-technical administrative structures of modern capitalist societies. Moreover, the manipulative force of modern rational-technical society enters into the formation of modern subjectivity. Through the relentless work of the culture industries, popular culture is commodified and fetishized. It manifests in what Adorno was to call 'the filthy tide of the entertainment industry' – a formulaic and barren system for crafting effects upon the body of the increasingly desociated, egoistic and narcissistic individual. The work of the culture industries, in the authors' analysis, is the very antithesis of their concept of genuine art. It stands on the side of totalitarian manipulation as surely as art – in its best modernist forms – stands on the side of resistance and freedom.

Myth and the mythic consciousness is the very vehicle with which Wagner himself recounts this story of the original separation from nature, a version of the lapsarian fall from grace. Like Adorno and Horkheimer, Wagner had set himself against the oppressive and rigid force of the bourgeois domination of the world. He identified freedom with spontaneity, with liberation from all the binding ties of that vast network of treaties and social contracts with which the bourgeois world had ensnared the individual. There were three principles stressed by Wagner here that were themselves key to Adorno and Horkheimer's critique of the Enlightenment: (1) the openness to change and renewal, to new formations, new experiences, new relations – an openness to the many-sidedness of life; (2) the social or collective aspect of life, of brotherhood, the importance of the 'folk' – Man's true nature is social, not egoistic, Wagner insisted; acting in concert and shared sympathy with others was mankind's natural state; (3) the falseness of 'fashion' and its divergence from art.

The development of Wagner's 'poem' sets forth the necessity of recognizing and yielding to the change, the many-sidedness, the multiplicity, the eternal renewing of reality and of life. Thus Wagner, like Adorno and Horkheimer, also locates the moral downfall of society in the principle of subjection, whereby individuals and particulars are subsumed within an abstract totality and lose the freedom to change and develop freely in relations with others. The threat posed by the development of the modern state to the freedom of the modern subject dominates Wagner's thinking in the construction of the *Ring* as it did that of Adorno and Horkheimer in the *Dialectic of Enlightenment*. In 'The Art Work of the Future', Wagner, too, clearly associates the 'over-administered' modern state with the development of science and Enlightenment thinking. Moreover, there is a remarkable resonance between his account, in this essay, of the development of the break with nature and the subsequent development of the mythic and religious consciousness:

> When he thus looked Nature in the face and from the first feelings of his dependence on her, thereby aroused, evolved the faculty of thought – from that moment did error begin, as the earliest utterance of consciousness. But error is the mother of knowledge; and the history of the birth of knowledge out of error is the history of the human race, from the myths of primal ages down to the present day.
>
> (Wagner 1993: 70)

In the same essay we can recover other claims resonant of those of Adorno and Horkheimer, for example in Wagner's insistence on the social nature of the individual and in his hostility to egoism:

> The impulse to loose oneself from commonality, to be free and independent for individual self alone, can only lead to the direct antithesis of the state so arbitrarily striven after: namely, to utmost lack of self-dependence . . . only in the fullest of communion with that which is apart from him, in the completest absorption into

the commonality of those who differ from him, can he ever be completely what he is by nature.

(Wagner 1993: 98)

The third aspect in which Wagner's essay resonates with Adorno and Horkheimer's study concerns the contrast drawn between genuine art and the world of fashion, what Adorno and Horkheimer label as the work of the culture industry. Adorno's later paper on jazz is subtitled 'perennial fashion' (Adorno 1993). Notwithstanding the poetic flights of Wagner's writings of a century earlier, it is not difficult to perceive a precursor of the type of analysis that culminated in the critique of the culture industry. In section 5 of the essay, entitled 'The Art-antagonistic shape of Present life, under the sway of abstract thought and fashion', Wagner identifies fashion with the cultivation of 'unnatural need', with perversity and tyranny:

Fashion is the artificial stimulus that rouses an unnatural need where the natural is not to hand; but whatever does not originate in a real need is arbitrary, uncalled for and tyrannical. Fashion is therefore the maddest, most unheard-of tyranny that has ever issued from man's perversity . . .

(Wagner 1993: 84)

Wagner contrasts the essential nature of fashion as slavish sterile uniformity with its restless striving after its antithesis in excess and deviation. There is a resonance here with Adorno's analysis of jazz as perennial fashion in which he sees it as an amalgam of rigid conformity and 'deviations' and 'interferences' that are never permitted to overcome the rigid structure established form the outset. There is a further resonance, too, in Wagner's polarization of art and fashion and his insistence that the needs that they satisfy are diametrically opposed to each other. If one substitutes the culture industry for fashion, the passage then clearly resonates with the thinking of Adorno and Horkheimer:

The soul of fashion is the most absolute uniformity, and its god an egoistic, sexless, barren god. Its motive force is therefore arbitrary alteration, unnecessary change, confused and restless striving after the opposite of its essential uniformity. Its might is the might of habit . . . Fashion's invention is, therefore, mechanical . . . the machine is the cold and heartless ally of luxury-craving men. Through the machine they have at last made even human reason their liege subject; for, led astray from Art's Discovery, dishonored and disowned, it consumes itself at last in mechanical refinements, in absorption into the machine, instead of in absorption into nature in the Art-work. . . . The need of fashion is thus the diametrical antithesis of the need of art; for the artistic need cannot possibly be present where fashion is the lawgiver of life . . .

(Wagner 1993: 84–5)

These structural resonances between the two projects do not imply that there were not real differences between these thinkers at the level of fundamental ideas. The fact is that Adorno and Horkheimer's study aims at telling a structurally similar story to Wagner but telling it differently, with its key concepts interpreted differently. But the resonances between the two projects identify them as rooted in a shared and complex cultural history.

Dystopian futures

Between Orwell's *Animal Farm* and *1984* there is a considerable gulf. Both works deal with oppression but the situation is not quite so desperate in *Animal Farm*. The pigs rule, exercising a cruel dominion over the other animals, but the possibility of resistance and rebellion is always present. What is demanded of subjects is obedience and not belief, and if criticism must remain mute for a time, it is still the case that it can, in silence, take form. It is a measure of the distance between the dictatorship of *Animal Farm* and the totalitarianism of *1984* that, in the latter work, the power of Big Brother is directed not to securing obedience or conformity but to obtaining absolute belief and submission; a surrendering of the consciousness and agency of the subject, a stamping out of even the possibility of 'silent insubordination'. The central character, Winston, is not simply required to say $2+2=5$ when the state says so, he must believe it with all his heart, and the torture is intended to secure just that ending of all resistance, of all personal agency and with it all history.

Atrocities – even atrocities on a large scale – are nothing new in human history; nor is the attempt to compel belief. However, when the terrified subject is offered 'the book or the sword', it is still his obedience that is being demanded. He is compelled to choose but the further step has not yet been taken of closing down either the imagination of alternatives or the power of choosing itself. That would require the erasure of the line dividing the subject from the state and the securing of the complete assimilation of the former into the apparatus of the latter. The possibility of resistance and revolution vanishes when a totalitarian and collective power exercises direct control over the consciousness and agency of the individual such that there is no longer any distinction between that power and the individual; when, that is, the latter is successfully ruled from within his own head.

It may be that none of these phenomena are new and that totalitarian pressures have appeared at different time throughout history. However, just as it is possible to argue that acquisitive economic behaviour and the profit motive are ancient but modern capitalism has a claim to be considered as historically unique, so the same can be said of modern totalitarianism. In the case of the latter, perhaps the decisive difference lies in the fact that the subject is not so much being indoctrinated into a set of beliefs as being made to reproduce within himself, in cellular form, the administrative apparatus of collective power, the reproduction of the means of administration now having become the immediate end of action.

Such a process demands fragmentation, the breaking down of every 'organic' action or experience into its elementary particles and the subjection of those particles to an anorganic process of organization, tearing object from subject in pursuit of a ruthless instrumentalism. Taylorist–Fordist production furnished the dominant model of industrial production during most of the twentieth century. The principles of 'scientific management' require that every productive action is broken down into its component parts and that each separate element is given to a different worker to perform. The organization of all these elements is then given over to a class of managers and administrators. The micro-division of labour thus secures the separation of all conception, design and control from individual workers, placing them in the hands of a superordinate agency. In these conditions, labour and action ceases to be intrinsically meaningful or to serve the expressive needs of a subject to realize, in action, a life-process. Labour is subject to a 'machine' logic and the labourer becomes an appendage to the machine. The rationale driving these developments derives from the pressures to maximize profitability throughout, down to the elementary units of the labour process itself. Taylorism, considered as an ideology, constitutes a techno-script for the most complete realization of Marx's theory of the alienation of the worker from the product and process of labour as well as from fellow workers. The worker is offered something in exchange for his soul. He, too, will receive benefits from the increased productivity in the form of higher wages that he can spend on the commodities produced by the culture industries.

The culture industry

It is to the area of consumption that all are encouraged to look for the spiritual freedoms that they have been deprived of at work. The sphere of leisure is deemed to be the domain of self-expression. The arts and culture are relegated to that sphere. Moreover, the contrast between work and leisure is maximized in public perception. Leisure is the domain of 'fun' and of liberation from the stresses of the workplace. The cultural artifacts that fill leisure space are supposed to manifest the variety, individuality and fertile imagination denied to individuals in their working lives. In short, the ideology of leisure would have it that men and women recover, in their leisure, the lives of which they have been robbed in the workplace. Adorno and Horkheimer set out to oppose this ideology in its entirety.

Liberal democracies lay claim to a freedom and individualism which they contrast with the totalitarianism of other types of society, theocratic, communistic, etc. In the *Dialectic of Enlightenment*, Adorno and Horkheimer rejected all such claims. Modernity had undermined the individual and all but extinguished the concept of freedom and autonomy, and it has done so in the late capitalist societies that called themselves liberal democracies as surely as it had in the so-called communist societies. Totalitarianism was the threatened future of a rational-technical development that was taking a hold everywhere in the age of monopoly capitalism. While Adorno insisted that the idea that society improves and progresses in a positive sense over time was an illusion and a lie, he did claim that a negative progression existed, a unilinear development 'from the slingshot to the megaton bomb'. The history of technology is the history of man's alienation from nature, of the efforts to master nature, to exploit and control it. The mastery over nature was achieved through the development of repressive social order.

Technology itself reflects the forms of control and social organization through which collective constraint is exercised in the social formation; the more total the exploitation of nature, the more total the self-domination of mankind (as the instrument of the domination of nature) through repressive social organization. The model of a world put together as a flawlessly functioning assemblage of separate parts – a machinery – was increasingly extended to the social world. Society ceased to approximate, at an ideological level, to the model of an organic social process – society as historical, biographical, an organic, developing whole – and became a fully programmed instrumental machinery, dispensing altogether with history. The image of the new totalitarian power was made visible in the rigours of assembly-line manufacture.

The more developed and global this antagonistic relationship to nature, the less viable were the residual forms in which freedom and resistance could be practised. In the dark vision of Adorno and Horkheimer, twentieth-century society had all but extinguished the individual. Its last refuges were to be found in certain centres of privilege such as the professions, among academics and scholars, for example, and among certain marginalized groups – most importantly, modern artists. Serious modern art offers a model of resistance to the totalitarian pressure of the world. However, the relentless process of eroding resistance continued through the totalistic organization of cultural production and reception, through mass culture, popular music, cinema, books and entertainment. In contrast to serious art, popular art was the very embodiment of the machine order. It was dominated by the model of mechanical assembly, of standardization and of repetition that was at the heart of industry. The culture industries even sucked the remnants of serious art into their mills, grinding its material down into the stuff of cultural goods that were not essentially different from all the other commodities produced by the culture industries.

Homes as 'machines for living in'

The ideology of liberal democracy took seriously the proposition that capitalism had produced, among its benefits, an increased freedom for individuals. What was formerly the freedom only of the wealthy, to own one's own dwelling and transport, became the province of the many in the post-war era. Winston Churchill built the image of the Conservative Party in Britain, after the war, on the notion of an extension of the property-owning democracy through the individual's ownership of the house in which s/he lived. Many have thought of the widespread ownership of the motor car as a similar extension of freedom for the individual. Finally, the development of mass media has given the majority access to the cultural goods and works of art that had formerly been the province only of the privileged minority.

For Adorno and Horkheimer, however, this is not the rich individuation of modern life that recovers, in the domestic sphere, what has been lost at work. They saw the type of 'individual' created by modern capitalism as an isolated (albeit massified) monad that is rendered, as a consequence, all the more subservient to the power of collective forces. To be genuinely individual is not to be self-contained in one of Le Corbusier's 'machines for living in' but to derive one's individuality from the dense interactions that make up living communities. Individuality is the product of sociality, of social interactions in and through which individuals change each other. Adorno and Horkheimer did not see the design of modern housing estates as anything but the antithesis of such an organic model. The domestic sphere of a modern urban existence was one constructed by the exigencies of capitalist production and designed both to facilitate the daily movement of a vast army of labour into the centres of business activity and to concentrate the same masses as consumers who spend their wages and salaries on buying the products of labour.

> ... Yet the city housing projects designed to perpetuate the individual as a supposedly independent unit in a small hygienic dwelling make him all the more subservient to his adversary – the absolute power of capitalism.
>
> (Adorno 1979: 120)

What was talked of by ideologues as the empowerment of individuals was in reality the securing of their utter sameness and conformity. The consumption of cultural products achieved the same result. Consumers were invited to exercise freedom of choice and expression in a world which no longer provided any genuine choices and in which expression and individual autonomy was all but extinguished. The cultural 'goods' that people buy are not essentially different from other commodities. They have been 'manufactured' for profit in accordance with the same laws that govern all commodity production in a capitalist society. In its monopolistic phase, capitalism is a vast interdependent system linking units of production, finance, energy and manufacturing in mutual dependence. The culture industries themselves – cinema, radio, popular music, TV and so forth – are part of this interdependent system and the relationship of cultural commodities to consumers partakes of the same fetishism that, in Marxist terms, characterizes the relationship of the consumer to all commodities. These industries themselves constitute very large enterprises and they engage in a highly organized system of marketing, promotion and distribution (that is, they behave like capitalist producers, observing all the requirements of commercial enterprise).

It is possible to conceive of an 'apology' for the culture industry that seeks to argue that culture is itself freely and (self-expressively) made by talented and creatived innovators and that the vast organizations of cultural producers such as the Hollywood film companies or the major broadcasting corporations, together with their complex systems of marketing, advertising and distribution, are merely instrumental in connecting a disparate mass of consumers to the cultural products of free creative individuals. The concentration of capital and size, in such a view, is only what is necessary to master the material conditions so that the consumers can enjoy what has been independently produced.

Adorno and Horkheimer rejected all such arguments that attributed some kind of ancillary role to technical organization. All technological rationales were manifestations of the rationale of domination itself, of the coercive nature of society alienated from itself. They were not an adjunct or support for ordinary creative action which was somehow different from them. They were present as the organizing process at work in the very cells of such action. The system as a whole, and in all its parts, has, as its primary aim, the making of profits through the successful production and marketing of commodities. Maximizing exchange value then becomes the central motive to which all else is subordinated and it enters directly into the formation of cultural artifacts as well as into every aspect of their marketing.

The fact that the culture industry relies on talented individuals does not mean that it does not own and control the production of culture by such individuals. The talented performers who are celebrated in popular culture, the film actors, jazz musicians, radio and TV personalities are themselves preformed by the culture industry that employs them. They are oriented to the industry and to meeting the demands of the industry to generate the commercial and marketable commodity. As Adorno and Horkheimer put it, 'they belong to the industry long before it displays them'.

If it is argued that the talents and creative spirit of the performers and artists, who are the primary producers of the cultural artifacts, somehow guarantee the artistic integrity of what is produced, Adorno and Horkheimer point out that that such primary producers are not only dependent upon the culture industries for work but the competition for such desired jobs and creative opportunities demands that they orient themselves, in advance, to meeting the principles of production that are key to the culture industry's operations. In short, no matter how talented the individual, s/he must repeatedly demonstrate the most valued talent of all, namely the talent to produce the cultural commodities through which consumers are made dependent. To be talented but incapable of commodifying one's work is a recipe for being unemployed.

Standarization of products, differentiation of markets

The central characteristics of the commodified work of art are 'standardization' and 'repetition'. One pop song is much like another, one film or TV programme is much like another and so forth. Such differences as appear are like the differences between the various models produced by the same car manufacturer and are superficial. Insofar as there are differences among the products, they are differences that reflect divisions within the market for commodities; that is, the subdivision of markets by the categories into which consumers fall (class, ethnicity, education status and so forth). A differentiation of products as between markets is matched by a homogeneity and standardization of products within markets. Massification demands nothing less. 'Marked differentiations such as those of A and B films, or of stories in magazines in different price ranges, depend not so much on subject matter as on classifying, organizing, and labelling consumers' (Adorno and Horkheimer 1979: 123). The lack of differentiation among products – the demand that all products should be essentially similar and only manifest superficially distinctive features – follows from the fact that the culture industry is oriented to the production of reliable *effects* that are to be worked upon the consciousness of the consumer. These have to be calculated in advance and to work for a disparate mass of consumers. In that respect the imaginative projection of the consumer in the reception of culture is minimized.

The lack of differentiation between whole and parts

The fragmentation of the sensuous life of the consumer is what is presupposed and secured by the commodification of culture. The sensuous continuum of life is reduced to the discrete sensations, emotions and excitations that are responses to the immediate stimulus world. This fragmentation of the sensuous life has as its correlative a process of de-sociation, a growing narcissism. In Adorno's ideal of serious art, the differentiated elements which make up the work all push each other, driving towards the construction of a larger whole, a totality. In modern popular culture, Adorno argues that the parts are no longer mutually determinative and interdependent in this way, developing in accordance with their own immanent and historically constituted tension. There is a draining of all dialectical relations from the construction of the work itself. Works of popular art are constructed of elements that are formed ahistorically in accordance with their predetermined effects upon the consciousness of the receiver. Maximizing the emotional appeal of the works to the audience is a key objective since maximizing this appeal and maximizing profits is one and the same thing. In this way, the subjectivity of the individual becomes transmuted into exchange values.

In a serious work of art there is a real distinction between the individual elements and the totality which is emergent from them and which transcends them. In a work of so-called mass or popular art there can be no such distinction because the whole is not the outcome of interaction among its elements but is a rigid frame that is no more responsive to its elements than they are to each other. The parts are therefore alike and like the whole. Moreover, if they fit smoothly together to produce a more or less harmonic effect, it is purely a manufactured effect that has been predetermined in advance and is not the outcome of an organic and historical development. The total form then becomes a container, not essentially different from the other parts and as unchanged by them as they are by each other. The harmony of the parts is a dead prearranged harmony that makes a mockery of the struggle to achieve harmony that occurs in classical art.

> The whole and the parts are alike; there is no antithesis and no connection. Their prearranged harmony is a mockery of what had to be striven after in the great bourgeois works of art.
>
> (Adorno and Horkheimer 1979: 126)

Leisure

Adorno and Horkheimer refer to 'light' art as 'the social bad conscience of serious art' (1979: 135). To the extent that serious art constitutes the cultural capital of the higher social classes its truth claims are compromised. This lack imparts to light art a certain legitimacy. The division between these two spheres is itself the truth that expresses the negativity of culture. The antithesis between them cannot be overcome by seeking to absorb light art into serious art or to sublate the latter in the former. According to Adorno and Horkheimer this is what the culture industry seeks to do; it is certainly part of the contemporary claim of postmodernity.

The newly marked distinction between work and leisure is one that the authors set out to deconstruct. They equate leisure with the mechanized work process itself. The final irony lies in the fact that the leisure sphere is intended as an escape from work but, in reality, the production of leisure is dominated by the same mechanized work process. The cultural goods to be consumed bear the stamp of that process and they do so to such an extent that Adorno says of the consumer 'his [leisure] experiences are inevitably after-images of the work process itself':

The escape from everyday drudgery which the whole culture industry promises may be compared to the daughter's abduction in the cartoon: the father is holding the ladder in the dark. The paradise offered by the culture industry is the same old drudgery. Both escape and elopement are pre-designed to lead back to the starting point.

(Adorno 1973: 142)

When Adorno and Horkheimer insist on the mechanized labour process as the schema behind the enjoyment of cultural goods, they are referring not to the decayed contents that stand in the foreground of popular art but the automatic succession of standardized operations (in jazz, in film or TV) that constitute the basic form of all amusement goods, just as they do of all modern industrial production. Thus the only escape offered to the tired worker is the chance to approximate to the work process in his leisure time. On the other hand, for the experience to be viewed as pleasure and not work it must not entail effort on the part of the consumer. Boredom is an inevitable consequence since the consumer is forced to step in the 'worn grooves of association'. It is a contradiction to seek to simultaneously escape both boredom and effort.

Amusement itself and especially laughter and comedy were viewed by Adorno and Horkheimer as permeated by sadism. Laughter appeared to be a shared expressive outburst that reflected a social feeling, to bring people together. Adorno and Horkheimer see comedy differently. The members of the laughing audience constitute a caricature of social solidarity. They are members of a collectivity made up of monads whose pleasure comes from a sadistic delight in the discomfort, humiliation or embarrassment of someone else. The undoing of others is the source of all such pleasure.

This is not to say that there was not comedy of which Adorno and Horkheimer approved. The test was always the same. Where the comedy embodied resistance to the rationalized force of the existent; where it was characterized by anarchic spirit or by absurdity, they gave it the seal of approval. The most obvious instance was that of physical clowning. Adorno saw the anarchism and resistance reflected in absurdity and clowning as the assertion of the physical over the intellectual. While he approved of a popular art in which these anarchic features were paramount and an intellectual art in which dialectical reason was paramount, he saw modernity as a draining away of both, such that low art became intellectualized and high art became intellectually impoverished. The consequence was a fusion of entertainment and culture. This is how Adorno would have seen the much talked about merging of high and low art or of news and entertainment, etc.

The culture industry does retain a trace of something better in those features that bring it close to the circus, in the self-justifying and nonsensical skill of riders, acrobats and clowns, in the 'defense and justification of physical as against intellectual art.' But the refuges of a mindless artistry which represents what is human as opposed to the social mechanism are being relentlessly hunted down by a schematic reason which compels everything to prove its significance and effect. The consequence is that the nonsensical at the bottom disappears as utterly as the sense in works of art at the top. The fusion of culture and entertainment that is taking place today leads not only to a depravation of culture, but inevitably to an intellectualization of amusement.

(Adorno 1973: 143)

Adorno and Horkheimer make two important claims concerning pleasure and its pursuit. To be pleased is to say yes. It is to go along with the collective programme. Pleasure is treated as synonymous with sensation, with the impact or effect produced upon the desociated body of the subject. It is only possible as a result of a process of fragmentation that insulates the individual from the total social process causing him or her to lose a sense of the whole. Amusement goods are designed to achieve just that and to the extent that they do so, the possibility of resistance is destroyed. Pleasure is therefore a form of helplessness, a flight not from reality but from the last remaining thought of resistance which vanishes with the larger picture.

Models of submission

Adorno and Horkheimer view modern culture as a training ground for those acts of submission and resignation through which one is promised some kind of survival. Absolute submission to the power that is threatening one is the *sine qua non* of jazz and of films, according to them. They see the products of the culture industry as inscribing models of the submissive process in which the helplessness and dependency of the subject, his or her surrender to social power, is made the object of repeated aesthetic demonstration. Films that depict desperate situations of the kind which crush people in normal life become a promise to the individual that s/he will be permitted to go on living provided s/he becomes aware of her nothingness and accepts defeat. Fate and circumstance will somehow ensure that s/he survives. The model is held to be present, too, in jazz music, where syncopation affirms the rigid unyielding beats that put down the effort to deviate or to strike out independently. Helplessness and emasculation are read by Adorno and Horkheimer into jazz, into radio crooning and into Hollywood comedies. All provide models of submission for those who must become whatever the system requires them to become. The illusory nature of individuality in the world of standardization and stereotypes is a ubiquitous theme. The culture industry's products are always standardized, formulaic and stereotypical; however, they

46

connect to their audiences through cultivating the 'distinctive feature' or accidental detail.

> personality scarcely signifies anything more than shining white teeth and freedom from body odor and emotions. The triumph of advertising in the culture industry is that consumers feel compelled to buy and use its products even though they see through them.
>
> (Adorno 1973: 167)

In short, cultural goods cultivate interest through disguising their utter stereotypy by introducing isolated effects or details that give the impression of something novel or individual. All such accidental details are instances of what Adorno and Horkheimer call 'pseudo-individualization'. We never cease to be in the grip of the stereotype and it is this generality that stands behind the accidental detail through which we connect to it. The culture industry has no problem with dealing with individuality because genuine individuality is all but extinct. In the emulation of fashion models and film stars the effort to achieve individuation has given way to the effort to imitate.

> The idolization of the cheap involves making the average the heroic. The highest-paid stars resemble pictures advertising unspecified proprietary articles. Not without good purpose are they often selected from the host of commercial models. The prevailing taste takes its ideal from advertising, the beauty in consumption.
>
> (Adorno 1973: 156)

The industry of mass deception

The stress on associating the word culture with industry calls to mind the planned, assembly-line method of turning out its products, all glossy and finished. In the original drafts, Adorno and Horkheimer had referred to 'mass culture'. They replaced the term with 'culture industry' because they saw the former term as suggesting a culture that arises spontaneously from the masses. It is from above that the culture industry seeks to process both high and low art and to assimilate them to a single schema, thereby integrating its consumers. The customer is not the master or the empowered element in all this; s/he is not the subject but the manipulated object.

> The entire practice of the culture industry transfers the profit motive naked onto cultural forms. Ever since these cultural forms first began to earn a living for their creators as commodities in the market-place they had already possessed something of this quality. But then they sought after profit only indirectly, over and above their autonomous

essence. New on the part of the culture industry is the direct and undisguised primacy of a precisely and thoroughly calculated efficacy in its most typical products.

(Adorno 1991c: 86)

Ultimately, the culture industry no longer even needs to directly pursue everywhere the profit interests from which it originated. These interests have become objectified in its ideology and have even made themselves independent of the compulsion to sell the cultural commodities that must be swallowed anyway.

the expression 'industry' is not to be taken too literally. It refers to the standardization of the thing itself – such as that of the Western, familiar to every movie-goer – and to the rationalization of distribution techniques, but not strictly to the production process.

Each product affects an individual air; individuality itself serves to reinforce ideology, in so far as the illusion is conjured up that the completely reified and mediated is a sanctuary from immediacy and life.

(Adorno 1991c: 87)

The more dehumanized its methods of operation and content, the more diligently and successfully the culture industry propagates supposedly great personalities and operates with heart-throbs. It is industrial more in a sociological sense, in the incorporation of industrial forms of organization even when nothing is manufactured – as in the rationalization of office work – rather than in the sense of anything really and actually produced by technological rationality. The compiling of cheap biographies, hit songs or documentaries has the same general 'manufactured' character. The individual features and accidental details that provoke interest are all detachable, all interchangeable and capable of serving ends external to the work in which they happen to be placed. They are the material of advertising. Adorno and Horkheimer argue that advertising and the culture industry merge both technically and economically. Both can be seen in multiple locations and the mechanical repetition of a car or a washing machine or a hit musical is not essentially different from the repetition of a propaganda slogan. This detachability and interchangeability of the elements of cultural goods is key to Adorno's critique. The elements of experience, be they sensations, emotions ideas, etc., can be ordered in accordance with an immanent and inherent logic, a meaningful dynamic interrelatedness or they can be detached and brought into play, not by an inner dynamic but by external pressure. To the extent that they are detachable, the consciousness of the subject becomes a reflex of an external force and any order that exists among the elements becomes a reflection of that external pressure. What is true at the level of the experience of the subject has its analogue at the level of the work of art.

The triviality of the culture industry ought to be more or less obvious to intellectuals. Adorno and Horkheimer argue that the fact is known not only to intellectuals but to many consumers as well. They accuse all such knowing individuals of a two-faced servility, of being aware of the deception that is being perpetrated upon them and of the worthlessness of the cultural goods that they consume, but of being afraid to live without the trivial satisfactions that are offered by the culture industry, sensing that the intolerable nature of their lives would become all too apparent without the distraction of mass cultural goods. The culture industry stands, for Adorno and Horkheimer, as the very antithesis of the Enlightenment, as an instrument of mass deception:

> The total effect of the culture industry is one of anti-enlightenment, in which, as Horkheimer and I have noted, enlightenment, that is the progressive technical domination of nature, becomes mass deception and is turned into a means for fettering consciousness. It impedes the development of autonomous, independent individuals who judge and decide consciously for themselves. These, however, would be the precondition for a democratic society, which needs adults who have come of age in order to sustain itself and develop. If the masses have been unjustly reviled from above as masses, the culture industry is not among the least responsible for making them into masses and then despising them, while obstructing the emancipation for which human beings are as ripe as the productive forces of the epoch permit.
>
> (Adorno 1991c: 92)

4

THE DECAY OF 'AURA' AND THE SCHEMA OF MASS CULTURE

In his pioneering series for television, *Ways of Seeing,* John Berger appears, in one of the programmes, standing before Leonardo da Vinci's painting *The Virgin of the Rocks* in the National Gallery in London (Berger 1972). He assures us, the viewers, that we are looking at Leonardo's famous painting. He then, teasingly, corrects himself. It is he who is looking at the painting by Leonardo; we are looking at a television image. More than that, this 'reproduced' image takes its place in the viewer's living room, perhaps beside other images, photos and so forth, that play a part in the formation of a local habitus. For the National Gallery itself, however, it is important to believe that it owns the *original* Leonardo, that the painting is 'authentic' and not a 'copy'. Pages of the catalogue are devoted to proving this point, to tracing its unique history, its various ownerships and so forth, to establish its authenticity. The fact is that there is another painting that looks just like this one in the Louvre in Paris. Which is the 'original', which is authentic, does it matter?

Benjamin

In this sequence, Berger provides a skilful dramatic evocation of a key part of Walter Benjamin's argument in what is, arguably, his most famous paper, 'The Work of Art in an Age of Mechanical Production' (Benjamin 1992: 211–44). *The Virgin of the Rocks* is not a simple image. Every effort has been made to see that it is not detached from its unique history. It possesses what Benjamin calls 'a presence in time and space', a unique existence at the place where it happens to be. The authenticity of such a painting lies in 'the essence of all that is transmissible from its beginning, ranging from its substantive duration to its testimony to the history it has experienced' (Benjamin 1992: 215). We respond not just to an image but to a history-soaked image, to a tradition congealed in the very 'presence' of the painting, a presence that always holds it at a distance, apart from everyday lives and experiences, as something beyond. An element of cult and ritual inheres in the act of attending to such an image. It is an attitude that Berger dismisses disparagingly as 'fake religiosity'.

This special authority that the unique object or work of art possesses and which sets it at a distance from us, is what Benjamin termed its 'aura'. When the work of art becomes reproducible and multiple copies are substituted for its unique existence, then the art object becomes detached from the domain of tradition; its history drains from it. Moreover, this detached image goes out to its receivers, enters their space and time and is activated there; its possibilities are realized in response to the exigencies of the local situation. With the decay of the 'aura' of the object, the distance between receiver and art work collapses; the art object is absorbed in the praxis and consciousness of everyday life, its meaning re-constituted:

> For the first time in world history, mechanical reproduction emancip-
> ates the work of art from its parasitical dependence on ritual. To an
> ever greater degree the work of art reproduced becomes the work of
> art designed for reproducibility . . . but the instant the criterion of
> authenticity ceases to be applicable to artistic production, the total
> function of art is reversed. Instead of being based on ritual it begins
> to be based on another practice, politics.
>
> (Benjamin 1992: 218)

Adorno's theory of the culture industry developed in tension with the ideas about art and modernity that his friend Walter Benjamin had advanced in this paper. It is clear from the correspondence between Benjamin and Adorno that the latter disagreed profoundly not merely with specific aspects of Benjamin's theory but with his treatment of modern art as a whole and especially his valorization of aspects of popular culture. He came to see Benjamin's paper as an apology for the culture industry and he claimed, in later years, that the popularity of this particular paper above all others in Benjamin's oeuvre was the result of its close alignment with, and reinforcing of, the claims of mass culture. Insofar as there was a Marxist project discernible in Benjamin's paper, it was of the type espoused by Bertolt Brecht and strongly disapproved of by Adorno. Thus, in his reply to Benjamin, Adorno refers directly and pejoratively to the paper's 'Brechtian motifs' (Adorno et al. 1980: 120–6).

Benjamin's examples centre particularly on the development of photography and of film. There is no doubting the positive sign under which he reviews these changes in his outline of a theory of modernity. In his view, the decay of aura is inevitably linked to a democratization of arts practice, to a heightened degree of participation by the 'masses'. Benjamin even offers a formula here. The more that an art declines in terms of its social significance, the more is criticism of the work divorced from its enjoyment. The conventional and banal is uncritically enjoyed and the truly avant-garde or new is criticized with real aversion. If the greater part of the population was reactionary in rejecting the art of Picasso, they were highly progressive in their response to Chaplin's films, argues Benjamin. The change from auratic to non-auratic art brought about a fundamental change at the level of the mental response to a work of art. The attitude of active concentration and study characteristic of the response to traditional art gave way to a type of distractive awareness, a kind of automatic apperception more characteristic of the 'habitual'; for example, the skill of driving a car, in which a great deal goes on below the level of explicit awareness. For Benjamin this kind of apperception was essential because events in a film could be very busy, changing very quickly, like everyday life; it was possible because events were assimilated to the ordinary consciousness of the subject; s/he does not have to continually point out to herself what is already part of herself. He locates the progressiveness of modern film media in the response of the typical cinema audience, which fuses visual and emotional enjoyment with the critical orientation of the expert. The film audience's identification with the actor, he argues, is really an identification with the camera. Because the audience takes the position of the camera, the role it assumes is one of 'testing'. It can become both the 'expert' prepared to comment on the production values of the work and the one who enjoys the effects produced.

However, if Benjamin's film audience is made up of 'experts' or 'examiners', their function is certainly not exercised with the type of focussed attention that is normally used to characterize the expert. They do not attend to the film in a way that can be identified as 'concentration': 'The public is an examiner, but an absent-minded one ' (Benjamin 1992: 234). To concentrate before a work of art is to enter its domain, to be absorbed by it. By contrast, the distracted individual absorbs the work of art. Benjamin turns to architecture as his example here. Buildings are appropriated both by use and by perception. Such appropriation cannot be understood, he argues, in terms of the attentive concentration of a tourist before a famous building. It is governed more by habit, both optical and tactile; by the kind of attention that the individual gives to a familiar building such as his own house. In everyday life, buildings are noticed in incidental fashion rather than studied with rapt attention. Benjamin associates this distractive process in art with the solving of problems by apperception. His notion emphasises that attentiveness which is below the threshold of explicit awareness; an awareness that can be likened to what Polanyi spoke of as 'tacit knowing' (Polanyi and Prosch 1975: 22–45).

Brechtian motifs

The kinship between Benjamin's idea here and that of his friend Bertholt Brecht is marked. Brecht sought to destroy the aura constituted by the nineteenth-century theatre of illusion. In that traditional ideal the play was constructed, on a proscenium arch stage, as a self-contained and self-sufficient world, complete with its own time and space, uniquely located, and with an unbridgeable distance between it and the ordinary consciousness of the members of the audience. The latter sat 'lamed and silent' in the auditorium, a 'universal witness' to the drama enacted before them. This 'distance', as with Benjamin's auratic work of art, resulted in a kind of religiosity, certainly a sense of the magical element in theatre. Brecht sought to destroy this pseudo-religiosity with his alienation effects. The actors demonstrated that they were actors putting on a play, that they were not to be identified with their characters, and the members of the audience were also encouraged not to identify with the characters portrayed but to consider the action on stage critically, in the light of their ordinary everyday experience – different for each individual. Once the drama has been relocated at the level of ordinary consciousness, fake religiosity disappears and the audience finds itself engaged in practical and personally situated reflection on the events before it. Instead of being enrolled as 'universal' man and woman, each member of the audience enters the auditorium as a fully situated individual in his or her real-life role and the drama is recontextualized at the level of that person's real-world experience.

Both Benjamin and Brecht were addressing the question of how art, traditionally elitist and more or less exclusively restricted to higher social classes, could realize its progressive potential in the consciousness of the masses. For both of these thinkers, liberation meant the destruction of the distancing of art objects from ordinary consciousness. It was that very distancing, the 'aura' of the work of art, which made of it a manifestation of the authority and power that higher social classes could recognize as their own. They could identify with the work, enter its temple and merge with its deity in a spirit of devotion. The auratic work invites the subject to enter and to make its life-process one with the inner movement of the work. Identification with the work confers an auratic distance on the receiver, herself, who assumes the mantle of the universal man or woman, responding to the material with 'how sad/ how marvellous/ how amusing/ life is like that'.

Benjamin, like Brecht, believed that the destruction of the aura of works of art and the falling back of the art object into ordinary consciousness liberated a critical and active imagination in which art would lose its exclusivity and become an instrument of the ordinary consciousness of ordinary people. Modern mass media could, of course, be reactionary or be used for reactionary purposes but the very possibilities of modern media, modern film, radio and so forth held out the hope of an aesthetic empowerment of ordinary people that extended deep into the praxis of everyday life. In themselves, they brought works of art closer to the ordinary consciousness of individuals.

It would be hard to overestimate the dismay Adorno must have felt in response to Benjamin's ideas in this paper (Adorno et al. 1980). Without perhaps intending it, Benjamin was striking at the very heart of Adorno's theoretical position. Adorno's whole argument concerning the fetish-object turns on the fact that objects of mass production and mass consumption are abstracted from the social relations through which they are produced and, therefore, from the constitutive activity of the subjects who both produce and consume them. It is this alienated condition of the object that results in its fetishization. Fetish-consciousness is thus produced, in Adorno's version of Marxist theory, by the disjunction (alienation) of the subject from its objects. The concept of 'fetish' and that of 'aura' share in common the fact that both reflect (albeit in different ways) a disjunction and distance between subject and object. Both appear in quasi-magical guise and both demand from the subject an act of 'submission'.

Benjamin had made several moves that were completely unacceptable to Adorno. He had relocated the problem of fetish-consciousness by transposing it from the realm of modern popular culture, where Adorno had located it, to the domain of so-called serious art, which Adorno looked to as an instrument of progress and of resistance to a barbarous world. Even worse, from Adorno's point of view, he had valorized the culture industry through his analysis of film, suggesting that popular culture was essentially free of aura and was already liberating a critical imagination in the masses who were somehow empowered by it. For Adorno, the overcoming of distance between the subject and the cultural goods of modern society was equivalent to 'identification with the aggressor', with surrendering to the overwhelming collective force represented by the culture industry as the agent of monopoly capitalism. No critical imagination or consciousness would be released by such an overcoming of distance because the individual would lack any means within himself to reach beyond the immediate pressure of events or to counter them.

If Adorno had identified the distance of alienation with fetish-consciousness when dealing with the culture industry, he dealt with the auratic distance of the work of art in an altogether different way. Alienation described the condition of all art in the modern world whether serious or popular. Serious modernist works, of which Adorno approved, expressed this alienated condition in their very constitution, in their inner cells. The distance they held from the world was both essential and integral to their critical force. To the extent that they preserved this disjunction from the world, works of art were islands of resistance. To destroy this distance was to sublate them in mass cultural kitsch. This was something that Adorno believed the culture industry was doing every time it played a Beethoven symphony over the radio. Thus the tendency of Adorno's thought was to insist, against Benjamin, both on the necessity for the integrity of the work of art – its capacity to hold its distance – and on the impossibility of a critical consciousness developing from participation in mass culture. Closely associated with both these critical points is Adorno's valorization of the attitude of concentration essential to genuinely experiencing and merging in consciousness with the distanced work of art. Non-identity between subject and world – the expression of alienation – is brought to mind in and through an identity between the consciousness and life-process of the subject and the formation of the work of art, an identity that demands concentration from its receivers. Adorno, in a clear reference to Benjamin, opposes the deconcentrative responses (distraction) of modern audiences as a regressive mode of reception, a weakening or undermining of consciousness and not in any sense a higher perceptual process as Benjamin appears to envisage it (Adorno 1991a: 26–84).

Adorno's critical response to Benjamin is often incorporated tacitly and indirectly in his writings. His strategy was to develop his own critique of the regressive features of the culture industry – and what he saw as debased cultural goods – in a way that incorporated a response to all Benjamin's key points. Not only had he read Benjamin's paper prior to setting out his now famous arguments about the culture industry but he clearly had it in mind when he was formulating his arguments against every aspect of the culture industry. Two of his most powerful papers on mass culture, 'On the Fetish Character in Music and the Regression of Listening' (Adorno 1991a) and 'The Schema of Mass Culture' (Adorno and Horkheimer 1991), can be read as a critical rejection of the key arguments of Benjamin's paper.

Recognition as a surrogate for meaning

It is often assumed by detractors of his work that, when Adorno attacked popular culture or recent developments in mass art, he was making judgements of taste. There were, after all, many contemporary critiques of mass culture that did, in effect, make claims about the lowering of standards and of good taste in the commercialized art of the day. Adorno was concerned to distance himself from all such critiques. Taste implies the existence of a subject capable of making authentic judgements; it also implies the existence of real choices for the subject to make. Adorno's cultural analysis led him to the conclusion that modernity had robbed the mass of individuals, both of an authentic selfhood that could serve as the arbiter of taste and of any *genuine* choices that could make the notion of a judgement of taste meaningful. Whenever Adorno spoke of a descent into barbarism he was referring to something different from, and very much more dangerous than, a decline in taste.

In an ideal sense, Adorno believed that culture with truth-value stimulated and empowered a process of active engagement, thinking, self-development and understanding in the subject. Engagement with a work of art, in the serious sense, is a journey of discovery, an enrichment of life and understanding. For the engaged subject, genuine appreciation of serious art is the very antipode of the sterile security provided by the process of 'moving in the worn grooves of the familiar'. The response engendered by mass cultural goods belonged to this latter pole. People were drawn to what they were able immediately to recognize; that is, to the recognition of what was familiar, of what had been repeated or played again and again, or to the recognition of new cultural goods that were more or less like other goods with which the individual was already familiar.

Adorno was doing more than identifying the response to cultural goods as one of recognition in the face of the eternally familiar; he was also identifying its regressive character as both an impediment to and a surrogate for the formation of meaning. To treat the response of the subject to the familiar and the habitual as the basis of a progressive relationship to art and culture, as Benjamin appears to do, meant that art would no longer be capable of a critical relationship to life. For music to become familiar, in Benjamin's sense, means only that music can no longer be perceived at all but remains a kind of background accompaniment to mundane life:

> It [music] inhabits the pockets of silence that develop between people moulded by anxiety, work and undemanding docility. Every-where it takes over unnoticed the deadly sad role that fell to it in the time and the specific situation of the silent films. It is perceived purely as background. If nobody can any longer speak then certainly nobody can any longer listen.
>
> (Adorno 1991a: 27)

The instant recognizability of the standardized products of the culture industry is also a result of the sensuous pleasure they afford in their characteristic details. Adorno argued that it was the emancipation of the elements or parts from any truly cohesive movement or development and from all moments that extend beyond their immediate present that destroyed meaning and replaced it with sensory pleasure (Adorno 1991a: 43). Musical truth or seriousness is found in the total movement to which the elements or parts contribute. The dissolution of music into its isolated details, climaxes and culinary moments is the mark of music's decline. The greatness of music – above all its involvement with values – resides in its power of synthesis in and through which all the elements acquire meaning only in the context of an emerging or developing whole. In that synthesizing power is an image of social formation. Without it there can be no serious art. Adorno recognizes, of course, that so-called great music has its moments of sensuous delight but he insists that such moments are always transformed by the movement of the whole in which they are caught up. In the standardized music of the culture industry and in the works of late Romantic composers such as Tchaikovsky and Rachmaninov, sensuous pleasure and the delight of 'featured' moments absolves the listener from having to give his or her mind to the whole. To Adorno, the capacity to give one's mind to the whole is the mark of autonomy and moral responsibility, of distance and therefore of the capacity for critical thought. To take the line of least resistance and to surrender to the delights of the musical moment is to have become a creature of the collective machine. The individual becomes an acquiescent consumer (Adorno 1991a: 29):

> The best-selllers here are the late romantics like Tchaikovsky and Dvorak for whom the symphonic form is simply a face. They already weakened symphonic form by turning it into a pot-pourri of melodies arbitrarily connected with one another. The symphonic schema no longer performs any real function here and all that is left of the dynamic form of the symphony, antiphonic motivic elaboration and thematic development, are the interludes of noisy excitement which unpleasantly interrupt the pot-pourri until it is resumed as if nothing had happened, as if everything could begin all over again.
>
> (Adorno 1991a: 63)

Musical fetishism

Adorno dismissed the argument that modernity had somehow brought about a destruction of aura. The 'star' principle at the very heart of the culture industry – the worship of glamour and celebrity – was marked by precisely that kind of cultic and fetishistic attitude on the part of cultural consumers that Benjamin had attributed to the traditional reception of serious works of art. Moreover, famous people were not the only stars. Stardom belonged also to cultural works themselves, to best-selling books or to cult musicals or records. The concert repertoire itself had its pantheon of best-sellers, its 600 endlessly repeated works. And even the composers acknowledged as great or famous have more attention paid to certain of their works than to others. Adorno points out, for example, that in the US, Beethoven's fifth symphony and his seventh are frequently played and performances of the ninth attract a special reverence, but the fourth symphony, by comparison, is rarely heard. Moreover, the selection of 'great and revered' works reproduces itself in a circular manner. The most familiar piece is the most successful and is played again and again, which is what makes it even more familiar and therefore more successful. Adorno thus applies the same logic to the concert repertoire of middle-class-taste publics as he does to popular or mass art. The principle governing both is that of the recognition of the most familiar.

There is very little in musical culture to which this fetishism is not extended. Musical instruments themselves are fetishized in the special reverence shown towards famous manufacturers – the Stradivarius violin, the Bechstein grand piano – for example. Adorno describes a contemporary radio programme that was centred around comparing not performances or interpretations of works but the famous instruments with which the music was played. The fetishization of the instrument is all the more absurd, Adorno argues, because none but the very expert can truly discriminate between these types of instrument and differences in performance and style of playing have far more impact upon listeners. The fetishization of the 'instrument' extends to the human voice. Whether the voice is that of Caruso or Gigli or Pavarotti, it is appreciated for its voluminous sound and for being capable of reaching and sustaining very high notes. These are what Adorno refers to as 'the holy properties of the voice' (1991a: 32). The quality of musicianship of the singer using this voice is a more or less irrelevant consideration. In the case of singers, the stardom of the voice as instrument and the famous person who owns it are brought together in Hollywood biopics about singers who become famous and who then lose their voices only to regain them before the end, thus weaving the double fetish into the standardized schema of the predictable Hollywood movie.

The conductor of the orchestra had also become a fetishized figure in the modern world as had the leader of a band or jazz group. The celebrity of Toscanini, as the world-famous conductor of his day, was a frequent target for Adorno. The reverential attitude shown towards the 'maestro' was not explicable by reference to the quality of musicianship or to the beauty of interpretation in his performances. One should look to the market and to the exchange values that such 'maestros' command for an explanation of this reverential attitude towards the Toscaninis of this world. The consumer has made the value of what s/he consumes not by appreciating it but by the act of purchasing it:

> The consumer is really worshipping the money that he himself has paid for the ticket to the Toscanini concert. He has literally made the success that he reifies and accepts as an objective criterion, without recognizing himself in it. But he has not 'made' it by liking the concert, but rather by buying the ticket.
>
> (Adorno 1991a: 34)

This transfer of the use-value of commodities to their exchange value ensures that the consumer comes to worship the very commercial success to which s/he, as consumer, contributes.

The commodification and reification of music performance extends well beyond reputation to the musical reproduction itself. The actual role of the modern conductor, as the type of modern virtuoso, is, according to Adorno, analogous to that of the totalitarian Führer, 'Like the latter he reduces aura and organisation to a common denominator' (1991a: 39). It is important to recognize that Adorno's arguments about classical music performed in the modern concert hall are no different from those he uses in connection with dance-band music. The model that guides performance becomes that of the brilliant, smooth-running machinery in which all the individual parts are perfectly meshed and everything is presented as closed and completed form the very outset. Certainly, the principle that brings about the reification of the music, namely its reduction to an organization of isolated parts is also the principle which makes it sound most appealing and romantic to audiences responding to its climaxes, themes and repetitions. The law promulgated by Adorno here is that the more reified the music the more romantic it sounds and the more it can be appropriated – can become the 'property' of the listener. To whistle the theme from a movement of a Brahms symphony is to appropriate it. Adorno argues that the symphony as a totality can never be appropriated. Property is here equated with the destruction of integral totality, with the inability to respond to the movement of the whole.

The authority of the familiar is reflected, too, in the extensive resort to quotation, to the cutting and pasting of the cultural goods of the past into the latest format. In recent times, quotation and the concept of 'double-coding' has been been made central to some definitions of the 'post-modern'. In Umberto Eco's formulation, lovers who can no longer speak to each other about love in a world when all such speech has become cliché, can nevertheless continue to talk to each about love in the form 'as Barbara Cartland would say . . .'. Not only did Adorno clearly recognize the significance of quotation in modern 'pseudo-culture', but he offered a different explanation of its connection to modernity. The identity between culture and reality, an identity in which culture simulates the 'real' to the point of standing in for it and life imitates art, deprives culture of anything external as a source of material and throws it back on itself, on its past decayed constructions for its contents; culture becomes an arrangement of quotations.

While Adorno never denied that there was sensuous pleasure to be had from the (distractive) enjoyment of the familiar 'standards' of popular culture, he insisted that the pleasure is a limited one. It easily turns into disgust when it is repeated endlessly. Consumers spring this cycle for themselves because they continually demand the quick thrill of recognition and the culture industry obliges by producing the same familiar goods each and every time. When recognition palls, the same goods are still produced but with an alteration of distinctive features in order to rekindle interest and revive the appetite.

The psychology of self-abandon

Adorno dismisses the question of what psychological effects are produced upon the audience by the features of music or by the impressions made by hit songs. Since he is arguing that individuals no longer belong to themselves, it would be inconsistent to view them as being influenced. He resorts instead to perceiving this assent to 'debased cultural goods' as an act of abandonment or surrender to the compulsive force represented by the culture industry, thereby securing the comfort that comes with conformity and avoiding the pain inflicted by non-conformity:

. . . it suffices to remember how many sorrows he is spared who no longer thinks too many thoughts, how much more in accordance with reality a person behaves when he affirms the real is right, how much more capacity to use the machinery falls to the person who integrates himself with it uncomplainingly so that the correspondence between the listener's consciousness and the fetishized music would still remain comprehensible even if the former did not unequivocally reduce itself to the latter.

(Adorno 1991a: 40)

The compulsion of collective force is also represented by the convulsive movements of people dancing. Adorno likens the responses to music to the stylized ecstasies characteristic of 'savages' beating war drums and extends the metaphor to embrace the convulsive movements characteristic of St Vitus' dance sufferers. This image of people responding with reflex movements to a compulsive force is an oft-repeated formulation of Adorno's. It appears not only in his analysis of popular music and culture but also in his analysis of the music of Stravinsky, especially *The Rite of Spring* and *Le Soldat*. Adorno applies the reasoning to sport. A few enthusiasts for sport still pay lip service to the idea that it is a domain in which individuals are able to get away from purposiveness and instrumental action and thereby to experience freedom. Adorno insists that the contrary is the case. The so-called play of sport is actually a complulsive purposefulness that wipes out whatever traces of freedom there might once have been in it.

Serious art

In defence of modern popular music, some have pointed to its technical musical innovations. Adorno argues that all these claims are falsely based. Popular music, he insists, has contributed nothing of significance to harmonic and melodic construction. The apparently innovative colouristic interplay in modern popular music in which one instrument replaces another without a break or one instrument disguises itself as another had already been developed and utilized ('more effectively') in Wagnerian and post-Wagenerian orchestral technique. Syncopation itself, so central to jazz technique, was, claims Adorno, present in Brahms and greatly improved upon in music by Schoenberg and Stravinsky. These techniques, while central in popular music, are not improved upon there, argues Adorno; rather, they are 'conformistically dulled'. Adorno makes the point that a technique is not progressive simply because it is invented or used (1991a: 50). Whether an innovation is progressive or rational is a matter that can only be settled by considering its meaning and purpose in the larger social process. A technical innovation can be a fetish and used in a regressive way to inhibit progressive development. This is actually how Adorno claimed syncopation was used as a technique in jazz. While purporting to introduce a break with conformity it was in fact used to reinforce the underlying rigidity and conformity of response.

Modern music of the type Adorno espoused, the music of Schoenberg and the second Viennese school of composition, was universally unpopular. It was music that observed a severe aesthetic restraint. In the past, Adorno argued, asceticism might have been viewed as a reactionary opposition to all aesthetic pleasure. Today, it was nothing of the sort; asceticism was the sign of the most advanced art. Its strict exclusion of all ornament and of all 'culinary delights' was a blow struck for seriousness, that is, for the rejection of the consumption of 'particulars', of exciting rhythms, romantic melodies and so forth, when the idea of a work of art is only truly disclosed in the whole rather than in any of its isolated moments (1991a: 29).

Moreover, the music of Schoenberg, Berg and Webern was rejected, argued Adorno, not because they were incomprehensible to contemporary audiences but because they were all too well understood. Theirs was a music that gave form to anxiety, loneliness and suffering, and reminded people of the uncomfortable fact that in this antagonistic and cruel world they are spiritually homeless. These composers recorded the catastrophe of the over-whelming power of the rational-technical machinery of modern collective institutions and they did so through the resistant spirit and suffering of the subjectivity mutilated by it. They resisted the collective liquidation of the individual that was taking place everywhere in late capitalist society including modern music. It was only the individual, argued Adorno, who was capable of representing the claims of the social in these times of collective oppression (1991a: 52).

Two torn halves

In 'On the Fetish Character in Music', as elsewhere, Adorno insists on the complementary nature of developments in both serious and popular music. They are both manifestations of the alienation of modern music. They are not complementary in the sense that one fulfils the needs that the other cannot attend to or that one enriches the other. However, the social condition of music as a whole is registered in different ways in changes brought about in each of them. Moreover, their combined effect is, rather, to double the negative consequences and to undermine totally the role of the 'individual':

> The unity of the two spheres of music is thus that of an unresolved contradiction. They do not hang together in such a way that the lower could serve as a popular introduction to the higher, or that higher could renew its lost collective strength by borrowing from the lower. The whole cannot be put together by adding the separate halves, but in both there appear, however, distantly, the changes of

the whole, which only moves in contradiction. If the flight from the banal becomes definitive, if the marketability of the serious product shrinks to nothing, in consequence of its objective demands, then on the lower level, the effect of the standardization of successes means it is no longer possible to succeed in an old style, but only in imitation as such. Between incomprehensibility and inescapability, there is no third way; the situation has polarised itself into extremes that actually meet. There is no room between them for the 'individual' . . . the liquidation of the individual is the real signature of the new musical situation.

(Adorno 1991a: 31)

In 'The Schema of Mass Culture', Adorno's critique strikes some of its darkest notes. In responding to popular culture, the impossibility of a genuine experience of art is compensated by a dreadful imitative identification with the power that has overcome the subject in late capitalist society. Adorno does not accept that when people dance to jazz, for example, that they dance for sensuous pleasure or in order to obtain release. Rather, he argues, their dancing merely depicts the gesture of sensuous human beings; these gestures, empty of genuine experience, become allegorical representations of modes of behaviour in general. In jazz, and in popular culture, what are proffered to the people are 'culture-masks', themselves the rigid emblems of collective power and terror:

> When people dance to jazz, for example, they do not dance for sensuous pleasure or in order to obtain release. Rather, they merely depict the gestures of sensuous human beings, just as in a film individual allegorical gestures on their own represent modes of behaviour in general, and that is precisely the release. They fasten on the culture masks proffered to them and practise themselves the magic that is already worked upon them. They become a collective through an adaptation to an over-mastering arbitrary power. The terror for which the peoples of every land are being prepared glares ever more threateningly from the rigid features of these culture masks. . . . Participation in mass culture itself stands under the sign of terror.
>
> (Adorno and Horkheimer 1991: 82)

Duplication

Nor is any of this lessened by modernity's obsession with facticity, with the empirical, with the appearance of reality. In the film age, popular culture does not oppose reality but slavishly imitates it to the point of standing in for it. Reality does not remain unaffected by this process. It absorbs its own simulation as its model. It imitates art. The commercialization of culture causes the difference between practical life and culture to disappear altogether (Adorno and Horkheimer 1991: 53). Ideology permeates everything, seeping into the material goods produced for exchange. Packaging, labelling and above all advertising pervade the very material of the commodities we buy. In this way, Adorno argues, commodities come to absorb the aesthetic sheen that commercial advertising lends to them:

> Reality becomes its own ideology through the spell cast by its faithful duplication. This is how the technological veil and the myth of the positive is woven. If the real becomes an image insofar as in its particularity it becomes as equivalent to the whole as one Ford car is to all the others of the same range, then the image, on the other hand, turns into immediate reality.
>
> (Adorno and Horkheimer 1991: 55)

The reproduction of reality on film, for example, is often massively costly in money and materials. Behind the product itself is an impressive power. Adorno was concerned to point out that the appreciation of the goods of the culture industry was as much a response to the awesome degree of power deployed. The aesthetic duplication of reality excites a certain 'tremor' which is a response not to art as such but to the excess power which technology and the power of capital exerts over every individual thing. The hype for a film such as *The Ten Commandments* is designed to elicit the experience of awe and excitement in audiences by testifying to the considerable expenditure of resources, technology and material in reconstructing, for the film, the armies and palaces and migrating population in all their hugeness. The notion that the actual appearance of all this massive material is authentically duplicated becomes important to those caught in the snare of the culture industry. When Moses parts the waters or an entire people is shown leaving captivity in Egypt this same tremor is stimulated.

At least in the cinema we are still obliged to acknowledge a certain difference between image and reality in that we are sitting in a cinema and not in Egypt or Sinai. However, the power of duplicating reality can engender a confusion that takes on the proportion of a real sickness. The depths involved in this collapsing of the distance between art and reality were plumbed by Orson Welles's experimental radio drama, *Invasion from Mars*. The trick here was to dispense with the difference between drama and newscast. The result is now legend.

> The affair of Orson Welles' broadcast 'Invasion from Mars' was a test performed by the positivistic spirit to determine its own zone of influence and one which showed that the elimination of the distinction between image and reality has already advanced to the

point of a collective sickness, that the reduction of the work of art to empirical reason is already capable of turning into overt lunacy at any moment, a lunacy which the fans who send trousers to the Lone Ranger and saddles to his horse already half effect.

(Adorno and Horkheimer 1991: 56)

Technique and content

Adorno notes that technique in classical music consists in the compositional process, in the inner relations among the elements that constitute the work. Technique, in the case of the goods produced by the culture industry, shows itself in the modish finish and hard-edged glossiness of the technically produced goods, the films and records and glossy magazines, etc. The sheen that marks the perfectly calculated, manufactured cultural article stands in a certain contradiction with its contents. According to Adorno the contents of modern culture goods are old-fashioned, traditionally individual, decayed and romantic. Again, he attributes this apparent contradiction to the faithful duplication of reality, and the loss of difference between practical life and culture. With the liquidation of its opposition to empirical reality, art increasingly cannibalizes itself. Inasmuch as it now (*l'art pour l'art*) stands in for the reality out there, it tends to relate back to culture as its own object, to the remnants of what has already been produced in the past – hence the decayed romanticism. The mass culture that expends itself in the duplication of reality is left only with itself for material, with the icons, voices and fetishized existences that fill its material repertoire (1991: 56).

The cultivation of the traditionally individual in art is not a mark of its progressiveness, quite the contrary insists Adorno. The totality of relations that constitutes late capitalist society tends to the annihilation of the individual. A truly critical art would have to be able to capture the truth of this horror and force expression from it, thereby securing, in the expression of suffering, the survival and resistance of the subject. What passes for something critical in a popular film is nothing of the kind, he argues. Mass culture treats conflicts as subject matter but in fact it proceeds in its formation as a work without conflict. The insistence on representing reality becomes a technique for suspending any development of reality. Representation, in the inner cells of mass cultural goods, becomes stasis.

So-called critical works of the culture industry actually heighten the lie of individuality and defeat any such critical purpose as a consequence. Adorno cites the case of a radical film director who wishes to portray the darker aspect of a merger between two corporations. 'Even if the dominant figures are revealed as monstrous, their monstrousness would still be sanctioned as a quality of individual human beings that would obscure the monstrousness of the system whose servile functionaries they are' (Adorno and Horkheimer 1991: 57). The very imputing of individual autonomy and responsibility implicit in such false critique belies the character of the system that has already eradicated it. The culture industry can boast many examples of works that are critical of war, capitalism and authority. One can see that for Adorno, most of these examples would be dismissed as instances of 'pseudo-criticism' much as cultural goods and popular art are labelled pseudo-culture.

The thief of time

The cultural goods of late capitalist society are irredeemably degraded in their inmost cells. The schema of mass culture can be exemplified by the 'variety act', a popular form of mass entertainment in Adorno's time. Variety was an entertainment that was essentially episodic. The audience is not required to remember anything that has already taken place earlier but is held in a continuous present. Every variety act – and Adorno has in mind here especially the juggler and the clown – involves a kind of suspense, an expectation or promise of something to come, a finale, a climax. It subsequently transpires, however, that the event itself is the very waiting for the thing in question. It lasts for just as long as the juggler keeps the balls in the air and it is brought to a sudden end in a kind of frozen tableau accompanied by the stilling of the music and a drum roll. The trick of the variety act, claims Adorno, lies in this betrayal of the temporal order. It doesn't actually get anywhere. The audience discovers that what was initially imagined to be a preparation for something else turns out to be the thing itself. The suspension of development, of the temporal and historical is the very essence of 'variety'.

This static and continuous production through time of what does not develop in time, is what Adorno sees as the 'allegory' of high capitalism, the magical repetition of the industrial procedure itself. It is the same critical formula that Adorno applies throughout his critical analysis of modern culture and modern art both serious and popular. The variety act demonstrates the rigid domination of technical repetition, appropriating it as the freedom of play. 'The act, the performance becomes the model of mechanical repetition and thus absolves itself of its nugatory historicality' (Adorno and Horkheimer 1991: 61). This vision of modernity as technical control over the temporal, as the abolition of history, is key to Adorno's entire oeuvre. It ties together his critiques of modern serious music as well as jazz and it runs throughout his critique of modernity. Thus 'variety' is linked by him to Impressionism in art. Adorno claims that both represent a process in which the concept of industrial procedure is made visible, abstracted and emancipated from every end, as the pure domination of nature. 'The representation of living reality becomes a technique for suspending its development and thus comes to occupy that static realm which revealed the very essence of varieté' (1991: 62). Impressionism is also linked, elsewhere, by Adorno, to jazz.

Adorno's critique of the undermining of temporality in variety and in the works of the culture industry is also a springboard for his attack on the arguments of Benjamin concerning film. Consider the very different conclusions that Adorno draws concerning the flow of imagery that Benjamin had theorized in his ideas on distractive apperception:

> Simply by virtue of what it does to the original the technique of mechanical reproduction as such already betrays the aspect of resistancelessness. Whatever problems of psychological fate the film may present, through parading the events past the viewer on the screen the power of the oppositions involved and the possibility of freedom within them is denied and reduced to the abstract temporal relationship of before and after . . . insofar as the individual images are played past in an uninterrupted photographic series on the screen they have already become mere objects in advance. Subsumed as they are they pass us impotently by.
>
> (Adorno and Horkheimer 1991: 62)

He extends the critique to the dramatic technique of Brechtian theatre, which he identifies clearly with Benjamin's theorizing. Brecht's 'epic theatre' embraced many of the techniques of modern art, such as montage, specifically for the purpose of social critique and for provoking a materialist dialectic. Adorno accuses Brecht of having cancelled the dramatic dialectic itself in his work. Again, the issue for Adorno concerns the killing of temporality and historicity in the inner cells of the work of art (elsewhere he is able to speak positively about montage as a technique where the aesthetic use made of it is different).

> The montage effects which Brecht introduced into drama implies the almost complete interchangeability of time and the explicit captioning which refers to 'Life' and 'Rise', for example, in the titles of his plays seems to deprive the dramatic characters of action and transform them into experimental objects of a pre-determined thesis.
>
> (Adorno and Horkheimer 1991: 64)

Intra-temporal conflict, the dialectical emergence of consequents from antecedents that concentrates past and future in the present and, through integrating time, attains transcendence, is precisely what Adorno sees as killed in the dramatic technique of Brecht as surely as it is in the variety act or in impressionist painting or music. It is important not to associate Adorno with any desire to revive an art in which the integration of time, the production of temporality, in this positive sense is possible. He was certainly opposed to any such regression. However, the impossibility of a positive temporality of the kind that was constructed by Beethoven in his major symphonies, meant, for Adorno, that the absence of this temporality, or temporality as loss, as suffering, as pure negativity, had to be the very form and content of the modern work of resistant art. Adorno's ideal dramatist was Beckett, not Brecht. In plays such as *Waiting for Godot*, *End Game* and *Krapp's Last Tape* the destruction of temporality is experienced in precisely this negative way. The attempt to integrate time and to master the temporal element is abandoned altogether. Beckett allows the dreadful weight of time and history to bear down upon the consciousness of the audience not as a presence but as an absence, as the revelation of the temporal in and through its negation.

The commodification of so-called serious culture by the culture industry ensures, argues Adorno, that these works can no longer be experienced as such. What becomes important is that they be correctly handled by persons whose involvement is at the level of information about cultural goods. To be well informed is to possess cultural capital and an entitlement to the status of being a cultured individual. And central to being well informed is to know the market value of something, its importance and the powers of those who are staging it. Being informed about culture is knowing your way around the culture market, argues Adorno; cultural knowledge is thus akin to advertising material. Adorno points out that a performance of Beethoven's ninth symphony is accompanied by publicity which is not intended to assist the audience with understanding the work or improving the musical experience it has but with persuading the audience of the historical importance of what is about to take place and of their good fortune to be part of a unique and great occasion.

5

STAR POWER

And that inverted Bowl, you call The Sky,
Whereunder crawling coop't we live and die,
Lift not your hands to 'It' for help – for It
Rolls impotently on as Thou or I
(Rubáiyát of Omar Khayyám)

Among the pleasures enjoyed by millions is the daily horoscope produced in the astrology column of newspapers and magazines everywhere. Most people know which star sign they are born under, that they are Taurus or Virgo or Leo or Scorpio, etc. Many people actually have an idea about what personal qualities and characteristics they are supposed to possess as a result of being born under a particular star sign. It is not uncommon to hear a person say of himself, 'I am a typical Taurean, I guess, home-loving, dependable and a bit boring'. The person hearing such a remark will not, on that account, be likely to conclude that the speaker is a superstitious or irrational person. The statement may even appear to convey a measure of objective self-awareness; it has nothing of the bizarre about it, no irrational excess, and its common-sense plausibility makes it appear 'normal'. Nor are statements such as these usually delivered with the conviction of the zealot, the true believer. Those who read such columns do not, as a rule, claim to be either believers or disbelievers. Indeed the whole question of belief is suitably clouded by a widespread disinclination on the part of the public to enquire too closely into the astrologer's system of justification with its claims about the movements and courses of the planetary bodies and their relations to each other. Authoritative and matter-of-fact references to the aspect that Mars presents to Jupiter and so forth may reassure the reader of horoscopes that there is, after all, some 'logic' underpinning the claims made but that usually suffices without the individual feeling the need for further investigation. The advice offered sounds broadly realistic and is couched in terms that are vaguely suggestive of a lay science discourse. However, there are many regular readers who would claim that they read such columns purely as harmless entertainment or fun and that they do not really taken them seriously.

In his long essay, 'Stars Down to Earth' (Adorno 1994a), Adorno performed an impressive deconstruction of one such daily horoscope, the column 'Astrological Forecasts' by Carroll Righter in the *Los Angeles Times* (Nov. 1952–Feb. 1953). His analysis aimed at exposing the social pathology that sustains indulgence in this particular form of the irrational. What others dismissed as harmless fun, he viewed, along with other products of the culture industry, as toxic:

> . . . the attitudes which the culture industry calls forth are anything but harmless. If an astrologer urges his readers to drive carefully on a particular day, that certainly hurts no one; they will, however, be harmed indeed by the stupefaction which lies in the claim that advice which is valid every day and which is therefore idiotic, needs the approval of the stars.
>
> (Adorno 1991c: 91)

The astrology column reflected, in his view, a widespread social pathology that he identified as 'ego-weakness', 'dependency' and 'authoritarianism'. The source of his explanation is broadly based in both his Marxist and his Freudian perspectives. These were brought together in a creative way in his most famous study, undertaken with collaborators, of *The Authoritarian Personality* (Adorno *et al*. 1982).

Authoritarianism

The astrology column purports to represent authority, the authority of the stars; the latter are assumed to influence and shape events in daily life and to provide the individual with opportunities that s/he can take advantage of, provided only that s/he acts appropriately and in a timely fashion. If s/he does so, s/he can feel reassured that all will go well and difficulties or frustrations will be overcome.

The stars represent authority over the individual's life that is not susceptible to being influenced; nor is it accountable in any way for the power it exercises. In Adorno's analysis, the authority of the stars is simply a projection of the dependency and powerlessness experienced by individuals in the face of the real collective forces in society that control their daily lives and over which they, themselves, have no control. Authoritarian dependency is fostered wherever there is a significant disparity in power and a corresponding lack of mutuality in social relations. In Adorno's analysis a monopoly capitalism leaves the majority of individuals more or less powerless in the face of the administrative machineries that control their lives. This situation can reproduce itself in households where the disparity in power between parents and children can, for some social groups, give rise to an authoritarian pattern of socialization. The type of personality that is developed as a consequence exhibits a marked tendency to invest irrational or supernatural forces with the power of determination over daily life. A second characteristic concerns the handling of information. Information, ideas and beliefs can be experienced as acutely threatening if they challenge the 'party line' or threaten to place the individual on the wrong side of a feared authority.

The closed mind

People differ in the degree to which they are flexible and adaptive in their thinking, receptive to new ideas and open to influence by others. Some people appear to be dogmatic and closed-minded, asserting beliefs and clinging to them rather than holding them tentatively and being prepared to alter them in the face of evidence that refutes them. For such individuals, the injunction to 'face the facts' is seldom ever complied with. They organize their beliefs about the world with an opinionated assertiveness. They do not approach the world with the desire to find out about it or to look and to discover how things 'really' are. Rather, their world is already 'scripted' and their personal security is founded upon knowing in advance how things 'necessarily are' and in never exposing themselves to perceiving anything that would undermine their pre-formed beliefs. This can be the case whether the belief system in question is of positive or negative value. A set of rigidly held beliefs may be impressive, profound, even aesthetically beautiful, just as it may also constitute a thoroughly distorted vision of the world. What matters most is that the set has been pre-formed, is resistant to change and opaque to perceptual process.

If an individual's basic anxiety level is high, there will be pressure towards a distortion of perspective, of perception. Veridical perception brings such an individual face to face with what may potentially weaken and crush her and thus truthful perception itself heightens the anxiety from which s/he seeks relief. By distorting perception, the individual can represent the world to herself in such a way that it appears to be a less threatening and less insecure place. Among the numerous studies by contemporaries published in the wake of the Berkeley study on the *Authoritarian Personality*, Milton Rokeach's investigation of *The Open and Closed Mind* narrowed the focus to the belief systems of the individual (Rokeach 1960). He, too, identified authoritarianism (closed-mindedness) with the experience of power disparity and threat and with high levels of basic insecurity. In Rokeach's formulation, authoritarianism is not something that is only characteristic of a few individuals. Most of us become more authoritarian if we experience high levels of threat or insecurity. In those circumstances, Rokeach argues, we have a heightened need to defend against veridical perception and to distort reality. There are many forms that such distortion can take, depending upon the nature of the threat that is sensed. One result of such defensive perceptual distortion is the formation of rigid belief systems that are not subject to empirical disconfirmation.

The dominance of rigid ideological systems is certainly not new in human history. Perception and action are always mediated by ideas that go beyond what is immediately given. We do not perceive innocently, attending only to what is actually there. Reality is always 'framed' or 'latticed' with the results of past perceptions and ideas. The door remains a rectangle when it is opened because we respond to it in terms of the idea we have formed of its shape and not on the basis of our immediate perception of what is actually there. If we only attend to immediate sense impressions then the open door would be better described as trapezoidal. If we were not able to respond to phenomena in a mediated way, however, we would have no means of bringing the results of past experiences in a variety of situations to bear upon the solution of present problems. Mediation thus plays a vital part in healthy social formation. The important difference here, however, is between that mediation of experience which is autonomously developed through experience and which represents genuine knowledge and understanding and that type of mediation which consists in rigid beliefs that represent the imposition of an external authority and which are the antithesis of understanding.

If ideology has often been viewed 'negatively', that 'negative' has to be understood as a rejection not of the role of ideas and of systems of ideas in perception but of the rigidity and reification of ideas, their lack of susceptibility to change. Viewed negatively, ideology consists in all those systems of ideas that are rigid and more or less impervious to change or development. Viewed positively, ideology is made up of ideas that are mobile, flexible and subject to reorganization through the immanent pressure of one element upon another in continuous engagement with new conditions and problems in the world. It is the closing off of the elements of an ideology (or a work of art) both from the world and from its other elements that renders it an object of critique. The critique of ideology thus comes to centre as much on the relationship of an individual to his or her beliefs – to a consideration of the way in which beliefs are held or discarded – as it does on the contents of belief systems as such. The typically open-minded individual is not someone who does not hold beliefs but, rather, someone who holds them tentatively and for only as long as they appear to accord with the 'facts'. Such an individual is always prepared to modify or discard beliefs when, in encounters with reality, they are found wanting.

This is essentially the position that Adorno held both in his discussions of the art work in terms of part–part and part–whole relations and in his understanding of culture generally. It allowed him to overcome the apparent contradiction of insisting on continuous openness and susceptibility to change, while at the same time admiring the enduring integrity of works of art and of philosophical ideas. In pointing to the fact that Beethoven's fifth symphony is a vast elaboration of the material that appears in its opening measures, Adorno was proclaiming both that systems of relations undergo change and development and that it is only in and through such develop-

71

ments that such 'systems' are conserved. The principle of change with him was used to buttress the idea of 'symmetry', that is of 'invariant relations' under continuous transformation. If systems of ideas endure in a positive sense this is only insofar as they are 'organisms' that continuously develop. Systems of ideas that endure without an immanent organic development are 'mechanisms' that come under the category of 'repetition' and in Adorno's philosophy represent the pathic aspect of ideology.

The individual resorts to 'mechanism' and to 'repetition' when his actions no longer express or realize his life-process, when they have become disjoined from that life-process. Alienated from the subject, the individual's actions become subject to the control and organization imposed by an 'external' authority; they become 'heteronomous'. This point is at the heart of Marx's theory of alienation. Capitalist production secures, for the capitalist, the greatest degree of power over the labour process, ensuring that the product of labour, the process of labour and relations among workers all bear the wounds of expropriation; all become subject to an omnipresent mechanistic organization. The repressive nature of society is reflected not only in the so-called relations of production but also in a repressive psychodynamics, in the repression of 'nature', of 'drive' or 'instinct' within the individual. Freudian theory is centred on this notion of 'repression'; as a concept, it operates in certain respects in an analogous way to the concept of alienation. The instinctual drives of the individual – conceived of as biological (in a broadly somatic sense, sexual) energy – are alienated from themselves and deployed (repressively) against themselves both to prevent them from reaching 'consciousness' and to distort them by attaching them to activities and goals that serve society's requirements. The alienation of man from nature is thus realised in both the expropriation and exploitation of external nature through modern systems of production and in the repression and distortion of internal 'nature' that results from the psychodynamics inherent in the organization of modern society. The individual comes to view his actions and circumstances as authored and controlled by external powers upon whom he is dependent. His personal security is bound up with lining up with those powers and acting in accordance with their 'will'. Those powers are present locally in the guise of authority figures such as parents, bosses, political leaders and so forth. More remotely, those powers are present in the heavens above, in the gods and in the stars whose courses are held to influence or determine the fate of the individual in his or her smallest daily acts.

The Berkeley study

If academic popularity is measured by the citations a publication receives in other works as well as the numbers of other works that are written about it or which criticize it or develop arguments from it, then only one book in which Adorno figured as an author can claim to have been instantly academically popular. The study of the *Authoritarian Personality*, published in 1952, did achieve instant recognition. Within a dozen years there were more than one thousand articles and books published on the topic and summaries of the study appeared in standard social psychology textbooks everywhere. It was arguably one of the most impressive social-psychological investigations ever carried out. Impressive in scale and in method as well as being theoretically sophisticated, it was the product of collaboration in which his three co-authors were all academic psychologists. Unusually, for a study in which Adorno features as a major author, the researchers employed a battery of (positivistic) empirical research methods such as questionnaires, Likert-type attitude scales, the use of correlation coefficients, formally coded interviews, projective techniques and so forth. Adorno had often been contemptuous of such methods and the claims made on their behalf. On the other hand, it would be wrong to see this book as having little to do with him or his perspective. Its topic and findings are thoroughly Adornoan and its central thesis concerning authoritarianism underpins all his work on popular culture including his critiques of jazz and popular music as well as astrology. By the time Roger Brown had written his extensive summary of both the study and its critics, in 1964, for his own widely read textbook, the *Authoritarian Personality* had achieved canonical status.

The topic was timely in that the study took place in the aftermath of the Second World War. Its ostensible aim was to investigate the potential for Americans to be influenced by Fascist propaganda. The pathology studied by the authors was the same social pathology, together with its psychological correlates, that Adorno sought to expose throughout all his writings. The Berkeley study was clearly the most American product with which Adorno was associated but for all that it is one that serves as a powerful expression of certain key ideas that were clearly part of his European heritage. The political theme was very much to the fore, which is hardly surprising given the important contribution made to this work by émigrés from fascism in the immediate aftermath of the Second World War. The study sought to identify a type of personality held to possess a number of disparate traits – punitive attitude towards criminals, belief in supernatural forces determining one's fate, dislike of minority groups, superstitious beliefs, instrumental attitudes towards work, manipulative sexual relations, hostility to introspection, etc. Despite the disparate nature of the traits, they were all held to be psychologically coherent and to hang together as parts of a 'syndrome' with a definite logic and causation.

According to Freudian theory, children develop through a process of identification with parent figures where identification has to be seen (as was argued in Chapter 2) as the internalization of an organized structure of 'ego-ideals' – in Riesman's terms, the introjection of an 'internal gyroscope' – and, therefore, as the source of personal autonomy. Conditions can prevail, however, in which the exercise of parental power is arbitrary and, as a result, no such internalized responsible agency is developed in the child. This tends to happen, the authors argue, when the child is subjected to a discipline that is arbitrary in its exercise, and which is determined by the single consistency that any opposition, resistance or aggression towards parent figures or other authorities is severely punished. Hostile feelings towards parents and authority figures are 'natural' given the disparity in power and the unavoidable violation of the will of the child. If such feelings are not allowed constructive expression but are severely repressed, the personality can become overwhelmed by them.

The authors reasoned that the young child subjected to this type of authoritarian discipline fails to develop an internalized set of ego-ideals, a superego. Rather, what is internalized, as a system of control, is the punishing and rewarding aspects of parental behaviour. To know what attitudes s/he should hold, the authoritarian must identify those beliefs and ideals that enable him or her to line up best with authority, to 'identify with the aggressor' and thereby to escape the threat of harm from the aggressor. Submission and obedience to authority is the only way in which such a personality can achieve any sense of security. Such obedience does not mean, however, that the individual is no longer hostile to authority or that aggressive feelings towards authority have gone away. Hostile feelings have simply been repressed and are all the stronger for that. Moreover, the individual is thrown into an anxiety state if s/he ever comes close to recognizing these feelings and their real target. Introspection is feared by such a personality because it threatens to bring these repressed feelings into consciousness. The personality is riven by conflict in that it is packed with aggression towards authority figures and at the same time filled with an overwhelming anxiety that such figures might harm her.

The psychological problem is to find an outlet for these feelings that will not incur the punishment of authority. This is achieved, argue the authors, through the disguising of the real target of the hatred – authority itself – and through displacing those hostile feelings onto minority and subordinate groups that do not have the power to threaten the individual. This is the psychodynamics through which the authors seek to account for the projection of hostility onto 'out-groups', Jews, Puerto Ricans and all minority groups, as well as the hostility projected onto criminals or political 'undesirables'. At a sociological level, the authors identify those classes and groups that experience the sharpest degree of alienation and insecurity in the modern world, the mass labour force and the marginal social classes such as the lower middle classes in pre-war Germany, as more susceptible to all the ills of authoritarian dependency. The authoritarian personality is thus marked by a potent cocktail of hostility and basic insecurity and by the lack of that kind of secure interior agency that permits of healthy and meaningful interactions with others. In place of such healthy interactions, the personality displays instrumental and manipulative attitudes towards others at work as well as in intimate relations. Also, because of that same lack of an intern-ally coherent formation that would permit the individual to be self-reliant and responsible, the authoritarian personality has a tendency to view people's lives as governed by the power of external and supernatural forces, the stars being among them.

The sense of personal inadequacy and threat experienced by an individual is heightened when others hold expectations of that individual that run counter to his or her experienced weakness, expectations that s/he will be an assured, competent, strong individual and be capable of making a difference in the world. Not only does the authoritarian individual lack ego-strength and the accompanying feeling that he makes a difference but the demands made upon him to be assured, constructive and positive continuously reproach him with the fact that his inadequacy is something for which he can be personally blamed, and this, of itself, becomes a source of further anxiety against which he needs to erect even stronger defences. Still more anxiety stems from the subjective feelings – principally, anger and self-hatred – that are aroused in the individual by the violation of personal will that inheres in this situation. For the individual to express that anger, to strike out against the forces oppressing him, would only heighten the sense of powerlessness, not only because such action would be ineffective but because it would also be dangerous and possibly injurious to the individual if he actually succeeded in provoking those forces. Thus, in addition to the heightened sense of personal inadequacy – and guilt over personal inadequacy – such an individual also has to contend with feelings of anger, hostility and hatred that cannot be safely discharged against the forces that are provoking them and which, therefore, build within the individual as a reservoir of bad feeling.

This cocktail of suppressed fear, anxiety and anger was central to what Adorno saw as the pathology of modern times. All those disordered and distorted perceptions that psychoanalysis holds to be characteristic of neurotic and psychotic illness – paranoia, projection, reaction formation, displacement of hostility – were viewed by him as being present to some degree in ordinary life. The lines along which perceptual distortion occurs are rational enough. The individual threatened by the overwhelming forces of an external power can obtain relief through 'identifying with the aggressor', thereby removing himself from the threat of harm while at the same time gaining some sense that he shares vicariously in the aggressor's power. Such a defence also allows the individual to conceal from himself and from the aggressor the fact that the latter is the true object of his hostility and hatred. These distortions reduce the degree of anxiety associated with the perceived threat and the low level of basic security and ego-weakness that accompanies it.

Identification with the aggressor can take another form, however, as when the individual projects the monolithic power of the collective order onto the stars in their heavenly courses or onto hypostatized 'spirits' or 'supernatural' entities. By colluding with the stars in their courses, by picking up the signs and auguries, the individual can be assured of allaying the worst effects of their dominion over him. The mechanisms at work here are not treated as essentially different from the paranoid-delusional psychoses, although they are clearly of a different order, both of magnitude and consequence, and are more circumscribed in their effects. However, the individual is still left with the problem of undischarged hostility. A further perceptual distortion is required to deal with this. One element in this concerns the attribution of both responsibility and blame. If the source of the threat is not the impregnable power to which one is subject but a relatively powerless group, then the latter can be safely blamed. Furthermore, to act against such a group not only discharges the accumulated aggression but it provides the individual with relief from his guilt feelings concerning his personal adequacy, his sense of himself as under-powered.

'Stars Down to Earth'

Adorno's essay 'Stars Down to Earth' discovers the roots of the 'irrational' in a process of rational self-preservation that has 'run amuck'. Adorno uses the analogy of secondary social relations, in which people are not related, as they are in primary family and community groups, in a direct, face-to-face way but are related through their membership of organizations and working groups, etc. Those believing in astrology are related to others through their 'membership' in the 'system' of the stars in an equally alienated way (Adorno 1994a: 33–5). The star-sign system itself is treated in astrology columns as something objective and thing-like. Its mechanics are not divulged to the readers of the column and the latter are more or less uninvolved and uninterested in the justification of the system. Adorno interprets this remote impersonality as a projection of the individual's relationship to the social system which is independent of the individual's will and interest and yet which is his fate and the entity on which he is dependent. The fundamental experience to which the column is oriented is the experience of helplessness. The reader of the column is able to invest this helplessness with a higher dignity by acquiring knowledge and personal advice from reading the stars. In this identification with the controlling 'powers' the individual can have the sense of somehow sharing vicariously in their authority. At the same time, the idea that the stars offer advice if only one can read them correctly, helps to alleviate the fear of the inexorability of social processes. The advice offered to the reader is oriented towards practical and relatively trivial aspects of daily life. The emphasis is put on the rational means-end control of one's inner and outer behaviour as the only assurance of salvation. It is only by the scrupulous observation of the requirements of rationality in the conduct of one's daily life that one can successfully cope with the conflicting irrational conditions of the existent world. In this way the column shifts the concern of the subject from the questioning of means and irrational conditions to the business of making the best of them from the viewpoint of maximizing the individual's own private interests (Adorno 1994a: 42–3).

All this might appear to imply that reading the stars betokens a fatalistic philosophy on the part of the astrologically inclined. In Adorno's deconstruction, however, Astrology avoids fatalism. While it is true that there are outward forces acting upon the individual's decision, including his/her own personality and character, the decision that will actually secure happiness, success or whatever is his or hers alone. S/he is continuously exhorted to take decisions, often of the smallest or most inconsequential kind, decisions that are practically oriented to making the best of things – the best, that is, of what a given planetary situation permits. This type of freedom is what Adorno calls the freedom to adapt and conform. 'It is as though the sphere of the individual were completely severed from that of the 'world' or the cosmos. The slogan 'business as usual' is accepted as a kind of metaphysical maxim' (Adorno 1994a: 49).

Adorno points to the fictive reasonableness of astrology. Like the culture industry, it overemphasizes realism and cultivates a matter-of-fact practical normality. In this way it obliterates the dividing line between the normal and the irrational. This very reasonableness, however, allows delusional urges to break through the defences erected by the ego. Supposedly irrational and magical forebodings are translated into the advice of being sensible. The stars are invoked in order to reinforce the harmless, beneficial but trivial admonition: 'Drive carefully!' (Adorno 1994a: 54).

All this practical advice is directed more towards avoiding things or not doing certain harmful things and less towards direct positive actions with outcomes. Fate will in the end take care of the individual if s/he acts appropriately and makes the right decisions (1994a: 54). In this way the column identifies with the reader's situation of dependency and exhorts the reader to be confident that things will work out OK. Fate stands in here for the interdependent social forces that confront individuals and control their lives. The very same powers by which they are threatened will see to it that they survive. The anonymous totality will take care of them in the end. Thus these 'elevated' collective forces become the object of identification and this secures for the subject a certain alleviation of anxiety as long as they concede their impotence. Of course, this promise that everything will turn out OK in the end is contingent upon the readers being 'good boys or girls' (1994a: 56). The reader must behave according to given standards but there are spaces in all this for a suspension of strict conduct, spaces for relaxation and for pleasure which is deemed necessary to balanced and reasoned conduct through the relief it affords from drudgery and the outlet it provides for otherwise irresistible urges.

The continuous exhortation to behave and act in accordance with certain private and individual interests generates the impression that those problems that are truly objective, that derive from the economy and from objective circumstances, are all somehow solvable by private individual behaviour or by psychological insight into oneself and others. This is not confined to the advice tended by astrology columns. It is a characteristic of film, television and of radio and the culture industry generally to attribute both the cause and solution of objective problems to personal or private capacities:

> On the one hand, the objective forces beyond the range of individual psychology and individual behaviour are exempt from critique by being endowed with metaphysical dignity. On the other hand, one has nothing to fear from them if only one follows objective configurations through a process of adaptation.
>
> (Adorno 1994a: 58)

The column's endorsement of the relentless pressure to succeed presupposes that success is to be equated with the pursuit of activity that is narrowly focussed on the personal and particularistic interests of the individual concerned. He has to pursue his personal interest ruthlessly. Paradoxically, he has to pursue adjustment by non-adjustment, by focussing upon his own private and limited interest to the virtual exclusion of all else. A spontaneous individuality implies, by necessity, adjustment to others. The result is a structure that Adorno unpacks as follows: the individual pursues adjustment through a commitment to his own narrow self-interest which sets him apart from co-operation with others. He can only realize himself as a personality, however, through co-operation with others:

> It is this complex structure which provides the column with the opportunity to somehow find a common denominator for the contradictory requirements of being a personality and being, as it is called euphemistically, 'co-operative'. The fact that one of the contradictory requirements often fulfils the other unwittingly is skilfully exploited.
>
> (Adorno 1994a: 79)

This structure is facilitated by the appeal to individuality itself which discourages the association of individuality with a self-possessed potency, with intrinsic powers, and which promotes, instead, the identification of individuality with personal qualities such as 'magnetism' and 'charm'. Individuality proves itself in and through the individual's functioning in a group set-up in which, because of his personal qualities, he performs as well as others do. 'In short, individuality show itself in holding one's own in the stampede to adapt. The column is no charter for outsiders. It is the supporter of levelling, of conformity with the status quo' (1994a: 81). Addressing individuals as though they are members of teams and the continuous injunctions to talk things over with others reinforces the (self-alienating) sense the individual has that lining up with the opinions of others provides him or her with more reliable knowledge about himself and his difficulties than he can have from within. The situation Adorno is describing here accords with Riesman's thesis concerning the 'other-directed' man or woman. The idea of problem-solving that is associated with this is the corporate notion of holding meetings and taking majority decisions. This stress upon being understood as well as understanding others, is itself a reflection of social atomization. Social psychologists such as Festinger have hypostatized this need as a drive for 'consensual validation', for associating with others who can offer reassurance concerning one's ideas about oneself and one's obligations and values.

> Psychological self-reflection is transformed into a tool furthering adjustment. Meekness toward the more powerful seems to do less damage to so-called self-esteem if cloaked in the outcome of a higher insight either into oneself or into those whom one obeys.
>
> (Adorno 1994a: 97)

The schema of adaptation lurks behind the astrology column as it does behind the culture industry generally. The column speaks to the ideal of the average well-adjusted 'normal' citizen. It does not present its readers with anything other than the utterly familiar, with what they are accustomed to in their daily lives. If anything, it brings them reassuringly closer to this already familiar world. Adorno points out that the stars appear to be in complete agreement with the established ways of life and with the habits and institutions of the age. The effect of the column is to reproduce in its readers precisely that state of mind that is engendered daily in them by the status quo.

The fictive image of its average addressee that the column projects is of a person in his early thirties, who is imagined to be vigorous in his professional pursuits, prone to romance and given to seeking pleasure or having fun in ways that should be held in check. The image is also of someone who holds a superior position in life, which obliges them to take decisions all the time. A great deal hangs on their reasonableness and the care with which they take decisions, on their ability to be decisive, to make up their minds. This fictive image is the opposite of the real image that is presupposed in the advice offered by the column. The real addressee is presumed to be an unimportant and more or less powerless or impotent individual who is not in a position to take decisions or to affect the course of his own life or that of others. Adorno argues that the mode of address deliberately disguises the reality that is presupposed by flattering the reader with this fictive image.

'While he creates the addressee in the image of the big shot with some worries, he reckons with an average lower middle-class reader' (1994a: 63). Continuous advice is given to take some action, to behave like a successful go-getter. The exhortation has nothing to do with the individual's real ego power but calls upon him to identify himself with a socialised ego-ideal. 'He is led to interpret his actions as though he were strong and as though his activity would amount to something' (1994a: 63). This is possible because the activities over which the individual is supposed to exercise control and initiative are what Adorno terms pseudo-activity, namely the spurious and trivial activity that is more or less meaningless with regard to important or significant ends.

> It is intrinsic to the astrological pattern itself: one believes he has to obey some highly systematised orders without, however, any manifest connection between the system and himself. In astrology as in compulsive neurosis, one has to keep very strictly to some rule, command or advice without ever being able to say why. It is just this 'blindness' of obedience which appears to be fused with the overwhelming and frightening power of the command. Inasmuch as the stars are viewed in astrology as an intricate system of do's and don'ts, this system seems to be a projection of a compulsive system itself.
>
> (Adorno 1994a: 64)

The bi-phasic approach

The astrology column carefully divides its advice in ways that are temporally specific as between morning, on the one hand, and the afternoon and evening, on the other. Adorno makes this a major aspect of his deconstruction of the column. In a society which makes the most contradictory demands on individuals, dividing them between work and leisure, between home and work, between commitment and feeling and impersonality, the column has to ensure that these contradictory requirements of life can be handled in the advice given. The device is labelled by Adorno as the 'bi-phasic approach'. Quite simply the device ensures that advice given by the column is assigned to different periods of the day, chiefly AM or PM. In this way many of the contradictions can be handled. AM is clearly identified with work and responsibilities, with go-getting, the pursuit of success and so forth. PM is closely identified with leisure and with domestic and family life, with fun and enjoyment. The bi-phasic approach of the column utilizes the temporal distinction as a basis for the fundamental dichotomous compartmentaliz-ation of life that occurs in modern societies, principally between the domestic and the industrial or workplace cultures. Advice to people to work hard or to pursue success or advantage is made consistent with advice to be supportive and co-operative by the simple expedient of splitting·the two pieces of advice between AM and PM.

> By dichotomies of this kind a pseudo-solution of difficulties is achieved: either-or relationships are transformed into first-next relationships. Pleasure thus becomes the award of work, work the atonement for pleasure.
>
> (Adorno 1994a: 69)

Work itself had been undergoing a continuous transformation and had moved a long way from the model of autonomous activity associated with an entrepreneurial phase of capitalism. The integration of utilitarian operations was increasingly holding people within an operant machinery to which each individual was required to adapt. The column advises people to fulfil little and insignificant tasks, implicitly acknowledging that what is required of the individual is that s/he fits in and adapts, performing as a cog in the machine. AM is filled with admonitions to attend to one's chores, to work without indulgence in instinctual gratification (1994a: 72). Adorno also points to the column's reinforcement of the libidinization of work tasks which is inversely proportional to the importance of those tasks. In an age in which individuals rapidly turn themselves into the appendages of machines, into things, so this libidinization extends to gadgets which are invested with a human aura, the personalization of cars and tools of all kinds. There is a narcissism involved here in that the close humanization of the gadget is identified with the ego's control over nature and the feelings of omnipotence that it foreshadows.

Adorno subtly points to the contradictory admonitions to be modern and to be conservative. When the column advises the reader to be modern it seems almost imperative that he should buy modern equipment, particularly for his home – an advice affiliated with gadgeteering. When he is advised to be conservative, it means he should watch his finances and control his expenditures. The column thus has to bring off the trick of capitalism itself, namely that of fostering discipline and restraint in its productive workforce and encouraging the same individuals to indulge their appetites and to buy the goods they help to produce. Among the strongest principles that Adorno detects in the column is the priority given to the ego over the id, to rationality over indulgence. All relaxation and indulgence can be tolerated and encouraged but only if it serves the ulterior purpose of enhancing one's chances of success or of self-promotion. This is the case even where it is recommended as a means of getting away from pressing work routines. The advice is given on the strict understanding that this will help the individual to go back fresh to the same routines that he is seeking to escape.

In this way the column promotes both sales and sales resistance, a trick that is neatly pulled off by spreading the conflicting advice over different periods of time (1994a: 93). The bi-phasic approach makes this possible to the extent that to be modern is clearly identified with work and with AM while it is the family background that is conservative and PM.

> The family is relegated to leisure; in the bi-phasic organisation of the column it is mentioned almost exclusively with reference to PM; in the same sphere in which the addressee is advised to fix his home or to go out . . . the prevailing idea is that the family is still the only 'team' knitted together by so strong common interests that one can rely on each other with little reservations and somehow make joint plans in order to cope successfully with a threatening and potentially hostile world. The family is constructed as a kind of protective organisation built exclusively on the principle of give and take rather than as a spontaneous form of living together . . .
>
> (Adorno 1994a: 99)

Adorno notes that family background provides a model of belonging and of collectivization that can be reminiscent of closed societies. His identification of the family–work dichotomy with a conservative–modern polarity is entirely reflected in the more ideological formulations of modern sociologists such as Parsons in his analysis of family structure. The concept of family also performs a more traditional role of providing a kind of narcissistic reassurance concerning one's status as 'deserving' and one's entitlement to privileges or to influential positions. The family, too, can be seen as a means of coping with the threatening disappearance of free competitive activity. The time-shifting that occurs in the column is reflective of the condition of weak and dependent egos that project their failings onto an abstract time dimension, holding onto the hope that these failings will all be solved in a future that will somehow make up for or remedy the ills of the past.

6

SITUATING MUSIC SOCIALLY

Adorno's critique of jazz and of popular music generally is widely read and frequently criticized in abstraction from (and often in ignorance of) his more copious writings on so-called 'serious' music. This has inevitably distorted the reception accorded his arguments since the latter depend crucially upon his analysis of the social situation of modern music as a whole. For Adorno the characteristics of all varieties of modern music have been conditioned by the same social situation, whether the music is 'light' or 'serious'. Hence his insistence, in a letter to Walter Benjamin, that 'high' and 'low' represent an integral totality with respect to the alienated condition of art in the modern world. Accordingly, it is not really possible to make sense of Adorno's structural critique of popular music without considering it in the light of his attempt to theorize the social situation of all modern Western music.

The proof of this has been there from the outset in Adorno's major writings on music. His first major contribution to the sociology of music was a paper published in 1932 when he was not yet 30 years of age. It was entitled 'On the Social Situation of Music' (Adorno 1978: 128–64). In it he analysed contemporary developments in both the production and reproduction of serious music as well as the social situation of light music. The paper represents something of a *tour de force* in the development of his ideas; it introduces most of the themes that constituted the project of his later work over a period of four decades of writing. Here, in outline form, is the basic argument of Adorno's later book *The Philosophy of Modern Music* (Adorno 1980) in which he contrasted the Schoenberg school with Stravinsky and the neo-classical composers. In the same paper he outlines the musicological argument he was later to develop against jazz and against popular music, and he theorizes the integral relationship between 'serious' music and 'light' music (as two torn halves of an integral totality). Here, too, he lays out the basic argument that he was to develop a dozen years after this, with Horkheimer, in the *Dialectic of Enlightenment*, as the theory of the culture industry:

The techniques of radio and sound film, in the hands of powerful monopolies and in unlimited control over the total capitalistic propaganda machine, have taken possession of even the innermost cells of musical practices; that is, of domestic music making . . . through the total absorption of both musical production and consumption by the capitalistic process, the alienation of music from man has become complete.

(Adorno 1978: 129)

However, in the papers on popular culture, notwithstanding frequent reference to Beethoven as his major exemplar of serious music and to a Marxist treatment of commodity production, Adorno takes much for granted about the reader's familiarity with both musicology and Marxism as well as Freudian psychodynamics. The highly developed Marxist perspectives on culture that were deployed by Adorno and his contemporaries owed a great deal to the brilliant theoretical work of Georg Lukács (Lukács 1971). In Adorno's own writings on popular culture, however, much is left implicit, especially with respect to the precise links (derivations or elective affinities?) between his structuration arguments with respect to music and a Marxist model of structuration in commodity production. Part of this may be due to the fact that the writings on popular culture belong largely to Adorno's years of exile in the USA. A certain restraint was definitely practised by Adorno and his colleagues at the time. The broad-brush references to the model are clear enough but it is in the (implicit) working out of an isomorphism between monopoly capitalism and music at the level of structural relations that gives Adorno's theoretic concerning popular music its sociological weight.

Alienation at every level of existence is the fate of the individual in capitalist society, according to Marxist analysis. The system of social production alienates the worker, destroying all organic connectedness and inner-directed initiative, subordinating all his action to mechanical operations. The market relations involving commodities and consumers complete this process. Everything is subordinated to and conditioned by the exchange of commodities in the market, including the exchange of abstract labour power. Music, as a social praxis, is part of social praxis, generally, and reflects its conditions. Just as organic relations among members of communities engaged in production decay with the advent of capitalism so, too, do the organic relations among elements in musical process and structuration.

In any expressive process the elements of the process would be open to each other, would push each other, change each other. Consequents would emerge from antecedents and would themselves be antecedents of further consequents. However, when such a dialectical and historical process is brought to a halt by the alienation of modern music, there is then a change in the inner cells of music, in music's internal relations. The elements become monads chained together by external design and calculation for the production of predetermined effects. Instead of the subject expressing herself through music, s/he becomes the recipient of the calculated effects that are worked upon her. Dependency and authoritarian submissiveness is built into the respondent's relationship to music and to all the products of the culture industries as surely as they are built into the consumer's relationship to commodities generally. Thus, for Adorno, the part–part and part–whole relations in music reflect directly the social condition of the individual in the world. When the elements of music lose their historicity, when they cease to interact together such that they change each other in a continuing process linking antecedents to consequents, then music can no longer be seen as a vehicle for the self-expression of the subject but becomes, instead, a machinery for generating effects that impact upon the subject. To the extent that these effects are desired and sought after, the relationship of the subject to commodities produced by the culture industry is a fetishistic one characterized by 'dependency' and 'authoritarian submissiveness'.

If alienation from man describes the condition of music in the modern world, the tasks facing serious music, and all serious culture, in Adorno's view, is both to reflect the truth of this condition and to use that reflection as a vehicle for the self-expression of the subject. If art is to be seen as a mode of knowing or understanding – and for Adorno this is certainly the case – it is not to be viewed as type of passive reception, a staring in horror at the world. The very condition of the world is known in and through actively resisting it. For art to become a repository of truth, that is of true knowledge, two things are necessary: it must reflect, at the level of its internal relations, the formal and technical development of social relations generally; it must also strike from those very relations an expression of the life-process that is distorted and mutilated by them. The language of art in the modern world becomes, for Adorno, a language of suffering 'music overcomes inward alienation only through the perfected expression thereof on its exterior' (Adorno 1978: 146). Thus the very alienation of music from man that annihilates expression is appropriated by the subject as a vehicle of expression and it is this appropriation which fuels the very resistance through which the human condition is truthfully comprehended.

This homology between social formation in the wider social sense and the aesthetic formation of works of art is a key assumption of all Adorno's writings on culture, including this early paper on the social situation of music. Objectification and rationalization in social processes, generally, had their counterpart in the thoroughgoing rationalization and objectification of modern music. The modern artist, as heir to the domain of subjectivity and sensibility, found himself exiled from a society in which the rationality and instrumentalization of social relations had effectively separated him from any meaningful relationship to the praxis of everyday life. The condition of a subjectivity overwhelmed by the development of rational-technical forces lead to a thoroughgoing rationalization of the musical material inherited by the artist.

Works of art in post-Renaissance Europe have been produced, typically by a single individual – the artist, musician writer or poet – rather than by a number of individuals working together. Nevertheless, works of art, even when made by an individual apparently working alone, are socially produced in two senses. The immediate producer of a work of art is really a participant in an 'artworld' that links a variety of actors in social processes from which such works are developed (Becker 1982; Baxandall 1988). Patrons, audiences, distribution agencies, markets and so forth all enter into the production of art works. Secondly, the social nature of the work of art inheres in its project, in the 'idea' it develops both in the formation of its material and in the explicit content of what is formed. It was certainly Adorno's position that aesthetic formation is an integral part of social action and that it participates in the character and development of social action generally. There is thus a direct link between the development of social relations in society, together with the development of the technical forces of social production, and the formative and compositional process in respect of works of art – that is, the technical development of the artwork. Social formation thus appears in the inner cells of a work of art, especially their part–whole relations, not as some mysterious parallel but as a thoroughly mediated process. In the being of the artist, the two spheres are united; working with aesthetic material that has been formed in the past (with the kinetic forces of past subjectivity), the artist seeks to develop that material in response to its inherent historical project but in a way that is conditioned by the need for the material to make sense of lived experience in the modern world. Thus, Schoenberg, as a twentieth-century composer, worked with aesthetic material bequeathed by Beethoven, Brahms and Wagner and sought to develop that material. His solutions to the aesthetic problems posed by the material are also responses to questions posed in the light of modern social conditions.

The social situation of music

The development of serious modern music of the type that Adorno himself composed was appreciated only by a minority of individuals – an intellectual elite. It was heavily criticized for its darkness, its intellectual coldness, its unpleasant dissonances and its lack of sensuous warmth. The composer is blamed for this as though the condition of music is something brought about by the composer alone; as though, that is, difficult modern music is the product of the 'perverse' will of the individuals who compose the music (Adorno 1978: 129). To claim that such music was advanced, progressive, and that it was high in truth-value (claims that Adorno frequently made and believed to be proven) was largely unacceptable to the majority of his contemporaries. Adorno insists from the start that the alienation of modern music from modern society has its origins not in the caprice or will of individual composers but in the alienated condition of modern capitalist social relations at the level of both production and consumption. It is important for him to establish that alienation cannot be overcome on the side of music alone. Any effort to produce within music or art, generally, a consciousness that is not alienated, that is somehow close to nature and to community, would be false because no such state can even be truthfully imagined independently of the social conditions necessary to bring it about; it would remain as unrealizable as any fantasy wish-fulfilment. The overcoming of the alienation of music can only be achieved through an overcoming of alienation in society (Adorno 1978: 130).

However, the fact that modern music is alienated from society does not mean that there is no such thing as modern music that is possessed of truth-value, quite the contrary. Adorno insists that for modern music to meet its responsibilities to society in an alienated world and to remain high in truth-value, it must take alienation into the inner cells of the work of art where it is transmuted into the coded language through which the subject expresses the suffering of a life disfigured by it. Adorno insists that the task of music is not to comment on society, not to tell a story about or to reflect on society as a content. Social conditions and problems present themselves immanently in the formal structuration of music as material. It is in diligently addressing the problems of structuration of music, in thinking in a formal and technical way about the development of music, that the composer effectively addresses problems originating in society and the social condition.

> . . . music is able to do nothing but portray within its own structure the social antinomies which are also responsible for its own isolation. Music will be better, the more deeply it is able to express – in the antinomies of its own formal language – the exigency of the social condition and to call for change through the coded language of suffering. It is not for music to stare in helpless horror at society. It fulfills its social function more precisely when it presents social problems through its own material and according to its own formal laws – problems which music contains within itself in the innermost cells of its technique.
>
> (Adorno 1978: 129)

The modern work of art that is high in truth-value for Adorno is one that perfects the expression of alienation on its outside and which, through this expressive negation, attains to a true understanding of the social condition, thereby banishing alienation and all illusion from its inside. If modern serious music is filled with shock and dissonance it is because music of this kind is the only music equal to the condition of the subject in late capitalist society – equal, that is, to the task of understanding that condition. Thus

87

Adorno assigns to music a parallel role to that of social theory. It is inherently critical and related dialectically to praxis. In the modern age, Adorno sees advanced musical composition as an assault on bourgeois categories such as the creative personality and the expression of the soul of this personality, the world of private feelings and its transfigured inwardness. All of these are invalidated and replaced in modern advanced music by 'highly rational and transparent principles of construction' (Adorno 1978: 131).

Bourgeois opinion was resolutely opposed to this development which was itself a product of the advanced technical rationality of bourgeois social relations. In effect, bourgeois society has always clung to the myths of individual autonomy, freedom and initiative and of the selfhood and inwardness claimed for the heroic individual of early capitalism. The ground for these claims was cut away with the development of the monopoly phase of late capitalism. The role of the ideology of individualism, which played a constructive role in the formation of bourgeois society, now came to serve the reactionary purpose of concealing from the members of that society the true facts of their social condition. The music of the Schoenberg school was hated because it stripped away this illusion and presented a modernity that appeared stark, abandoned and emptied of the spiritual substance of bourgeois mythology.

> Schoenberg has annulled the expressive music of the private bourgeois individual, pursuing – as it were – its own consequences, and put in its place a different music, into whose music no social function falls – indeed, which even severs the last communication with the listener. However this music leaves all other music of the age far behind in terms of immanently musical quality and dialectical clarification of its material. He thus offers such a perfected and rational total organization that it cannot possibly be compatible with the present social constitution, which then unconsciously, through all its critical representatives take up an offensive position and calls upon nature for assistance against the attack on consciousness encountered in Schoenberg.
>
> (Adorno 1978: 134)

The lack of popularity of the music of Schoenberg was closely associated, according to Adorno, with the fact that it was high in truth-value. There were other instances of altogether more popular composers of so-called serious music; their very popularity was seen by Adorno as marking the lack of truth-value in their music. The late Romantic music of composers like Rachmaninov, Tchaikovsky and Sibelius perpetuated the decayed contents of bourgeois ideology, conjuring the appearance of spiritual values, inwardness and heroic individualism that had been all but extinguished by modern social conditions. The music itself bore all the scars of this. It was only able to present the outer appearance of these qualities, their showy exteriors. It was music that cultivated large motives and themes, expressive details that it hammered it out in large repetitions. It was not able to bring off an integral totality in which all these details were subordinated to a developing whole, something Adorno insisted that Beethoven's music achieved in its day. The richness of expressive detail in late Romantic music was counteracted by the structural poverty of the music. This brought it, in Adorno's musicological analysis, into the orbit of the products of the culture industry. While such music purported to be serious and formed part of the concert repertoire, it was essentially similar in character, in the way it worked and in its impact, to mass cultural music. Like mass cultural music it perpetuated the same bourgeois myths about the individual and transfigured inwardness and it clung to the same musical means, the remnants of the diatonic system of tonal music, which Adorno saw as a mode of structuration—a musical formation – lacking in truth-value. Like mass cultural music, the music of the late Romantics was music that oriented itself to the demands of the market, it was commodified music.

Much of Adorno's polemic against varieties of modern music that he sees as lacking in truth-value – or music that colludes (unwittingly) with socially oppressive or socially reactionary forces – is directed against the music of Igor Stravinsky. It is Stravinsky (and behind him the neo-classical school of composition that included composers such as Hindemith) that provides Adorno with the dialectical polar opposition to set against Schoenberg. It would be a mistake here as elsewhere to treat Adorno as making a judgement of musical taste. His is a theory that concerns the functioning of music in relation to society and in that sense his personal tastes are not really the point at issue. It would equally be a mistake to imagine that Adorno did not respect or admire the musicianship of composers such as Stravinsky. Adorno's late essay on Stravinsky should convince one of the falseness of such a point of view (Adorno 1992: 145–78) and his recognition of Stravinsky's technical accomplishments appears even in the early papers. One finds Adorno, on occasion, using words like 'magician' and 'conjurer' to capture Stravinsky's technical skill (Adorno 1980).

Nevertheless, technical accomplishment *per se* is never the issue with Adorno. Stravinsky's skills are used to develop a type of music that is both peculiarly modern and, in Adorno's analysis, anti-subject. His is music that recognizes the fact of alienation as the isolation of music in the modern world. Adorno accords respect to Stravinsky (who he differentiates from, and views as superior to, his followers), because of the latter's negativity, the critical orientation he developed in respect of the alienation of modern music. However, Stravinsky's musical handling of the problem of alienation is quite different from Schoenberg's (as theorized by Adorno). Alienation is viewed by Stravinsky as a product of the excesses of 'individualism'. The isolation of the individual from the community and of music from society had to be raised to the level of consciousness in music so that it could be overcome and so that a music more suited to the natural and bodily constitution of man and of his social being as a part of community could be brought about (Adorno 1980). When music is stripped of intentionality, of all those expressive residues and of the subjective individuation that is responsible for its alienation then it can become a pure music crafted to produce objective musical effects. Purified of subjective expression, of intentionality and freed of alienation, such music can evoke the experience of non-alienated life, of life in which individual and community are one. Adorno rejects any such attempt to cope with the problem of the alienated condition of modern music. He identifies, as the principle flaw, the fact that the neo-classical composers seek to eradicate alienation within music 'in aesthetic and form-immanent terms' (Adorno 1978: 132–3) without relating musically in any way to the problem of change at the level of social relations. In short, these composers seek to banish alienation in and through music alone.

How did these composers hope to purify modern music, which, in its forms and techniques, bears the imprint of the intentionality and individuality that has congealed in it? The solution chosen was to resort to the models provided by an earlier music that antedated the division of labour and the development of industrial society. Neo-classical music resorts to stylistic forms drawn from the past and which it views as immune to individualism and alienation. The resort to pre-bourgeois musical forms is held to be necessary in order to affirm some supposedly natural state of music that can be applied to modern musical material. This accounts, too, for the resort to dance forms which are held to be somehow above historical change and accessible to every age.

Adorno insists against Stravinsky and the neo-classical movement, that it is quite impossible to reconstitute what belongs to an earlier time within a completely changed society and through completely changed musical material. Stravinsky's project is clearly distinguished by Adorno from a 'Romantic stylistic history' which dreams of restoring some past style to its former glory. Stravinsky's music does not aim at a revival of some older pre-bourgeois music. His resort to pre-bourgeois musical models does not lead him to seek to turn the clock back. Rather, the object appears to be to apply these supposedly eternal or pure models to modern material that he and the neo-classical composers have gleaned form the Schoenberg revolution.

> The ideal of musical objectivism is the formation of a highly differentiated material, manifesting all the signs of the division of labor, but doing so in a static naturalistic manner pre-dating the division of labor.
>
> (Adorno 1978: 139)

The project involved in Stravinsky's music is actually likened by Adorno (this is prior to Hitler's ascendancy to power) to the fascist project, to 'estate corporatism'. It appears, argues Adorno, that the sovereign composer stands in free control of the supposed musical organism, in much the same way as in fascism a leadership elite appears to be in control while in truth real power over the social organism lies in the hands of monopoly capitalism. While Adorno holds only tentatively to the fascist analogy, he is certain of the role of neo-classical music in diverting attention from real social conditions:

> All objectivist music has the intention of diverting attention from social conditions. It attempts to make the individual believe he's not lonely but, rather, close to all others in a relationship portrayed to him by music without defining its own social function; it attempts to show the totality as a meaningful organization which fulfills individual destiny positively merely through its transformation into the aural medium.
>
> (Adorno 1978: 144)

Adorno presses to the limit the contrast between Schoenberg and Stravinsky and makes it his model of the fault line in respect of all modern music. There are two possibilities open to the musician here. S/he can refuse to submit to the commodification process and as a consequence be exiled to a hermetically sealed world that has been emptied of its contents and of all social responsibility. Adorno saw this as the fate of the music of the Schoenberg school and of all modern music high in truth-value. Or s/he can submit to the commodification of life and can find conditions for being included by skilfully fulfilling an ideological role in support of the collective force of capital. This was the fate of all effect-music that abandoned the subject and made of the individual an object of manipulation.

This leads Adorno into a straightforward opposition between music that accepts the demands of the market, unconditionally recognizing its commodity character, and that which does not accept the demands of the market. However, Adorno is careful not to reduce this question of the market nature of the music as a basis for a simple division between light and serious music. That distinction, though relevant, is not adequate to capture the dichotomy he has in mind. A great deal of so-called serious music is as much oriented to the demands of the market as is popular music. Stravinsky's popularity is attributed to this.

> An effort is made to exempt 'serious' music from an alienation shared to an equal degree by Stravinsky's *Symphony of Psalms* and the latest hit song of Robert Stolz. . . . For this reason, the distinction between light and serious music is to be replaced by a different distinction which views both halves of the musical globe equally

from the perspective of alienation: namely, as halves of a totality which to be sure could never be reconstructed through the addition of the two halves.

(Adorno 1978: 132)

Adorno's insistence on the manipulative market-dominated character of a great deal of modern music, including so-called serious music, did not mean that he believed such music did not orient itself to real needs. The need for music is real enough and, he argues, it is made all the greater by modern society which continuously frustrates the desires it stimulates, impeding their real-world satisfaction. Faced with this, the individual seeks, all the more fiercely, a substitute in musical culture for the satisfaction s/he is denied in reality. Such satisfaction can only be provided by a music that lines up with the bourgeois tendency to flee from all genuine social reality and to project upon the world contents that it never possessed. By providing this kind of escapist projection and encouraging audiences to cling to the decayed contents of a defunct bourgeois Romanticism, music meets the ideological aim of offering emotional gratification in and through a process of avoiding all change. This argument which appears in the 1932 paper is at the very heart of the later thesis about the culture industry.

Vulgar music

Music in the past may have had a folk tradition to draw on but that is no longer the case. There are no longer any 'folk', insists Adorno. The bourgeois process of rationalization has subordinated all society to bourgeois categories. According to Adorno, the material of vulgar music is 'the obsolete or depraved material of art music' (Adorno 1978: 161). Because this music stands below the level of what belongs to the realm of education and to representation – because it is mere entertainment – it is looked upon as being harmless and as a source of pleasure and relaxation. Equally, as music and art lacking in seriousness, it is also considered unworthy of serious criticism. The most important factor in bringing this about is the changed mode of production of light music, its subsumption, as a kind of 'handicraft', within the industrial process. In a passage that clearly prototypes the argument of the *Dialectic of Enlightenment*, which appeared more than a decade later, Adorno says:

It is the decisive factor in the history of recent vulgar music that the definitive break, the sacrifice of its relationship to independent production, the growing vacuity and banalization of light music corresponds exactly to the industrialization of production. . . . The industrial development of light music annulled the last aesthetic responsibility and transformed light music into a market article.

(Adorno 1978: 161)

This mass-produced music draws upon the decayed contents of past art music not only for its melodies and hits but for its techniques. Already in the 1932 paper Adorno singles out jazz for special treatment, identifying and disparaging its claims to be more than light music or to have discovered techniques that were not previously invented by classical composers and used by them to 'better' effect. The centrality of his concern with jazz becomes apparent in the backing up of his general claims by a musicological analysis, clearly a preparation for the 1936 paper 'Uber Jazz'. The arguments concerning the conditions of success in light music are thus applied as much to jazz as they are to popular music generally. In order to dominate the market, a 'hit' tune has to marry its standardized banality to some sort of attention-grabbing individual quality, something that makes it appear to be different or unique – a 'cute' rhythm, motive or ornament – when in reality it is nothing of the kind. In the case of film music, however, it does not even have to do that:

> The totally rationalized factories of sound film hits with their capitalist division of labor are excused from such efforts. No matter how their products looks and sound they are 'successes'; listeners are forced to sing them to themselves, not only because the most finely tooled machinery hammers them into them, but above all because the monopoly of the sound film prevents all other musical commodities – from which they might choose something else, from reaching them.
> (Adorno 1978: 161)

There is no doubting that Adorno's polemic drives his argument towards a dialectical polarization at the expense of musical variety. In a Marxist fashion he does recognize intermediate cases and other musical claims – for example he approves of Kurt Weill's musical experimentation with Brecht and of Bartok's folklore idiom – but these remain quite secondary to the overall polarization of modern music which is what he views as dialectically decisive.

Music reproduction

Adorno uses the 1932 paper to set out the elements of his theory of music reproduction and music consumption. The alienation of music from society is reflected in the antinomies of musical reproduction. Given that Adorno sees the work of art itself as a coded script, the meanings of which are not fixed in eternity but change over time in encounters with the historically changing conditions of the work's reception, it is clear that the reproduction of the work is a key factor in mediating between the work *per se* and the consciousness of its audience. Reproduction has somehow to be true to the work itself while bridging the gap between the work and the consciousness of the listener for whom the work must be intelligible in a world that is quite different from the one in which the work was made. Reproduction is thus concerned neither with the eternal work *per se* nor with a listener dependent upon constant natural conditions.

> Not only is the consciousness of the audience dependent upon the change in social conditions and not only is the consciousness of those involved in reproduction dependent upon the state of the total musical constitution of society at a given time, the works themselves and their history change within such constitution. Their text is merely a coded script which does not guarantee unequivocal meaning and within which changing thematic contents appear, along with the development of the music dialectic, which in turn encompasses social impulses. The change within works themselves is portrayed in reproduction.
>
> (Adorno 1978: 146)

Looking back at the conditions of pre-capitalist musical production dominated by the tradition of the music guilds, Adorno argued that there was then a more or less stable relationship between the works and their public in which the consciousness of those producing and those receiving were very much attuned. There was no sharp division between production, reproduction and improvisation. The boundaries and strictures that have been placed on music reproduction are of relatively recent origin. A modern can be startled by the seeming casualness of no less a composer than Carl Philipp Emanuel Bach when he advises musicians reproducing his work not to bother playing a particular passage if they find they do not like it or to play it over again if they find they do. Adorno points out that interpretive freedom was the rule in Beethoven's day and for Beethoven himself. He makes the important point that what a later period came to regard as the inherent structural logic of a particular work is something that may not have occurred to audiences at the time nor, necessarily, to the composer himself. We should see it as a product of the later experience that audiences and interpreters living under changed conditions have had with the work.

> If an early Beethoven piano sonata were to be played today as 'freely', with such arbitrarily improvisational changes – changes of the basic tempi of individual movements – as it was – according to contemporary reports – by Beethoven himself at the piano, the apparently authentic manner of interpretation would strike the listener as contradictory to the meaning of the work in the face of the constructive unity of such movements. This unity has become clear only today and largely through the efforts of later production in music.
>
> (Adorno 1978: 149)

In the course of the nineteenth century, with the rise of bourgeois individualism, the conditions for production and reproduction clearly changed. Nevertheless, the bourgeois conductors reproducing a work could still rely on a certain alignment of consciousness between themselves as interpreters or reproducers, the producers and audiences. *Interpreters* such as Franz Liszt could still fall back on the notion of being the interpretive personality in which the demands of being true to the work and those of making the work intelligible to its audience, mediate each other. They were able to do this because interpreter and author were both bourgeois individuals and both perfected the expression of bourgeois individuality for an audience equally constituted in terms of bourgeois individuality. In the celebration of the virtuoso, the interpretive personality, the conductor, the nineteenth-century bourgeois society celebrated itself.

In the twentieth century, with the advent of monopoly capitalism, no such alignment between producer, interpreter and audience could be relied upon. Increasingly, the work of serious artists parted company with the consciousness of audiences and the task of mediating between the demands of audiences and those of the producers of the works became a more or less impossible one to bring off. The result was the advent of a sharp polarization or bifurcation sending musical reproduction off in two opposite directions. Adorno argues that the history of musical reproduction in the twentieth century destroyed reproductive freedom. It meant that the interpreter either had to pursue a strict realization or decoding of the 'exact language of musical signs' (Adorno 1978: 147) or he had to adjust to the demands that society, as market forces, made upon him and sacrifice the configuration of the work itself. The development of monopoly capitalism upset the nineteenth-century balance between individualistic production and individualistic society.

For serious avant-garde artists, resistance to the pressures of the market became so decisive in the early decades of the twentieth century that it brought into being a music that asserted its independence of the market through demanding the total subordination of the interpreter – 'the interpreter becomes the executor of the unequivocal will of the author' (Adorno 1978: 148).

Modern reproduction in the music of the Schoenberg school constitutes a thoroughgoing rationalization of music that accords with the rationalization of economic life to which it is a response. However, this does not mean that the capitalist classes approve of such music. Bourgeois society equates the 'spiritual' with the private individual. Thus technical rationalization of music that gives rise, ultimately, to its autonomy status, its separation from society, is feared as de-spiritualization. True reproduction brings the overwhelming and shocking forces of atomized life into the work of art. Consumer consciousness, wishing to protect itself from the force of true reproduction, from the realization of its true condition, seeks instead to secure a type of music-making, the major function of which is to conceal reality through a cocktail of dreams, intoxication and inward contemplation. Through such reproduction the bourgeoisie are offered, in aesthetic images, the very satisfaction of drives that are denied to them in reality. Throughout Adorno's writings on music this is a recurrent preoccupation. Intoxication was what Wagner offered his audiences – Stravinsky, too. It is what the culture industry offers. To a committed Marxist, all such wish fulfillment and intoxication kept the individual from waking up to face the real world. How can one experience, through music, the shocks that constitute genuine suffering, when one is immersed in a well of despondency that has been sweetened with romantic music.

> In relentlessly pursuing to the limit, the technical rationalization of the work of art, the music of Schoenberg threatens to hold up to bourgeois society an image of its own spiritual bankruptcy. The bourgeois thus defends against what he perceives to be the despiritualization of art and the extinction of the individual. He seeks to preserve and reinforce the ideal of the bourgeois independent private person in an age of monopoly that has extinguished such persons and undermined the basis of all the associated claims concerning spiritualization, inwardness and so forth.
>
> (Adorno 1978: 149)

The majority of the music played in the concert halls of the world is still the five or six hundred works making up the classical canon. The interpretive personality in the modern age – the 'great conductor' – was a figure about whom Adorno made many disparaging judgements. S/he had to fill two functions, both of them a lie, in his analysis. The work – say a Beethoven symphony – is now quite removed from the consciousness and concerns of the modern audience. The interpretive personality has to re-establish that lost communication, make it appear intelligible and so forth. This is done through establishing the sovereignty of the interpretive concept (which is also associated with the grandeur of the reputation of the conductor) and through sacrificing the configuration of the work by imposing upon it a larger-than-life image that may be quite unsuited to the work. This falsehood is further compounded by another, in that the interpreter must also project the work as the expression of individual human dynamics which, in the modern age, it no longer is nor could be.

> Above all other qualities it is the ability to present works in a configuration long since absent from them – indeed which they perhaps never expressed at all – which distinguishes the 'prominent conductor'. The dream image of vital fullness and uninhibited verve, of animated organic quality and direct non-reified inwardness are provided by him, corporally for those to whom capitalist economy denies in reality the fulfillment of all such wishes.
>
> (Adorno 1978: 150)

Finally, in a discussion of the modern opera house, Adorno anticipates aspects of the argument of Bourdieu concerning the use of art and art venues as status markers (Bourdieu 1984). Among the lesser bourgeois circles that fill the opera house are the small merchants and the representatives of artisan professions. They may command a certain standard of living and of economic advantage but they are excluded from the fruits of this by background, education and training:

> This is the type of opera-goer who is naturally delighted to hear the march from Aida and the aria of Madame Butterfly again – familiar to him from movies and coffee houses and on a level with his musical education. At the same time, he feels that he owes it to his actual economic position and to the possibility of social ascent to receive these bits of commodity in the place consecrated by the old bourgeois ideal of education and which grants the opera-goer, at least in his own eyes – through his presence in the opera house, something of the dignity of that education.
>
> (Adorno 1978: 152)

This ambiguity of property and education also receives ideological reconciliation in the concert hall. It is reflected in the differentiation between philharmonic and symphony orchestras, often within the same town or city, the former catering to the tastes and demands of higher social classes than the latter, a fact reflected in the repertoires.

7

ON POPULAR MUSIC

The line between 'serious' and 'popular' music can be drawn in different ways. Serious music may be viewed as more complex or more difficult or more refined than popular music or as it may be seen as a spiritually higher form – highbrow as distinct from lowbrow. Adorno rejects all such categories as a basis for distinguishing between serious and popular music. Although he might well agree with the implications of some of them, others are plainly wrong. For example, to view classical music as more complex than popular music is in some respects untrue. He points out that all the works of early Viennese classicism were, 'without exception' rhythmically simpler than the most common arrangements of jazz. Melodically, the wide intervals of a good many hits (he offers 'Deep Purple' and 'Sunrise Serenade' as examples of the day) renders them more difficult to follow than most melodies of Haydn. 'Harmonically, the supply of chords of the so-called classics is invariably more limited than that of any current Tin Pan Alley composer who draws from Debussy, Ravel and even later sources' (Adorno 1990: 305).

The category on which Adorno fixes to distinguish what he might call good serious music from popular music is *standardization*. The term is deceptively simple. The connotation of regularity and repetition are clear enough but this needs qualification. In Adorno's treatment, standardization is an entire theory of popular culture in itself. At a superficial level Adorno is referring to the stereotypical forms and schematic formulae of popular music – to what he holds to be the rules governing its composition – for example, that the chorus should consist of thirty-two bars and that the range should be limited to one octave and one note. Standardization is also used to embrace the content-types such as the various dance types, or songs about mother or home, laments for a lost girl/boy, nonsense or 'novelty' songs and so forth (1990: 304). Adorno was certainly not alone in pointing to the role of standardization in the music produced by the culture industry. Most contemporary writers on jazz did so. Unlike, Adorno, however, they distinguished between the polished commercial article marketed to a mass record-buying public and the raw music improvised and developed by passionate groups of musicians working in small venues in the poorer black neighbourhoods.

Moreover, these writers saw the commercial world as both parasitic in its appropriation of this vital and energetic music and as destroying its vitality through smoothing and standardizing it. Because Adorno was concerned to root out what he saw as the ideology and mythology that surrounded all jazz production he was not careful to distinguish between the more and less commercialized types of jazz nor was he prepared to recognize in so-called primitive jazz any kind of authentic popular music to which his charge of standardization might not apply in the manner in which it applied to the more commercial model.

The term 'standardization' becomes less obvious in its meaning when we try to apply it to forms in serious art that exhibit a certain regularity. After all, it can be argued that standard forms are ubiquitous in all art. Why should a sonnet by Shakespeare be considered less standardized than a popular song by Irving Berlin? Surely painting genres and the forms of classical music – symphony, sonata, minuet, rondo, scherzo and so forth – all exhibit their regular features in different works. Why should these not also be labelled as instances of standardization? Certainly, if all Adorno meant by the term 'standardization' was the formal regularities *per se*, then his concept would have little value as a category for distinguishing between serious and popular music. In fact he meant much more by the concept of standardization than this.

If we identify the form of a work of art with its organization as a whole, we can conceive of that organization as being either a fixed and static form that is simply repeated in each new work or as a mobile and dynamic structure that engages actively with its object and is open to being developed and changed. If the latter is the case, then the form, be it the novel-form or the form of the fugue, will develop in response to the changing life-world in which it is created and with which it engages. We may acknowledge that *Robinson Crusoe* and *Crime and Punishment* are both examples of 'novels' but the category 'novel' is not an instance of what Adorno means by standardization. While these two novels may share a number of general features which allow them to be classified as belonging to the genre, the genre has itself undergone immense developments between these two instances. To the extent that this development is gradual and occurs within the broad parameters of the form-type without radically contradicting it, the form-type is conserved.

There are broad regularities that allow you to say something is a symphony or a fugue or a sonata, but the form itself – sonata-form, fugual-form, etc. – undergoes change and development over time; it has an historical evolution or development that is responsive to the problems that a given historical moment sets for its composers. The formation of material must undergo this development if it is to constitute a truthful and meaningful reflection on experience because conditions change and the composer has to confront them with material that has been formed in the past; material that s/he must adapt when faced by the challenge of the present and the demands to project a future. Only when the artist develops these materials in contact with the life-world on which they reflect can meaningful form be constituted. For this to happen, all the parts and elements constituting the form must be open to each other and must develop through mutual interaction. Equally, the form itself, which is the product of these inter-actions, must develop in response to them. Recurrence of a form-type, however, is not the same as repetition or standardization. Ultimately, the form-type gives way to something different when it is no longer capable of meaningfully ordering its contents in response to the challenge of the present. When experience no longer answers to the form-type, the decay of the latter is certain. Thus in his analysis of the music of Alban Berg, Adorno speaks of an unfettered assault on every aspect of the sonata-form.

By contrast, where the form-type is not a living process but a finished or completed result, a 'ready-made', which is not subject to change or develop-ment in response to the pressure of its elements, then it can best be thought of as a 'mechanism' – a schema that clicks automatically into place when cued. The parts or elements that constitute the schema are equally closed, completed and not subject to being changed in response to each other. Because there is no mutual mediation, there is no development in the events that constitute the form, no consequences for the form from whatever takes place in it. Historicity is banished from such a form-type and so too is any notion of a genuine subject who can realize or express a life-process. A form-type with these characteristics is an instance of what Adorno terms 'standard-ization'. If, as in the example Adorno gives below, any specific event in a Beethoven symphony gains its entire meaning and force from the total con-text in which it occurs, no such thing is possible in the standardized forms of popular music:

> Nothing corresponding to this can happen in popular music. It would not affect the musical sense if any detail were taken out of the context; the listener can supply the framework 'automatically' since it is a mere musical automatism itself. The beginning of the chorus is replaceable by the beginning of innumerable other choruses. The interrelationship among the elements or the relationship of the elements to the whole would be unaffected. In Beethoven position is important only in a living relation between a concrete totality and its concrete parts. In popular music, position is absolute. Every detail is substitutable; it serves its function only as a cog in a machine.
>
> (Adorno 1990: 303)

Development versus ornamentation

The 'details' in popular music – the striking chord sequences, melodic themes, harmonies, rhythmic motifs, the breaks, blue notes, dirty notes and so forth – are no less standardized than the form despite the fact that they are regarded as individual effects and are supposed to introduce something characteristically different and to display individual flair or expertise. Certainly, the details are dependent upon the whole but only in the most limited way. Some details are likely to be more easily attended to or remembered simply because they occupy a musically strategic position within the framework. Adorno cites as his example the musical material at the beginning of the chorus, or its re-introduction after the bridge, as being more noticeable, whereas details occupying the middle bars of the bridge have less chance of attracting attention (1990: 302). To this limited situational extent the detail depends upon the whole. But, Adorno insists, no stress is ever played upon the whole as a musical event, nor does the structure of the whole ever depend upon the details.

There is no disputing, of course, that some of these details are complex and demand musical flair and skill for their successful execution, but because they are not mediated by the whole but are more or less independent of the context, they function only as an embellishment of the threadbare schema of the form; the latter can always be perceived behind the ornamentation. Again Adorno contrasts the situation with what happens in classical music, where the detail derives its meaning entirely from the context and where, as a consequence, the whole is present in the detail. Here, the detail is itself dense with meaning and is never a mere adornment or embellishment. The listener has to concentrate. The average listener to popular music does not have this problem. Confronted by the complex, s/he perceives only the simple schema behind the detail; the latter serves as a digest or summary statement. Again and again Adorno returns to this fundamental distinction between so-called serious and popular music, the presence or absence of a mediating relationship between parts and whole:

> To sum up the difference: in Beethoven and in good serious music in general – we are not concerned here with bad serious music which may be as rigid and mechanical as popular music – the detail virtually contains the whole and leads to the exposition of the whole, at the same time, it is produced out of the conception of the whole. In popular music the relationship is fortuitous. The detail has no bearing on a whole, which appears as an extraneous framework. Thus, the whole is never altered by the individual event and therefore remains, as it were, aloof, imperturbable, and unnoticed throughout the piece. At the same time the detail is mutilated by a device that it can never influence and alter, so that the detail remains inconsequential. A musical detail which is not permitted to develop becomes a caricature of its own potentialities.
>
> (Adorno 1990: 304)

Adorno's treatment of individuation within the work of art or music is subtle. Individuation is the very antithesis, in his theory, of the notion of the monad or self-contained or isolated entity. The individuation of the parts is a function of their thoroughgoing sociation. It is insofar as they interact with and are mediated by others that they develop an individual character; each element is uniquely itself and the more highly organized the music, the less possibility there is of substitution among the details.

Adorno argues that certain complex harmonies are more easily grasped in popular music than they are in serious music simply because of this difference at the level of the individuation of the parts. Because the scheme in popular music is more or less abstract and exists independently of the course of the music, the complicated in popular music, at the level of the details, never functions as itself but only as a disguise or embellishment behind which the scheme can always be perceived. The jazz listener, Adorno suggests, can always replace a complex harmonic sequence with the schematic one which it represents and which it still suggests no matter how daring or elaborate this ornamentation appears to be. The ear deals with complexities in popular music through making substitutions derived from knowledge of the patterns:

> The listener when faced with the complicated actually hears only the simple, while it represents and perceives the complicated only as a parodistic distortion of the simple.
>
> (Adorno 1990: 305)

Music and meaning

The substitution of complex ornamentation for simple musical schemas is something that Adorno holds to be distinctive of popular music. Adorno argues that in serious music no such substitution of the complex for the simple is possible. The detail must be grasped immediately in all of its complexity. It will not do to summarize it vaguely and, to achieve this, takes real concentration of a kind that is rendered unnecessary in popular music where the listener never really leaves familiar ground, no matter how elaborate the ornamentation. In serious music the whole and part are intricately and dynamically interwoven with each other. This dense articulation of part–whole relations thus has its antithesis in popular music where the rule is disarticulation and a stress on 'effects'. Popular music in Adorno's analysis is a more or less mechanical arrangement of effects:

> In popular music the composition has done the listener's listening for her. It has pointed up the path whereby the listener can escape the complex by providing him with norms or models of the simple. The schematic build-up dictates how the listener must listen and makes effort unnecessary.
>
> (Adorno 1990: 308)

Adorno argues that all industrial production generates standardization. However, while he refers to culture as industry, he limits the term industrial to the process of distribution, promotion and marketing of the product rather than production *per se*. The latter he likens to a handicraft level of production, pointing out that it would not increase the costs of producing a hit song if composers did away with standardization, whereas that is clearly not true for the production of cars or any other such item where costs might increase markedly if they were not standardized. Popular culture is made by an industry that is principally engaged in imitation:

> The most successful hits, types and 'ratios' between elements were imitated, and the process culminated in the crystallisation of the standards. The original patterns that are now standardised evolved in a more or less competitive way. Large-scale economic concentrations institutionalised the standardisation and made it imperative.
>
> (Adorno 1990: 307)

Thus, Adorno argues, rugged individualism is outlawed and everything become subject to a uniformity and standardization. Escape is sometimes sought in the form of 'revivals' and these appear to provide something fresh and less outworn than the standardized product because there is something alive within them. 'On the other hand the famous old hits which are revived today set the very patterns which have become standardised. They are the golden age of the game rules' (Adorno 1990: 307).

Natural music and pseudo-individualization

The necessity for standardization derives from the fact that the popular music must meet the demand of grabbing the individual's attention and it must also fall within the category of what the listener views as natural music. By natural music, Adorno means all the conventions and formulas to which the listener has been accustomed since early childhood and that s/he believes to be the natural language of music.

> In terms of consumer demand, the standardisation of popular music is only the expression of this dual desideratum imposed upon it by the musical frame of mind of the public – that it be 'stimulatory' by deviating in some way from the established 'natural', and that it maintain the supremacy of the natural against such deviations. The attitudes of the audiences towards the natural language is reinforced by standardised production, which institutionalises desiderata which originally might have come from the public.
>
> (Adorno 1990: 307)

Each hit song or item of fashion trades on distinctive features that marks it out from other hit songs or fashion items. These distinctive features in no way alter the rigidly standardized frame that underpins these items, ensuring that they are all more or less identical, but they help to disguise the fact, to rekindle interest and to covey the impression of there being something new when there is not. In a television programme exploring the history of popular music, the successful song-writer Neil Sedaka described the method he used for the composition of his first big 'hit' song, 'Oh! Carol'. He studied the successful songs of several different countries and worked out which were the features that regularly seemed to have consumer appeal, from the use of girl's names to the harmonic, rhythmic and musical features that were 'ear-catching'. He then selected a number of those features that he judged to have been truly market-tested and threw them all into the composition of 'Oh! Carol'. Adorno can be said to have written Sedaka's recipe for the construction of a commercial hit thirty years before the song-writer in question was born.

Adorno applied the label 'pseudo-individualization' to the distinctive features that served to brighten up the product without altering it in any material way. Pseudo-individualization is a necessary correlate of standardization. Standardization alone would produce response fatigue that would endanger the market for future cultural goods. The public can be kept going with those little shots of inessential novelty that help to revivify the standardized schema. If standardization effectively predetermines the experience the listener will have, thereby doing the listener's listening for her, pseudo-individualization is the drug that effectively makes her forget that what she listens to has already been pre-digested and all her responses calculatedly pre-figured.

> The paradox in the desiderata – stimulatory and natural – accounts for the dual character of standardisation itself. Stylisation of the ever-identical framework is only one aspect of standardisation. Concentration and control in our culture hide themselves in their very manifestation. Unhidden they would provoke resistance. Therefore the illusion and, to a certain extent, even the reality of individual achievement must be maintained. The maintenance of it is grounded in material reality itself, for while administrative control over life processes is concentrated, ownership is still diffuse.
>
> (Adorno 1990: 308)

Improvisation

Jazz improvisation provided Adorno with a challenging opportunity to develop and extend his theory about standardization and its links to pseudo-individualization. There was a whole culture supporting the model of the jazz musician as live and inventive, improvising music in different ways for different occasions. Some jazz musicians claimed that no two performances of a piece of music even by the same musicians could ever be the same and by this they were not referring to differences that were trivial but to differences that were essential and that contributed to the liveness and spontaneity of the music. Adorno was unrelenting in his denial of these claims. Jazz was for him an example of thoroughly standardized music. It lived off an amalgam of utterly rigid and standard schemas and a variety of 'deviations' or 'excesses' which never overcame the fundamental conformity of the basic structure but which lent it a certain quality of excitement (Adorno 1989). These were instances of what Adorno meant by pseudo-individualization. So-called improvisations were the quintessential examples of pseudo-individualization. Because of the rigid framework within which the musicians are operating, so-called improvised passages in which spontaneity is permitted are tightly delimited and constrained by the standardized harmonic and metric scheme. The solo 'breaks' in pre-swing jazz were not examples of unbridled creativity. They could be easily perceived, by the musically knowledgeable, to be functionally determined by the underlying scheme and to be nothing other than 'disguised cadences'. A whole terminology developed to describe improvisations – in itself a mark of the standardized nature of improvisation, of the pseudo-individualized deviation – and facility in using this terminology became a badge of expertise for the growing army of jazz-wise aficionados (Adorno 1990: 308).

Adorno explains the complete subservience of improvisation to standardization as fulfilling the psychological function of reassuring the listener that s/he is secure and on safe ground. Deviations from the normal in themselves invoke a strong sense of the standard frame behind them and from which they deviate so little. The improvisatory features cannot be grasped as musical events in themselves. They can only be experienced as embellishments and ornaments. They 'substitute' for the underlying schema that can always be perceived behind them. Adorno points to the prevalence of 'dirty', 'false' or 'worried' notes in so-called daring jazz arrangements; these are experienced as exciting, he argues, only because they are connected by the ear to the correct note. (In another context, Adorno wrote about Wagner's uses of dissonance in a similar way, arguing that Wagner's dissonance was not autonomous or genuinely revolutionary because it gained its force solely from its relationship to the implied consonance from which it deviated.) Adorno claimed that that this type of substitution occurs in all cases of individualization in popular music:

> Any harmonic boldness, any chord which does not fall strictly within the simplest harmonic scheme demands being apperceived as 'false', that is, as a stimulus which carries with it the unambiguous

prescription to substitute for it the right detail, or rather the naked scheme. Understanding popular music means obeying such commands for listening. Popular music commands its own listening habits.

(Adorno 1990: 309)

Adorno also extended the concept of pseudo-individualization to embrace both the differences in style between types of jazz and popular music and the differences among the bands or groups playing the music. Again, the enthusiasts and aficionados appropriate new terminologies that delineate all the finer points of these differences and display them as badges of expertise. Adorno recognized two basic styles in his day, those of 'sweet jazz' and 'swing'. The average listener can distinguish between the basic styles even though, Adorno insists, the material is basically the same; s/he can differentiate also between the bands playing the music even though the presentations are essentially the same apart from the deliberately emphasized trademarks. These distinguishing trademarks are instances of pseudo-individualization. Audiences learn them and thereby learn to differentiate between the actually undifferentiated. It is as though the audience has been presented with a multiple-choice questionnaire with which to register likes and dislikes with respect to these distinguishing brands. The culture industry can market test the brands and trademarks and learn more of what works best for the marketing of future products

Popular music and 'leisure time'

Adorno theorizes the mental attitude for listening to popular music as one of inattention and distraction. He saw distraction as a withdrawal from life and responsibility, from the demands of reality. He treated distraction not as a psychological category but in sociological terms, in its relationship to modern production. Most people were involved in boring, deskilled, mechanical and rationalized operations from morning to evening. If the fatigue and boredom of the working day were not sufficiently exhausting, there were the anxieties generated by work itself – fears about unemployment, loss of income – and by the threat of war. The strain of living and working in this way meant that individuals sought relief in their spare time, simultaneously from boredom and effort, both of which were endemic in the capitalist labour process. People want to have 'fun'. Commercial entertainment (unlike serious art) induces relaxation precisely because it is patterned and pre-digested. For the same reason, the listener or viewer needs to make no effort in order to participate. His or her listening and viewing has been done for them, in advance, so to speak. At the same time, the distinctive features, trademark deviations and other aspects of pseudo-individualization provide a sufficient degree of interest and excitement to enable the individual to escape boredom at least temporarily and partially.

Adorno is equally scathing about the defence of the culture industry that claims that the industry is only giving the masses what they want. He points out that this ideology of providing what the customer wants has a commercial logic to it that is not always obvious. An audience that has been entrained out of making any genuine discriminations has, as a consequence, been prepared to purchase cultural goods indiscriminately. While it is true that mass audiences want these cultural goods, Adorno claims that they only do so because they are driven to seek, in their spare time, 'after-images' of the very mechanized existence to which they have been subjected in their working lives. They want standardized goods and pseudo-individualization because their leisure is an escape from work that is at the same time moulded by the same mechanical, rationalized, disciplines that characterize the world of work.

> . . . there is justification for speaking of a pre-established harmony today between production and consumption of popular music. The people clamour for what they are going to get anyhow.
>
> (Adorno 1990: 310)

As Adorno perceptively points out, there is a contradiction in seeking to obtain relief simultaneously from both boredom and effort. The mechanized work process denies to many an experience of novelty or genuine change. They crave novelty in their leisure time but the strain experienced at work leads people to avoid making the effort which is necessary to any genuine experience of change. In place of this the individual craves 'stimulation'. Popular music is one of the forms that this craving for stimulation takes. Each stimulus, each pseudo-individualized sensation, is quickly worn out and the cycle of boredom begins again. The demand for permanent renewal of stimulation feeds the commercial interests that have brought about this situation in the first place. The culture industry is always there to bury yesterday's excitement beneath the sheen of today's. To stimulate the public is to stimulate the demand for stimulating the public.

> In this situation the industry faces an insoluble problem. It must arouse attention by means of ever-new products, but this attention spells their doom. If no attention is given to the song, it cannot be sold; if attention is paid to it, there is always the possibility that people will no longer accept it, because they know it too well. This partly accounts for the constantly renewed effort to sweep the market with new products, to hound them to their graves; then to repeat the infanticidal manoeuvre again and again.
>
> (Adorno 1990: 311)

Response types

The dependence on continuously renewed stimulation still leaves open the question of what music can actually mean to an audience that Adorno characterizes as generally inattentive and distracted. Lack of attention interspersed with flashes of recognition does not provide a basis for actually following the music as a sequence of events that is integrally meaningful in itself, and in which each moment is grasped in relation both to what has gone before and what is to come after. Such music does not appear to the listener as a language sui generis. Nevertheless, the audience to whom any kind of musical meaning, in the above sense of an internal coherence or logical development, is inaccessible, seizes on music as a means of adjustment, a psychological adaptation to the demands of present-day life. The adjustment Adorno has in mind here is one that corresponds to one of two major social psychological types of response to popular music. There is what Adorno labels the 'rhythmically obedient' type and the 'emotional' type (1990: 312–13). Individuals of the rhythmically obedient type are categorized by Adorno as susceptible to a masochistic adjustment to authoritarian collectivism. However, he does not identify the authoritarianism and crowd-mindedness of this type with any particular political attitude since it can appear on the left or the right of the political spectrum. In his 1936 paper 'Uber Jazz', Adorno identified the importance of the march, as the model of a fictive community, in the tradition of modern popular music. He noted the tendencies of young people everywhere to develop the rhythmically obedient type of response (Adorno 1989).

Adorno dismissed the idea that it might be possible to express political convictions through such means. Those who ask for a song that has social significance ask for it through a medium which deprives it of social significance. The use of popular musical media is inevitably repressive *per se*. Much of the critical literature that followed the publication of the *Authoritarian Personality* accused Adorno and his colleagues of identifying authoritarianism with the political right rather than the left, a conclusion that is hardly justified by Adorno's writings either before or after its publication. In respect of the authoritarianism that he attributes to the rhythmically obedient type of response to music, Adorno moves easily between claims about music to claims about the general psychology of the individuals responding to the music:

> This obedient type is the rhythmical type, the word 'rhythmical' being used in its everyday sense. Any musical experience of this type is based upon the underlying, unabating time unit of the music – its 'beat'. To play rhythmically means, to these people, to play in such a way that even if pseudo-individualizations – counter-accents and other 'differentiations' – occur, the relation to the ground meter is preserved. To be musical means to them to be capable of following

given rhythmical patterns without being disturbed by 'individualiz-ing' aberrations, and to fit even the syncopations into the basic time units. This is the way in which their response to music immediately expresses their desire to obey. However, as the standardized meter of dance music and of marching suggests the co-ordinated battalions of a mechanical collectivity, obedience to this rhythm by overcoming the responding individuals leads them to conceive of themselves as agglutinized with the untold millions of the meek who must be similarly overcome. Thus do the obedient inherit the earth.

(Adorno 1990: 312)

This adaptive response – obedience to authority – is associated by Adorno with the experience of disillusion, of an anti-romantic response to life, a feeling that fulfilment and self-expression is not possible. He cites both Stravinsky and Hindemith as examples of serious composers whose music is marked by this sense of disillusion, claiming that they orient themselves to achieving, through their music, an adaptation to a reality understood by them in terms of the 'machine age'. The raw adjustment to collective force through the cultic simulation of the machine, which Adorno sees as represented by the rhythms of jazz, is an act of self-renunciation that is only possible in an age in which men and women have become appendages to machines and the machine can thereby appear as an end of existence and not simply a means.

In the adaptation to machine music necessarily implies a renunci-ation of one's own human feelings and at the same time a fetishism of the machine such that its instrumental character becomes obscured thereby.

(Adorno 1990: 313)

The other response-type, which Adorno labelled the 'emotional type', is no less based upon disillusion than the 'rhythmic type'. It involves an idealiz-ation of personalities and situations with which the individual identifies These represent human relations that are marked by the ideal qualities that are largely missing from ordinary life. Adorno offers as an example 'the shop-girl who identifies with Ginger Rogers, who with her beautiful legs and unsullied character, marries the boss'. Wish-fulfilment is the guiding principle involved here, claims Adorno, as it is in the appreciation of neo-romantic music and emotional–erotic music. However, Adorno does not see the wish-fulfilment of this type as unmarked by disillusion. The shop-girl does not really equate herself with Ginger Rogers nor does she believe her life will be like that portrayed in the film:

What does occurs may be expressed as follows: when the audience at a sentimental film or sentimental music become aware of the

109

overwhelming possibility of happiness, they dare to confess to themselves what the whole order of contemporary life ordinarily forbids them to admit, namely, that they actually have no part in happiness. What is supposed to be wish fulfilment is only the scant liberation that occurs with the realization that at last one need not deny oneself the happiness of knowing that one is unhappy and that one could be happy.

(Adorno 1990: 313)

Adorno's argument is that the appeal of sentimental music lies in the temporary release that the glimpse of happiness affords to the individual who is made aware that he has missed fulfilment. The emotional listener is drawn to late Romanticism and to all the modern cultural derivatives put out by Tin Pan Alley. They consume music in order to weep. What captures them is the musical expression not of happiness but of the frustrating of happiness. The intense wish to feel is the predominant characteristic of this orientation to music but the feeling is of a world that is lost or happiness unfulfilled. Adorno argues that the emotionality elicited in this type of response is as conformist as it is in the case of the rhythmic type:

It is catharsis for the masses, but catharsis which keeps them all the more firmly in line. One who weeps does not resist any more than one who marches. Music that permits its listeners the confession of their unhappiness reconciles them, by means of this 'release', to their social dependence.

(Adorno 1990: 314)

Winthrop Sargeant

If Adorno is viewed as a classical musician mounting a critique of jazz, the question immediately arises as to whether there were any contemporary writings from within the jazz tradition itself that provided any support for his position at the time he was writing. There was certainly one well-known writer on jazz who is cited enthusiastically by Adorno. Winthrop Sargeant's authoritative text, *Jazz: Hot and Hybrid*, was published within two years of Adorno's 1936 paper on jazz (Sargeant 1959). Adorno was clearly pleased to cite Sargeant as an authority and as the 'only reliable writer on jazz'. He claimed to find, in Sargeant's analysis of the differences between jazz music and classical music and Sargeant's overall analysis of jazz form, an impressive degree of accord with his own views about structure in music.

Winthrop Sargeant, internationally known today as the art editor of *Life* magazine, is responsible for the best, most reliable and most sensible book on the subject [of jazz]; twenty five years ago he wrote that jazz was in no way a new musical idiom but rather 'even in its most complex manifestations a very elementary matter of incessantly repeated formulae'. This kind of unbiased observation seems possible only in America.

(Adorno 1967: 121–2)

It is a pity that Adorno himself did not exhibit some of the objectivity he attributed to Sargeant when he wrote that passage. The truth is that he was highly selective in the matter of what he credited in Sargeant's work. The latter was, of course, an enthusiastic advocate of jazz music and celebrated its creative energy and vitality, seeing it as essentially a folk music. Notwithstanding his citation in support, Adorno would not have agreed with Sargeant's conclusions or his basic analysis any more than Sargeant would have agreed with him. In the first place, Adorno did not accept the notion that there was even a folk left to make folk music and he certainly did not treat jazz as folk music. He opposed, too, the idea that jazz was in some way vital, creative, spontaneous or genuinely improvisatory, all claims that are clearly made by Sargeant. Moreover, Sargeant also expressed scepticism about certain 'readings' of jazz. His critical remarks on that subject can easily be applied to Adorno:

> . . . the attempt to link up jazz to moral and social ideas, or to the Weltanschauung of modern civilization has proved on the whole a rather barren intellectual pastime, and has tended to disappear from most recent writing on the subject. It has never contributed an iota of clarification to the musical and aesthetic question 'What is jazz?'
>
> (Sargeant 1959: 26)

However, Adorno did find impressive support for his own position in Sargeant's musicological description of jazz, in his discussion of jazz harmony, rhythm and melody, and especially in his discussion of the differences between jazz and European concert music. Sargeant was concerned to oppose a fashionable line of thinking that made claims for jazz as the music of the future, one which would displace the classical European tradition (1959: 23–5). Such an argument would effectively rob jazz of everything that he considered to be important to it as music. It is important to recognize that when Sargeant attacks the identification of jazz with art music he does so in the interests of jazz, which he sees as threatened by such an identification. Jazz, as he saw it, was quite different from European art music and it could never satisfy the drives of those who participate in that tradition. Sargeant sees jazz as completely lacking in the intellectual and structural features that sustain the interest of a cultivated highbrow musical audience over time (1959: 23).

Repeatedly, Sargeant is concerned to stress the primitive untutored and musically illiterate origins of jazz. Jazz, he claims, is a genuine Negro folk music. The very vitality of the music, its improvisatory and spontaneous character, derives from this and without it, jazz dies. Sargeant is effectively identifying spontaneity and improvisation as being of the essence of a musically illiterate folk music. The lack of a formalized technique and tradition of composed music, written notation, a developed canon, etc., allows of a kind of liberated and spontaneous musical response to everyday situations and griefs and relationships, one that is fully of the situation in which it is performed. Jazz is music made for participation; Sargeant speaks of 'get-together music' as the antithesis of music that is composed and then faithfully executed for audiences that listen in a darkened auditorium in rapt concentration.

In a chapter dealing with jazz as a 'fine art', Sargeant equates jazz to the skyscraper, the baseball game and the 'happy ending' movie (Sargeant 1959: 250–64). Like the skyscraper and unlike the Greek temple, jazz is not built for permanence but for continuous replacement. Its continuous movement is everything. The skyscraper finishes when it can go no further, just as a piece of jazz finishes when the musicians are tired or want to go onto something else. There is a difference between this and the inevitability of the ending of a piece of classical music or architecture that fulfils some internal logical development.

> [the American's] most characteristic arts – the comic strip, the skyscraper, journalism, jazz, the tap dance, the 'happy ending' movie – all lack the element of 'form' that is so essential to tragedy, to the symphony, to the novel, to the opera, to monumental architecture and even to some of the less pretentious arts of other nations . . . The European 'composition' is a complex structure of organized sound, fixed more or less immutably as to form. It perpetuates the message of a creative mind through generations, even centuries. The understanding of this message presuppose a tradition – -guarantee that men will, to some extent, think and feel alike from generation to generation. The form in which the message is cast is subject to a process of intellectual development. Its composers themselves are highly trained professionals, the greatest of them capable of extraordinary feats of technique which average people marvel at but can scarcely hope to duplicate.
>
> (Sargeant 1959: 252)

In claiming that jazz lacks all of these characteristics, Sargeant must have appeared to Adorno to be making his case for him. However, the conclusions that the two wish to draw from their common insight are radically divergent. Adorno draws the conclusion that the standardized and repetitive harmonic and melodic formulae used by jazz musicians is a mark of a sterile cliché-ridden music that is all fashion and lacking in genuine style. Sargeant, however, sees this type of standardized structure as a necessary skeletal basis for a genuine improvisatory and spontaneous music; a music that he identifies with performance and not with composition. The jazz musicians, even in a piece of commercial 'sweet jazz', 'worry and cajole' the rhythms and phrases of their solos, extemporizing here and there and 'ornamenting the printed skeleton that has been provided for their collective guidance' (1959: 25). In an account of a 'hot ensemble', Sargeant writes of the soloist:

> He varies the pattern of the melody, tortures it this way and that, leaves it for melodic inspiration of his own, returns to it again, tosses it back and forth among his colleagues who tear it up into all sorts of unrecognisable melodic shapes. . . . The composer, that towering artistic figure of concert music, occupies here a very lowly if not entirely unnecessary role. In the end his 'composition' is almost completely lost sight of, or at best serves as a mere framework on which more interesting things are hung.
>
> (Sargeant 1959: 24)

In his discussion of the characteristic jazz 'break', the differences between Adorno and Sargeant can be clearly seen and there is little doubting which thinker has provided the richer and more informed discussion. Again, the starting point is one of initial agreement. Both of them identify the jazz break with the cadenza in classical bravura music. Both of them, too, identify it as an ornament and as a divergence from the rigors of strict structure. Both, too, recognize that the fundamental rhythm is always there, implicitly, behind the dizzying solo and that the audience holds on to it in imagination. For Adorno this is a clinging to safety, to the absolute authority of the beat; it is an acceptance of conformity and security; everything that is played on the surface is a trivial fireworks display that leaves the threadbare schema of the music unaffected and which is, in itself, devoid of meaning. With Sargeant the matter is quite different. The tension created by musical deviation in jazz most certainly requires the continuing imagination of that from which it deviates. It is that ground which makes genuine spontaneity, originality and creative improvisation possible. The tension at the heart of the solo break is the tension created at the heart of all good jazz according to Sargent:

> The phenomenon of simultaneous rhythms, playing against each other, is, of course, not limited to the break. . . . The break merely represents the principle of syncopation operating on somewhat larger spans of musical structure. . . . Indeed certain types of hot jazz may be said to consist of an indefinite series of breaks.
>
> (Sargeant 1959: 240)

The creative exhilaration felt by musicians and audiences alike, suggests Sargeant, comes from the battle between the unexpected, restless challenging rhythm played against the fundamental regularity of the stated and implied pulse:

When players, dancers and audience alike are hanging desperately on to their sense of rhythmic orientation on one hand and are violently disturbing it (or listening to it being violently disturbed) on the other, the result is jazz in its purest form.

(Sargeant 1959: 241–2)

If Sargeant is concerned to differentiate jazz sharply from European classical music he is equally concerned to make comparisons and to discover its similarities to Indian music. In particular he discusses the type of music known in northern India as gath. Like jazz, this music has a fundamental rhythm, the pulses of which are always kept in mind by the player even though they may only be stated at very wide intervals in the music. Moreover, this fundamental rhythm is not restricted as in jazz to 'four quarter or two quarter time' (1959: 242) but may be measured in several different metres. On this basic framework the instrumentalist improvises a type of composition, syncopating in very subtle and complicated ways. These deviations last so long that most Western musicians trying to follow them would lose track of the fundamental rhythm. Added to that, the syncopating musician is often accompanied by a drummer who is developing a different chain of complex 'breaks' built on the same fundamental rhythm but developed against those of the melody line. Quite emphatically, Sargeant claims that this type of musical structuration is only possible in an improvisatory art. Surprise and suspense are integral to both Indian music and jazz, and Sargeant concludes:

. . . in psychological effect, and in essential qualities of rhythmic structure, there are certain resemblances between the two. And in these peculiarities, jazz invades a dimension totally foreign to the music of the West.

(Sargeant 1959: 245)

Taking up this latter theme, Sargeant proceeds to question the usefulness of the type of musicological comparisons that Adorno and others favoured:

The formal layout of jazz phrases and routines is thus a fairly simple matter compared with the corresponding structure of concert music. But, . . . the form of jazz is not wholly explicable in terms of cut-and-dried formulae. Some of its more characteristic elements invade a musical dimension that is quite alien to Western musical culture. This dimension to the Southern Asiatics and North Africans, is peculiar to improvised music. To compare the phraseological structure of jazz with that of European music is to point out re-semblances that are to a certain extent superficial. The phraseology of jazz is related to a wholly different functional plan, characteristic of an art that is essentially unpredictable and impulsive.

(Sargeant 1959: 249)

There is little doubting that the breadth of argument and evidence adduced in support is impressive in Sargeant's work. Most particularly, however, the ethnomusicological perspective that he adopts in order to see jazz in a larger cultural context is something that is almost entirely missing from Adorno's work. While Sargeant's characterization of the structural features of both classical music and jazz accords rather closely with that of Adorno, his use of these is to secure a very different set of conclusions. Certainly, he recognizes something akin to Adorno's idea of a sterile standardized music, but he associates that with the mass cultural music of radio and record companies, with commercial music. He insists on a distinction that has often been made since between the genuinely improvisatory social contexts in which new vital musics are developed and the parasitic appropriation of these musics by a commercial industry that drains them of vitality as it standardizes them and disseminates them to mass audiences. Sargeant went further. The culture industry was more or less dependent, for any revitalization, on this type of spontaneous development that occurred outside its design initiative. He argued that every twenty years or so, the culture industry goes in search of a new wave of vital folk jazz to revivify its tired schemas. Adorno's thinking led him to include everything that belonged to popular music within the design initiative of the culture industry. Sargeant insists that truly spontaneous and creative music is made on the margins of the culture industry and is then appropriated and marketed and transformed in the process into the perfectly predictable and pre-digested commercial article. Not only did Adorno fail to recognize the distinction between these two domains, he denied that a music that he would claim to be structurally impoverished could ever be capable of generating anything genuinely creative and spontaneous. What Adorno called structural poverty – standardization – was nothing of the kind in Sargeant's analysis. The constant reference to an underlying uniformity was, in any case, essential to the liberation of a genuine creative vitality in music. Sargeant, who was concerned to insist on the difference between jazz and European art music, nevertheless drew attention to their similarity in this respect. The amalgam of deviation and conformity which Adorno attributed to jazz is, for Sargeant, a fundamental principle that applies widely to art and to life:

> Unrest followed by relief, in one form or another, is fundamental to a great deal of art. It has been an essential element of narration from the Greek drama to the detective story . . . Symphonic form, with its 'recapitulation' of original themes following an adventurous 'development section' is another [form of it].
>
> (Sargeant 1959: 236–7)

8

ADORNO'S RADIO DAYS

Adorno's critique of modern media, of radio, television and film is especially associated with the papers he wrote on the subject during his exile in the US from 1938 to 1949. His views concerning the development of music and its social situation in the modern world had been more or less fully developed years before he began to work with Paul Lazarsfeld on what became known as the Princeton Radio Project. His part in the project concerned the broadcasting of music. Adorno's arrival in the United States coincided with the golden era of radio: the days before television, when radio was a powerful and influential arm of the culture industry. Its influence was felt at the heart of every home and it provided an endless stream of entertainment, information, quiz programmes, gossip, drama and music. Adorno saw the effects of all this in a negative light. Radio represented commercial interests. It was an instrument of propaganda and it pandered to the regressive tendencies of mass audiences, serving up an unremitting diet of undemanding 'baby food'.

Insofar as radio claimed to disseminate so-called 'serious' culture, Adorno was scathing in his dismissal of the claim. Radio was complicit in the degrading and extinguishing of the serious work of art. The attitudes it encouraged its mass audiences to hold in respect of art and music were, for the most part, reactionary, serving only to impede any serious engagement with art. When Adorno arrived in America to take up a position as a member of Paul Lazarsfeld's team his task was to carry out research into radio music. The studies for which he was directly responsible concerned the broadcasting of 'serious' music over the radio. Two of the papers he wrote in the early 1940s dealt with the broadcasting of symphonic music and the third and largest study focussed on a well-known series of programmes that introduced young radio listeners to classical music. The latter paper remained unpublished during Adorno's lifetime.

Paul Lazarsfeld was an empirical sociologist with a strongly positivistic bent and had an impressive track record not only in mounting empirical research but also in writing texts on the subject of research methodology. On paper, at least, Adorno was the most unlikely of collaborators for such a researcher. His antipathy to empirical survey methods and what he called 'administrative research' with all its claims to 'scientific' findings had been fully formed by that time. He was generally sceptical, if not outright contemptuous, of all such research, together with what he saw as its covert or latent agendas and its pretensions to scientific truth. Empirical survey methods in administrative research were no better than instruments of market-testing, in his view. It was not that they did not provide genuine information about people; what concerned him was that the research itself was part of a social machinery for controlling its subjects. The information obtained about people's habits, practices and tastes provided a means for manipulating them.

The Princeton Project thus brought Adorno into a difficult relationship with a type of research that he found distasteful. His compromise with the aims of the project was hardly a compromise at all. In the papers he produced for Lazarsfeld he mounted a critique of the treatment of serious music on the radio which drew only slightly and in an illustrative way on the actual empirical content of radio programmes. It has to be said that whatever the merits of these papers as critical theory, it would be difficult to defend them in a sociological context as making effective use of available methods of research. It is unlikely that Adorno's content analysis in his study of the *NBC Music Appreciation Hour* would have met the methodological standards current in his own day (Adorno 1994b: 325–77). This situation contrasts dramatically with the later collaborative study in America of the 'Authoritarian Personality', in which Adorno and his colleagues deployed an armory of 'positivistic' survey methods, questionnaires, interviews, attitude scales, projective tests and the like.

In the radio papers one would be hard put to see Adorno seeking to discover something new or approaching the medium with any kind of openness. Adorno 'knows' in advance that radio is bad and that its attempts to transmit serious culture degrade that culture. There is an already worked-out theory concerning the mass media and the part they play in a monopoly capitalism. One does not have the sense, reading any of Adorno's forays into the domain of 'conventional' empirical research, that he is seriously testing his theory or opening it to empirical disconfirmation. It is true that Adorno did sometimes alight upon findings that surprised him; he occasionally responded in a fresh and open way to previously analysed phenomena, allowing himself to find new possibilities and to see them in a changed light. However, when he operated with the type of research represented by the radio studies, he was at his least flexible. The research is used essentially to *illustrate* his theory, not to test it. The reader is in little doubt from the beginning, as soon as he discerns the authorial voice, that radio is not likely to come out on the right side of this study. If Adorno's analyses are, nevertheless, effective, it is because he was able to bring to bear his great knowledge of music and music culture, his perception of modernity and his well-honed positions concerning the commodification of cultural goods. The radio papers provided him with an opportunity to apply these ideas directly in what is really a critical reflection on, rather than a sociological study of, the medium.

In 'A Social Critique of Radio Music' Adorno sets out his explicit rejection of the ideology of what he calls administrative research (Adorno 1945: 208–17). He sees the latter as a matter of asking people questions about their likes and dislikes or responses to experiences in order to better manipulate them in the future. Even though the purpose may not be commercial, Adorno makes no distinction between this type of audience research and what is normally called market-testing. While he appears to withhold this judgement from the type of research that Paul Lazarsfeld was engaged in by referring to the latter as 'benevolent administrative research', the qualification somehow lacks conviction. Benevolent research is guided by such aims as 'how can we enable the largest number of people to have access to really good music?' However, Adorno's whole approach is antithetical even to the formulation of such a question and his understanding of the character of modern media and their function precludes him from accepting that anything good can come of the dissemination of so-called good music by radio.

For a start, there is the problem of the relationship of the classics in music to modern problems and modern society. Given the seriousness with which Adorno views the relationship of music and the arts to modern society – their kinship with 'knowledge' and 'understanding' – the test of authenticity for him lies in the degree to which a given work addresses the problems presented by its own time. But Adorno's meaning here is a sharply delimited one. It can easily be shown that much popular music and jazz is relevant to its time. Adorno even describes it as suited to accompanying mundane everyday acts. The lyrics of many pop songs are unmistakably of a given time and appear to express or convey affective or emotional states with which individuals in modern society identify. Yet all of these constitute examples of music or art that, in Adorno's theory, have failed to address the problematic of modern times, and he contrasts them strongly with the unpopular works of serious modernist art that he claims do rise to the challenge of their time.

Adorno questions the claim that classical music, of the type played over the radio, can address the problems of the time. Should we see Beethoven's music as 'good music' and if so why? Is music that is labelled good always good for all times or does it change its status over time? Does music designated as good music in one period cease to be so in another? Beethoven's music, in the problems it sets itself, is no longer linked to our own situation. Constant repetition of his music has smoothed it out and familiarity with its themes has reduced it to being a source of well-known tunes. Even if that were not true, argues Adorno, the transmission of a Beethoven symphony by the radio actually changes it in ways that are consequential for the entire listening experience. The latter is most certainly affected by the very musical culture into which radio listeners are inducted. It was a culture dominated by popular music and, in Adorno's day especially, jazz music; on the classical side it was a music culture then highlighting late Romantic composers such as Tchaikovsky and Rachmaninov.

Music is not simply played on the radio. Radio teaches its audiences how to listen and which composers to value and so forth. Audiences listen to and hear music in the way they are overwhelmingly taught to do by the culture. Adorno insists that audiences are encouraged to isolate the emotionally gratifying moments – what Adorno called the 'culinary moments' – in so-called great music, 'to wait for the solo on the French horn in a Brahms symphony in much the same way that they might listen for Benny Goodman's solo clarinet in a jazz piece' (Adorno 1945: 210). Adorno never ceased to deprecate any type of response to art that isolates specific details and loses the mediated tension between part and whole. Again, the underlying theoretic extends way beyond the empirical investigation and holds his observations on music and the media in place.

When Adorno accuses the modern listener to radio music of fixating upon isolated details and of being incapable of appreciating the structured web of sound that constitutes the whole, he is not simply talking about the state of music or even about the effects of radio but about an atomization of society together with its psychic correlatives. Under the pressure of late capitalist society, social life itself fragments into isolated details that no longer add up or provide a meaningful psychic coherence. This broken life made up of elements alienated from the sensuous social formation gives rise to an abstract subjectivity, a complex of egoistic desires and impulses seeking gratification. The commodities promising that gratification are equally alienated from the social process through which they are produced and manifest as an abstract objectivity that is the counterpart of the reified ego. Such an ego is not an authentic subject in Adorno's theory and the heightened self-consciousness it exhibits signifies only the gestures of selfhood performed by individuals without selves.

Radio is viewed by Adorno as an integral part of the highly organized and overwhelmingly powerful machinery through which a monolithic capitalism degrades and disfigures social life to the level of egoistic drives and collective narcissism. He saw its institutional structure as thoroughly pervaded by commercial interests and permeated throughout by the rhetorical registers and techniques of advertising. Radio dealt in commodities and commodified everything. That this was the case was presupposed from the outset by Adorno and was not itself a question put to the research. In 'A Social Critique of Radio Music' he laid out his presuppositions in a thinly veiled version of Marxist theory. The task he set himself was to flesh out some of the ways in which radio degrades so-called serious music, as Culture, in the very process of transmitting it to mass audiences.

In an age in which music of all kinds has become increasingly commodified, the individuals that hear it become less and less able to experience it in a concentrated way. Concentration is a key concept for Adorno. It is associated with inner directedness, with autonomy. It is an active and subject-centred process that involves effort and struggle. The modern radio listener, Adorno argues, seeks to appropriate music, reducing it in two ways: to cultural goods or cultural capital that offers those extrinsic gratifications that have been identified by Bourdieu as status markers – *music as quotations from and knowledge about music*; radio listening also reduces music to the isolated themes – the 'hit tunes' that can provide some kind of instant gratification for minds that lack the inwardness and interiority required to appreciate the structural integrity of music as a meaningful totality:

> A symphony of the Beethoven type, so-called classical, is one of the most highly integrated musical forms. The whole is everything; the part, that is to say, what the layman calls the melody, is relatively unimportant. Retrogressive listening to a symphony is listening which, instead of grasping that whole, dwells upon those melodies, just as if a symphony were structurally the same thing as a ballad.
>
> (Adorno 1945: 213)

Concentration demands precisely that inwardness that Adorno saw as having been seriously eroded, if not all but destroyed, in late capitalist society. Radio plays an important part in pre-figuring the consciousness of its listeners. It feeds them on a diet of modern popular music, delivered in packets that favour the fixation on sensuous detail, climaxes and isolated moments. These listening habits are overwhelmingly established not only through the continuous radio transmission of light music but the careful selection of 'lollipop' classical pieces. Those classical composers who become the ideal composers for radio transmission, according to Adorno, are those that provide a wealth of sensuous details allied to structural poverty and there is no doubting that the two principal names he had in mind here were those of Tchaikovsky and Rachmaninov.

Radio entrains its listeners to respond in this fractured way to music and has engendered an entire musical culture with its distractive and, in Adorno's view, regressive listening habits and modes of appropriation. When radio attempts to transmit so-called 'serious' music – often accompanying the transmission with a kind of fetishized reverence towards these works – the music is easily assimilated and shredded by the radio-entrained listening culture that goes out to meet it. The corruption of serious music is not the product of modern mass media alone, however, but is part of the wider social process of modernity which transforms the consciousness of audiences in ways that destroy the potential for genuine self-development and change. Adorno saw this as characteristic not only of radio but also of the modern concert hall and of the appropriation of classical music by middle-class taste publics. Music has ceased to be a human force and becomes instead a commodity and is consumed like other consumer goods.

> The listener suspends all intellectual activity when dealing with music and is content with consuming and evaluating its gustatory qualities – just as if the music that tasted best were also the best music possible.
>
> (Adorno 1945: 211)

This commodified listening even extends, argues Adorno, to an obsession with the differences in quality between musical instruments, such as the Stradivarius violin as opposed to one produced in modern times, differences which might be meaningful to experts but hardly to lay persons. He refers to a radio company that arranged a cycle of broadcasts as an acoustic display of the properties of famous instruments in which the music played or the quality of the performance was merely incidental.

The charge of being an 'opiate of the people' is never far from Adorno's critiques of mass culture. Radical resistance to society does not come from those who have been made smug and self-satisfied. A sense of self-importance, of belonging to the cognoscenti, to a class that can appreciate things, is not least among the effects that radio is accused of cultivating in its listeners. Radio gives people access to cultural goods from which they had formerly, by reason of class and social status, been deprived. It encourages them not so much to appreciate music as to recognize the importance and value of their new claims to possessing knowledge about music and to see themselves as better persons for being able to make these claims.

In response to those that might protest that many of the audience actually feel enriched and benefited by such programmes, Adorno draws on his content analysis of the cards and letters sent to a radio station expressing enthusiasm and gratitude for its introduction of a 'serious music' hour. Adorno describes them (we are not given any details of how many there were nor how they were categorized and coded etc.) as being instances of standardized enthusiasm, generalized and unspecific, lacking any references to particular features, details or musical elements. He sees the respondents as being under the spell of the announcer, responding to his call to prove themselves cultured by their appreciation of good music. The fact that the writers do not discuss the specific details of the work indicates to Adorno that there is no coherent structure to frame the listener's experiences; it is only when there is such a coherence that all the details emerge in their constructive contributions to the larger whole that makes sense of them.

However, Adorno is presupposing here that these listeners are simply incapable of hearing the symphonic music played to them and that the poverty of their musical experience of what has been transmitted to them by radio is reflected in the poverty of the language with which they express their pleasure and gratitude for the programmes. It may be that Adorno's conclusion makes sense but no acceptable justification for it is provided by his research. Indeed one might want to conclude that that this kind of argument is the product of a cultural ethnocentrism. Adorno presumes that an individual who has been moved by a work of art will also have the language, vocabulary and repertoire of linguistic expressions for discussing art. The same cultural ethnocentrism characterized some of the questions in the later famous study of the 'Authoritarian Personality'. If a subject chose General MacArthur rather than Beethoven as a person who had contributed the most to civilization then that choice was categorized by the researchers as an authoritarian response. As critics have pointed out, however, the answer probably reflects the numbers of years of education the subject has had and his or her degree of cultural sophistication (Brown 1965).

'The Radio Symphony' is something of a curiosity among Adorno's papers in that he constructs his argument about the degrading of serious music in radio programmes in terms of the technical features of radio transmission and their deficiencies (Adorno 1941: 110–39). There is no doubt, of course, that many of these technical deficiencies have now been diminished if not altogether overcome with the invention of FM and digital broadcasting. The acoustic properties of the best modern equipment are very different from what they were in 1940. For example, Adorno notes at the outset of the paper the problem of the 'hear stripe', the continuous thermal noises that can be heard in the background and which disappear from the musical surface as soon as the broadcast begins but which can still be heard underneath the music, playing its part in the apperception of the whole even if the listener is unaware of them. Adorno likens the effect of the 'hear stripe' to the awareness of the screen in the cinema. At the same time, in a footnote to the paper, he acknowledges the fact that technological improvements such as the advent of frequency modulation might well change matters.

The degradation involved in the appropriation of serious music is really based, in Adorno's consciousness, on a theory about capitalism and commodification; it is presumably coincidental that the technical deficiencies of radio as a medium for sound transmission in 1940 conspired (in his analysis) to reinforce those same degrading effects. And yet, notwithstanding the changes in technical development since that time, Adorno's argument provides an insight into the interesting way in which he views the physical aspect of sound production and its relationship to meaning in the musical work:

> We are primarily concerned with pointing out the fact that serious music as communicated over the ether may indeed offer optimum conditions for retrogressive tendencies in listening, for the avalanche

of fetishism that is overtaking music and burying it under the moraine of entertainment.

(Adorno 1941: 112)

Radio, as a physical medium, he claims, is unable to reproduce the intensive dynamics that is associated with the performance of symphonic music. This is a matter of the sheer scale and volume of sound intensity and its character of surrounding the individual, of being sound that is huge in scale, sound that the listener can enter. This, too, is bound up with what Adorno claims to be radio's preference for symphonic music over chamber music. He accounts for this preference in terms of what he calls 'the primitive and spectacular strength of sound, its publicity character'. He also points out that the structure of chamber music of the 'classical' period is actually more complex than symphonic music of the same period, particularly with respect to its polyphonous texture. Adorno claims that there is more polyphony to be heard in chamber music than in symphonic music and that it is the polyphonic structure of the music that is the principle obstacle to the understanding of the listener.

Beethoven is key to Adorno's argument and method here as elsewhere. Because Beethoven exemplifies, for Adorno, the quintessence of symphonic form, the change a Beethoven symphony undergoes in the process of radio transmission provides him with his theoretical 'test'. It is the structural aspect of Beethoven's music that is key to the analysis. But not just any description of structure will do here. By structure, Adorno is not referring to the conventional understanding of the sonata as having a subject, an exposition, a development and a repetition, nor is he referring to the typical antagonism of the two main subjects of the exposition, their 'bridge, their conclusion, the way they develop and undergo their modified recurrence in the work' (1941: 114). Adorno insists that such constituents of form are essential in the context of a Beethoven symphony only in terms of the dynamic interplay of the specific contents of each work. Each work gives rise to a unique realization in which the form itself is responsive to and is developed by those contents. Adorno's argument is important here in the context of what he has to say about popular music. He insists that popular music is formulaic and standardized and that the form of the music is completely unresponsive to its contents, from which it does not differ in any essential way. In his comments about the formal constituents of the Beethoven symphony, however, he anticipates and rejects the critical rejoinder that the sonata-form is no less standardized and formulaic than the thirty-two-bar popular song. That would be to argue that any symphony could be replaced by any other which has the same formal characteristics. Adorno denies that this is the case for the symphony (see Chapter 7) while insisting that it accurately describes the substitutability of popular songs.

Adorno's analysis here is entirely consistent with all his other writings on music.

The symphony is differentiated by Adorno from chamber music or from other forms such as the orchestral suite or the tone poem by its 'particular intensity and concentration'. There is a greater density and economy of thematic relationships in the symphony:

> . . . a truly symphonic movement contains nothing fortuitous, every bit is ultimately traceable to very small basic elements, and is deduced from them and not introduced, as it were, from outside, as in romantic music.
>
> (Adorno 1941: 115)

Adorno returns again an again in his writings to the importance of the developing totality of the symphonic work which absorbs every detail, no matter how spontaneous. Beethoven's symphonies achieve a level of integral organization such that 'one hears the first bar of a Beethoven symphony only at the very moment when one hears the last bar' (1941: 116). This is what Adorno referred to as 'the nothingness of the parts' in a Beethoven symphony. The Beethoven symphony is contrasted by Adorno with the symphonies that were created by the later Romantic composers such as Tchaikovsky or Rachmaninov. In these latter works, the importance of the expressive details are asserted over and against the whole such that each moment of the work can no longer be determined by the totality. The expressive details in the work thus become extraneous to the structure. It is precisely this assertion of the parts over the whole that Adorno resisted. The integral work of art with its thematic density produces what Adorno calls 'a suspension of time consciousness'. Time becomes contracted through the very density of relations among the elements. There is not a multiplicity of moments but one moment. The effect upon this contraction of temporal relationships on the consciousness of the listener is such as to obliterate the contingencies of the listener's private existence and to summon that experience of the 'intentionless whole' that is marked by a characteristic elatedness (1941: 117).

His point about the integral interdependence of the parts over and against the assertion of the parts and their lack of integration within a whole is the very pivot on which Adorno's musical and aesthetic analyses turn. His method in the case of the radio symphony is simply to fit this position to the conditions of radio transmission. If late Romantic music engendered structural poverty in its superimposition of novel and expressive details, Adorno views radio as bringing about the same kind of disintegration of the integral work of art by virtue of both the physical characteristics of radio transmission as well as the culture of radio. In place of the contrast between Beehoven's densely integrated music and the comparative structural poverty of late Romantic music, radio is held to actually bring about the structural impoverishment of Beethoven's own music, its regression to being a collection of striking melodies and themes.

Adorno likens the factor of absolute dynamics in music to that of absolute dimensions in architecture. The cathedral we can enter, the vast interior, impresses us in quite a different way from any scale model. So it is with the symphony, he argues. The power of the symphony to 'absorb' its parts into the organized whole depends in part upon the volume of sound. Only if the sound is 'larger' than anything that the individual might produce with his own body, will he be able to enter the sound and become aware of the possibility of merging with the totality 'that has been structurally prepared to leave no loophole' (1941: 118). What is key, here, suggests Adorno is the experience of the enveloping symphonic space:

> To 'enter' a symphony means to listen to it not only as something before one, but as something around one as well, as a medium in which one 'lives'. It is this surrounding quality that comes closest to the idea of 'symphonic absorption'.
>
> (Adorno 1941: 118)

All of these qualities, argued Adorno, are radically affected by radio. Because of the diminution of sound dimensions and the monaural condition of radio broadcasting (at the time Adorno was writing) the 'surround' quality of the music disappears and one is left with what Adorno calls a chamber symphony. Adorno shifts the critical argument at this point. In destroying the surround quality of the symphony the listener is unable to achieve that entry into the work which enables him to immerse himself in the structural web of the work. But Adorno insists that this loss of the surround character of the symphony has its progressive aspect too in that it is this very hugeness of scale that gives rise to the functioning of music as a source of intoxication, as a drug. In Wagner's music the hugeness of sound clearly exemplifies this intoxicating effect.

Adorno now shifts the argument once more. Wagner's music is subject to the drug effect because of its hugeness. But Beethoven's music is not. The formula that Adorno provides makes the intoxicating effect of the large sound inversely proportional to the density of articulation of relations among the elements of the work. To the extent that Wagner's music lacks the tightly integral structure of a Beethoven symphony it is subject to reliance on intoxication for its effect while the structural density of a Beethoven symphony causes the largeness to absorb the listener in a very different way. The largeness of the sound serves to realize the density of structure. In Beethoven's fifth symphony, Adorno argues, the famous opening bars are nothing in themselves but the entire movement is built from the repetition and variation of this one motif. The 'nothing-in-itself' is the 'all' of the entire work. The positing of this motif at the outset such that the oak can be perceived within the acorn demands the utmost dynamic intensity. Without this hugeness of sound, the larger whole can no longer be grasped in the opening measures:

> . . . the simple, no longer emphasized in its paradoxical nature as Nothing and Everything, threatens to degenerate into the trite if the 'nothingness' of the beginning fails to be absorbed into the whole by the impetus of the statement. The tension is broken and the whole movement is on the verge of relapsing into time.
>
> (Adorno 1941: 122)

Not only the diminution of the magnitude of the sound but also the compression of the dynamic range is key to the loss of meaning in Beethoven:

> Only if the motif can develop from the restrained pianissimo to the striking yet affirming fortissimo, is it actually revealed as the 'cell' which represents the whole even when exposed as a mere monad. The more the gradation is compressed – which is necessarily the case in radio – the less this tension is felt. Dynamic repetition is replaced by a mere ornamental, tectonic one . . . the Beethoven tension obtains its true significance in the range from Nothing to All. As soon as it is reduced to the medium range between piano and forte, the Beethoven symphony is deprived of the secret of origin as well as the might of unveiling.
>
> (Adorno 1941: 123)

If the Beethoven symphony becomes a kind of chamber symphony as a result of all these reductions and compression of its dynamics, that does not mean that it now acquires the positive virtues of chamber music. It becomes simply a bad work of chamber music. Symphonic simplicity ceases to function in a symphonic way and becomes poverty of musical texture, lacking, as it does, 'polyphonous interwovenness of parts characteristic of the Chamber work'. The whole effect begins to approach that of the 'salon orchestra' (1941: 123).

If symphonic simplicity becomes structural poverty, there is a similar fate for symphonic richness. Adorno describes the way in which Beethoven articulates the symphonic texture by attaching the smallest units of motifical construction to as many different instruments and instrumental groups as possible. This colouristic differentiation realizes the most complex structural interrelationships beneath the surface. Beethoven generates a richness of finely graded colours equal to the structural complexity of motivic development within the work. The subtle colourific gradations tend to be effaced by radio, argues Adorno, and crudely conspicuous contrasts are emphasized.

Radio's neutralization of the sound colours 'practically blots out precisely those minute differences upon which the classical orchestra is built as against the Wagnerian, which has much larger colouristic means at its disposal.' (1941: 124). Beethoven's articulation of symphonic texture which subdivides a melody between first and second violins such that the decisive elements are given to the former and the more incidental to the latter, is lost in radio, which eliminates this difference between first and second violins. Such colourific values are an integral part of the composition and of the articulation of its meaning. Their elision by radio does not merely make the work less audible; in Adorno's view it destroys the work by slackening its structural articulation. It *reduces it to a collection of neat tunes whose interrelation is of no real importance at all.* This is, in any case, how Adorno tended to think of the regressive character of the music of Tchaikovsky, Rachmaninov and the late Romantic composers.

Thus behind the argument concerning the specific effect of the auditory aspect of radio transmission in the 1940s, there is the same general model concerning progressive and regressive modern music that informs all Adorno's aesthetic studies. Radio is held to trivialize a Beethoven symphony, and the classical tradition generally, by transforming it into a type of music that approximates to late Romantic compositions, to being a potpourri of hit tunes with something more or less inessential in between. This produces a type of atomized listening in which the meaning shifts from the totality to the individual moments; the latter become semi-independent monads that are then organized chiefly by temporal succession.

Adorno's argument discloses the most fundamental axiom of his theory of temporality in music. A dense structural articulation annihilates empirical time by making an entire work into one moment. A work that is a simple succession of key moments knows only empirical time. Adorno makes a distinction here between a work which constitutes an intensive totality – an instantaneous focussing of an idea, something he attributes to a Beethoven symphony – and an extensive totality – an unfolding within empirical time. He claims that the radio symphony resembles the narrative as a kind of unfolding or unpacking of details in empirical time. The details retain something of the context from which they have been torn; they acquire the character of 'quotation'. Quotation listening belongs to what Adorno has termed regressive listening. When Beethoven's fifth symphony is reduced to a series of quotation themes from the symphony it is trivialized. The quotation theme has no power to transcend the specific and to show its generality. Adorno offers the following example which underlines the distinction he wishes to make between the structural aspect and the details:

From the point of view of symphonic construction it would be possible to imagine a substitute for the second famous theme of the first movement of Schubert's B minor Symphony (the unfinished).

127

The radio listener who has no grasp of the symphonic structure would be deeply shocked if the tune he was waiting for had been replaced by another which performed its musical function equally well.

(Adorno 1941: 130)

To such a listener the theme is all, whereas to Adorno when the theme is all, it can no longer fulfil its truly musical function of serving only as material for what is to follow: 'Hence in the isolation of the symphonic theme only the trivial remains' (1941: 131). Moreover, this trivialization is nevertheless the mark of authority:

Only what is established and accepted as a standard social value is quoted, and the anxiety of the listeners to recognize the so-called Great Symphonies by their quotable themes is mainly due to their desire to identify themselves with the standards of the accepted and to prove themselves to be small cultural owners within big owner-ship culture.

(Adorno 1941: 131)

In an important reflection on the status of 'quotation', Adorno argues that the substitution of quotation for genuine reproduction does not imply fidelity to the original but the very opposite. In a statement that is surely worth considering in relation to a so-called postmodern aesthetics, Adorno insists that 'Quotation is reproduction in its decline'. Genuine reproduction reproduces a form in all its tension with its object; 'quotation-reproduction', he argues, dissolves all tension towards the object and seizes upon its particulars as fixed and reified items.

The disintegration of classical music into its themes or atoms is also associated with a romanticization of the music. In the history of the develop-ment of Romantic music after Beethoven, the disintegration of the totality in favour of the emphasis on the detail was fostered in pursuit of a greater lyrical and expressive quality in music:

The weight that falls upon the isolated detail conveys to it an importance that it never has in its context. And it is this air of importance that makes it seem to signify or express something all the time, whereas in the original that expression is mediated by the whole . . . It is the romantic notion of melodic inventiveness which radio projects upon classical music strictly so-called. Details are deified as well as reified.

(Adorno 1941: 133)

Adorno identifies 'musical thinking' with the structural element that goes beyond the mere presence of a sensuous stimulus. Radio impedes musical thinking and replaces it with an emphasis on the sensual side of music, its 'culinary aspect'. And yet the atoms (themes and tunes) that are debased by radio through a combination of trivialization and expressiveness generate their own mystique. It is the same mystique which Marx labelled 'phantasmagoria' in referring to the spell cast by the desired commodity.

While much of Adorno's argument in this paper deals with the degradation of Beethoven's symphonic music through radio transmission, the same factors account for the widespread popularity of radio broadcasts of late Romantic music, particularly Tchaikovsky. Adorno also sought to demonstrate by his arguments the pointlessness of taking seriously the listener's own accounts of the effect of the music on them through some positivistic interview or questionnaire study: 'There is no justification for unqualifiedly accepting the listener's word about his sudden delight in a Beethoven symphony, if that symphony is changed the very moment it is broadcast into something closely akin to entertainment' (1941: 136).

As with all other entertainment products of the culture industry, the radio symphony transforms the living process into ready-made piecemeal product. The ready-made, in Adorno's philosophy, indicates a passive mode of reception. The individual wants the object 'to do something for him' preferably without having to do anything himself and certainly without having to think it through.

Pedagogy

The degrading of works of serious art into the consumer goods of the culture industry reaches from the performance of serious music on the radio into the role that mass media assume as educators. Radio prided itself also on the contribution it made to introducing young people to music and to teaching them about music. For Adorno this was an extremely sensitive issue. He saw radio, at its benevolent best, as failing to bring people into an actual life relation with music and as encouraging a false understanding and appreciation of music as well as reinforcing snobbish attitudes concerning cultural knowledge as capital.

The 'Analytical Study of the NBC Music Appreciation Hour' is the least known and the longest of the radio papers (Adorno 1994b: 325–77). It was never published in Adorno's lifetime and was found among Lazarsfeld's papers after the latter's death. However, it is probably the most ambitious of the three studies. The *NBC Music Appreciation Hour*, conducted by Walter Damrosch, was a popular and highly regarded series of programmes that ran over several years in the 1930s and 1940s. Its explicit aim was to develop an appreciation of good music in the young and it was accompanied by a published guide. Adorno's critique of the programmes drew, for its empirical base, upon the accompanying textual material in the published guide (published in 1939). These included the *Teacher's Guide* and four *Student*

Worksheets. The piece is notable for providing one of the clearest insights into Adorno's own philosophy of music and his approach to pedagogy. Not the least remarkable aspect is the glimpse we get of Adorno's positive side beyond his critical demolition of the 'musical Babbitry' of the programme. He cites with genuine approval the following description of music provided in Charles B. Farnsworth's 'Introduction to series C':

> The basis of all music is the feeling of movement that the rapid passing from one tone or chord, to another produces in us, called 'ideal motion'. The way this ideal motion is put together, produces what we call form in music. In other words it gives sense to music. The mind must tie up, as it were, that we have heard with what we are hearing.
>
> (Adorno 1994b: 326)

Adorno offers concrete suggestions of his own as to pedagogic procedures that would be proper to employ, that would genuinely help to improve musical appreciation in a radio programme. He even offers alternative suggestions for the test materials used by the programme.

Here, as in the earlier 'Social Critique of Radio Music', Adorno insists at the start that the faults he will find with the programmes stem not from individuals who should be criticized but from the very conditions under which radio operates at the heart of an ownership culture forced to promote a naïve enthusiasm for any material it offers. It is clear that Adorno is not altogether comfortable in his research role. The obvious choice open to him as a critical theorist is the one he takes, that of performing a deconstructive analysis of the written materials associated with the programme. His critical deconstruction can be viewed as a confrontation between his entire orientation to culture and to music, and these written materials. Adorno samples the material primarily to illustrate the points he wishes to make. However, there are some concessions to the conventional research form. For example, there are elements of systematic exposition here; an analytical scaffold is provided for the exposition of the argument in the text.

Adorno sets out the main pedagogical aim of the makers of the series as moving from a concern with the more physical (outer) aspects of music such as the sounds of the instruments, through their imaginative associations (that is, the ideas with which they become associated such as the thunderstorm, the brook and so forth) to (inner) intellectual and spiritual aspects focussed on expressing the life-process of the composer. Such a strategy does not appeal to Adorno but he opts to take the programme's aim seriously and to set up six postulates with which the programmes would need to comply in order to meet their own objective of producing a deepening level of participation by young people in the appreciation of music. It is important to recognize here that the real arbiter of this is going to be Adorno's own certainties about what constitutes serious participation in music. He interprets the pedagogical aim of the series in terms of what that aim would mean to him and the criteria he sets up to test the success of the series are those that disclose the extent to which the programmes fail to meet their own specified aim but this is done on Adorno's terms. There is nothing necessarily wrong in this; Adorno's is a very considerable musical intelligence and his knowledge of music is profound. Nevertheless, there is a need for clarification at the level of the implicit claims made concerning research method and the role of content analysis. Notwithstanding concerns one may have at a methodological level, there is little doubt that a considerable insight is offered by Adorno into his own approach to music culture and to pedagogy generally in this paper. Above all, those who have struggled with the philosophical texts on music will find some of his most lucid statements here where he is attempting to outline an alternative pedagogy for the education of children with his discussion of the nursery rhyme, 'London Bridge is falling down'. Here, his treatment of the vital integrity of a work, which is never a mere aggregate of motives or themes, is made crystal clear.

In his first postulate, Adorno insists that if the programme series is to begin with the outer aspect of music, with the musical instruments and sounds themselves, then this should not be done in such a way that the external features of music do not become in themselves an impediment rather than an aid to genuine musical understanding. In discussing the concern with the sounds of instruments, which are given 'personalities' in the programme materials, Adorno observes that in 'serious music' the instrumental sound is a mere function of the structure of the whole 'with no intrinsic value as an individual sound'. He criticizes the programme for distracting pedagogy at the outset from the important to the subsidiary. The pedagogical objection Adorno is making here is that a child waiting to hear the individual voice of the flute in a Haydn symphony is going to be disappointed because the flute, for Haydn, has no such voice and no such message. Far from children being led to experience good music in this way they are led into the realization that adults only talk nonsense to them or into the infertile process of trying to produce in themselves the experience that is expected of them. Both poles of the child's response lead away from a genuine appreciation of serious music that is obscured and not helped by a pedagogy that points in the opposite direction.

Adorno continues his critique of the way in which the series develops from the outside to the inside of music in an analysis of the pedagogical use made of the theme as distinct from its development, the form, in a piece of music. As with all his studies of the media, Adorno argues that under the guise of making music attractive or easier, educators encourage an atomistic listening centred on themes or tunes.

> The theme is one element of the composition and an important one, but when the element is hypostatised as the composition's content, the stream of music is destroyed and replaced by the automatic recognition of what is, after all, one of the composition's tools among others.
>
> (Adorno 1994b: 333)

In his second postulate, Adorno asserts that if actual musical understanding is to be developed (something he counterposes to the dissemination of information about music), an education from the 'simple' to the 'complex' must be well-planned and all juxtaposition of divergent or non-cohering materials should be strictly avoided. Adorno thus applies to pedagogy the same criterion of structural articulation that he applies to music itself. The series authors, for example, have presumed, he argues, that by and large the historical development of music coincides with the development from the simple to the complex and that therefore an historical view of musical form leaps step by step to actual understanding. Adorno dismisses the idea as 'palpably absurd'. For example, the fugue is historically an older form and it is therefore introduced earlier in the series. Adorno insists, however, that the fugue is actually one of the most difficult forms for the layman to understand.

The third postulate concerns the relationship between theoretical explanations, their accuracy and their relationship to the concrete musical examples chosen to illustrate them. Above all, the examples must not contradict the explanations or confuse the young person. Adorno's example here refers to the programme on the fugue where the difficulty for the pupil is compounded by the fact that it uses confusing and uncharacteristic examples and does not proceed from the elementary and characteristic form. The pupil cannot get anything in the way of musical understanding from the programme but s/he can certainly absorb a lot of academic talk and its implicit claims to being cultural capital.

The fourth postulate asserts the need for the use of examples that are characteristic and explanations that are specific. An example of what Adorno has in mind here is the programme that deals with *three-part and rondo-forms*. The listeners are given an explanation of rondo-form as a logical extension of three-part form. The explanation is technically correct but Adorno insists that it is pedagogically empty. It is an unspecific explanation that can be used to explain every form – the sonata, as well as the fugue – which is unrelated to the rondo. As to the selection of characteristic examples, Adorno – in other contexts the critic of jazz – here castigates the programme for failing to illustrate the rondo form by examples of jazz, the most immediately familiar model of music for American youngsters and an appropriate one for discussion purposes. In similar vein, Adorno criticizes the inappropriate and unspecific theorizing of sonata-form.

The fifth postulate asserts that everything told to the child must be truthful. Erroneous information or partial explanations or inadequate and forced examples are not justifiable. From a programme devoted to Wagner's music, Adorno quotes this *NBC Music Appreciation Hour's* description of the plot of *Tristan*, which refers specifically to the second act of the opera:

> There the unhappy pair meet to seek brief moments of joy in each other's presence, while Isolde's maid, Brangane, stands guard in the watch-tower above. But even such momentary happiness is marred by the knowledge that night conveys only fleeting oblivion, that the stark reality of day will soon return, and that death alone can bring them liberation from these now-hateful bonds which they cannot honorably break – his as loyal liege of King Mark, and hers as Mark's queen.
>
> (Adorno 1994b: 345)

This, for Adorno, is a travesty of meaning, a 'purged Tristan'. The lovers do not 'seek brief moments of joy in each other's presence' nor do they have any twinges of conscience about 'breaking these now hateful bonds'. The programme conveys to young audiences the idea that the lovers simply suffer because the demands of conventional morality mean they cannot get together. Adorno comments that the lovers in fact do get together and that adultery is the presupposition of the whole Tristan plot. If the programme was afraid to speak about adultery, it should not have tackled Tristan or presented a dishonest account of it to young people. Needless to say, this section on false and erroneous information given to young people by the programme is the largest of the paper, as Adorno brings all the weight of his considerable musical understanding to bear in a critique of pedagogy.

The sixth and final postulate asserts that the series should not employ notions or associations contradicting the essence of the musical material or the background of the material. To select but one example, the programme states that Haydn is often referred to as the 'father' of the symphony. For good reason, it is argued, because he developed and standardized the form which has been in constant use ever since as the accepted form for symphonies, concerts, quartets, trios and sonatas. Adorno responds sharply to the use of the word 'standardized' in that account and in so doing, as stated above, he makes a distinction that is pivotal in the justification of his own use of the term in relation to popular music and jazz 'hits'. Adorno views the term 'standardization' as applicable to industrial mass production and it is for him a central category in his analysis of jazz and of all the works of the culture industry. Haydn's development of the sonata rendered it a highly dynamic framework, more capable than ever of responding to any impulse of the composer in any specific work s/he was writing. Adorno insists that sonata-form is dynamically mediated by and responsive to its constitutive elements whereas a pop song is a more or less rigid schema, unaffected by its distinctive elements, and ever shining through them.

In the second part of the article, Adorno discusses the *NBC Music Appreciation Hour* as a promoter of musical pseudo-culture. He attacks the emphasis on 'fun', on the idea that music should be appreciated because of its effects upon a listener. The fun referred to is somehow identified with the listener's recognition. While recognition is important in understanding music, it is not identical with understanding. The *NBC Music Appreciation Hour* shifts attention from fun as a life-relationship to music, to a fetishism of ownership of musical knowledge. The authoritarian nature of this type of music education promotes a cult of personalities and its accompanying veneration of the successful. This is reflected in the actual test materials developed by the programme which turn out to be essentially that of a musical spelling bee.

> The Music Appreciation Hour destroys respect for the work, its meaning, and its achievement, by transposing it into the effect it has upon the listener and inculcating in him composer-fetishism which becomes virtually identical with the 'fun' he derives from viewing a world series baseball game.
>
> The Music Appreciation Hour first cheapens music, and then teaches its pupils to adore musicians as spiritual leaders. This contradiction, basic to the whole approach, makes any destruction of fetishes impossible.
>
> (Adorno 1994b: 358)

9

FILM AND TELEVISION

Adorno once remarked that he seldom came out of a cinema without feeling that he had been made that little bit more stupid. It would be wrong to conclude from this that he detested all popular culture or that he admired none of the products of the mass culture industry. Adorno was scathing, for example, in his critique of the cruelty and conformism that he saw reflected in the laughter that filled the cinemas. This did not prevent him from being an admirer of the work of both the Marx Brothers and Charlie Chaplin – surely among the most popular entertainers ever marketed by the culture industry. Moreover, during the years of his exile in California, he was sufficiently well connected to have become aquainted with many leading luminaries of the Hollywood entertainment business, including Chaplin. In a beautifully crafted memoir (Adorno 1996: 57–61) he pays tribute to the century's quintessential clown, identifying, as his precursor, a comedian of the 1830s named Beckmann, of whom Kierkegaard had said: 'He is not only able to walk but he is also able to *come walking* . . . and by means of this genius he also improvises the whole scenic setting' (Kierkegaard, *Repetition*, cited by Adorno 1996: 58).

> The one who comes walking is Chaplin, who brushes against the world like a slow meteor even where he seems to be at rest; the imaginary landscape that he brings along is the meteor's aura, which gathers here in the quiet noise of the village into transparent peace, while he strolls on with the cane and hat that so become him. The invisible trail of street urchins is the comet's tail, through which the earth cuts almost unawares. But when one recalls the scene in *The Gold Rush* where Chaplin, like a ghostly photograph in a lively film, comes walking into the gold mining town and disappears crawling into a cabin, it is as if his figure, suddenly recognized by Kierkegaard, populated the cityscape of 1840 like staffage; from this background the star only now has finally emerged.
>
> (Adorno 1996: 58)

Mime and mimetic improvisation, so central to Chaplin's art, is the aspect of aesthetic work that Adorno revered. He saw in mimesis that purposive purposelessness Kant had claimed for the realm of the aesthetic; in a Schopenhauerian sense mimesis describes a relationship to the world that is non-exploitative, non-antagonistic. In the pure mimetic impulse there is a renunciation of all that belongs to the 'grown-up, purposive life' with its antagonisms, conflicts and ambitions in favour of a 'primitive sympathy', a play of 'semblance' through which the subject assimilates itself to its objects. Brought hard up against the purposive world, the innocence of mimesis manifests as a cruel redeemer. Chaplin was a master of this art. Adorno appreciated being one of the few intellectuals that Chaplin had actually imitated. That particular mimesis took place at a party in Malibu at which they were both present:

> While Chaplin stood next to me, one of the guests was taking his early leave. Unlike Chaplin, I extended my hand to him a bit absent-mindedly, and, almost instantly, started violently back. The man was one of the lead actors from *The Best Years of Our Lives*, a film famous, shortly after the war; he lost a hand during the war and in its place bore practicable claws made of iron. When I shook his right hand and I felt it return the pressure, I was extremely startled, but sensed immediately that I could not reveal my shock to the injured man at any price. In a split second I transformed my frightened expression into an obliging grimace that must have been far ghastlier. *The actor had hardly moved away when Chaplin was already playing the scene back* [emphasis mine]. All the laughter he brings about is so near to cruelty; solely in such proximity to cruelty does it find its legitimation and its element of the salvational. Let my remembrance of this event and my thanks be my congratulations to him on his 75th birthday.
>
> (Adorno 1996: 60–1)

Chaplin's brutal objectivity in this scene, his ability to make visible all that belongs to a moment, is no mere simulation of the phenomenal surface of a gesture or the mechanical reproduction of a sequence of acts. Mimesis springs from relatedness, from a primitive sympathy and identity with the world; all its play is insight, understanding. In the face of the world's cruelty, mimesis – absolute fidelity – brings a sense of suffering, of pathos and of longing. In a genuine mimesis, the 'copy' redeems a life and a truth that is lost to the 'original'.

Cinema has always had the power to reproduce the phenomenal surface of the world, to fill the screen with the objects, place, faces and gestures of an everyday reality. However, for the most part, this appropriation of the phenomenal surface of reality is the very antithesis of what Adorno meant by mimesis and he made this antithesis a key feature of his critique of both film and television. The typical film is a manufactured commodity. Its reproduction of the recognizable surfaces of the world represents the purposeful and skilful construction of calculated and predetermined effects upon the psyches of the mass of consumers. Adorno termed this the 'pseudo-realism' of film.

The presence of everyday reality in films – cities, bars, furniture, faces, talk and gestures – hardly equates to the 'natural' experiences of ordinary life in which presence is mediated by the specifics of the subject's life-world relations. There is a sense in which objects appear more vivid, more real in films, precisely because technique has alienated them from their life-world contexts, their 'subject relations', and re-deployed them as the material substructure of manufactured cultural goods. What was once real now partakes of the intensity of a pseudo-reality that manifests as the siren appeal of the fetish-object. Drained of any connection to the real life-world relations of the subject, objects and faces lose that specificity, that ordinary eccentric and accidental quality that stamps them as authentic. The appeal of the Hollywood phantasmagoria is a powerful one. Millions have been drawn to the box office, attracted by 'stars' who have been manufactured with even rows of teeth, flawless complexions, formless features, and with the pupils of their eyes enlarged by belladonna. The characters portrayed – gangsters, sweet heroines, bitch heroines, avenging cowboys – are rigid stereotypes and the plots of the film dramas are standardized cliché-forms that deliver calculated and predetermined messages.

Modern mass culture was also associated with changes in the audience for cultural goods, with the decline of the cultured elite and its replacement by a mass of new consumers of culture. Moreover, argues Adorno, the modern intellectual minority does not equate to the old cultured classes. The crucial factor in the change in the audience for cultural goods is the decline of *inwardness* inherent in that change. The concept of an inner agency, of a subject that stands back from the world, that has distance and is not identical with the existent, is crucial for Adorno. The autonomous individual is heir to a 'Culture' that mediates his or her relationship to the world, realizing itself in his projects. The mechanism for conceiving of the internalization of such a culture, for Riesman as for Adorno, is essentially that developed by Freud: the child's identification with parent (authority) figures, which results in the internalization of his/her ego-ideals as a structuring agency within the personality. Paradoxically, the theory holds that it is identification with authority figures that gives rise to the introjection of Culture as an autonomous agency within the personality (Riesman's 'internal gyroscope'), thereby enabling the individual to distance himself or herself from authority through internalizing authority. It is this that is key to the possibility of resistance.

Within the hard glossy surfaces of commodified cultural goods is what Adorno referred to as the soft centre of a decayed romanticism. Values that were developed in an earlier time by a class that celebrated individualism and honoured the claims of an interior world of subjectivity were now disseminated to mass audiences who lacked both individuality and inwardness and whose lives were stamped by an increasing anxiety to conform. The tenets of bourgeois idealism could not serve to make sense of the real-world relations of such audiences. They lacked the autonomy or internalized agency necessary for that. These ideological remnants were now external to and superimposed on the consciousness of mass audiences. Thus, the alienated tenets of bourgeois decency, enshrined in filmic clichés, assumed an authoritarian relationship to individuals in whom traits of dependency and conformity were continuously reinforced by cultural goods.

In the days before television, Hollywood movies of the 1930s and 1940s unashamedly fed the demands for 'escapist' entertainment. They provided regular relief from the seedy drabness of the Depression years, from the degradation of unemployment and domestic insecurity. The masses of cinemagoers were able to pass easily and quickly from the stresses of modern life into the vision of a glamorous and seemingly more 'desirable' life; all for the price of admission to the local 'flea-pit'. The up-close, larger-than-life realism of adventure films and musical romances conjured a vivid presence for silent dreamers in a darkened auditorium. For a few hours at a time, the fretful could exchange the drabness of their surroundings for all this. They could identify with the characters and relations that appeared so vividly present and could draw on these identifications to feed a fantasy-life outside the cinema. This did not mean, of course, that the average cinema-goer was unable to distinguish between reality and fantasy. On the contrary, the pleasure of experiencing what was on offer in the Hollywood dream only served to make reality's deficit more visible. The relief on offer was never more than a temporary 'fix'.

Nevertheless, there is a sense in which reality and fantasy do become confounded. Insofar as the medium of cinema appropriates the material of everyday reality – the images of men and women speaking and smiling and acting much as people do in everyday life, of furniture, furnishings and textured material – so everyday reality itself comes to take on the associations that have been acquired from the world of cinema; life imitates art. More than this, the business of constructing reality in everyday contexts comes to resemble the making of a film or the writing of a script. It has been said that when the film *The Godfather* achieved cult status, real criminals and Mafia bosses took on some of the appearances and gestures of their film counterparts. When an English princess mounted the steps of St Paul's Cathedral with her long bridal train billowing behind her, it was tempting to see Walt Disney's princess as having made some contribution to the scene.

Everyday life has been affected by cinema and by all the associated meanings that have come to permeate commonplace venues, pubs, bars, nightclubs, street corners, etc. A table is so much more than a physical surface that is rigid, smooth and rectangular or round in shape. It appears also in terms of its uses, the disposition of bodies with respect to it – people sit around a table; they do not, typically, walk on it. The table may be an instrument of work or of commensality, the site of business meetings or family gatherings. Culture, the record of experience, permeates the phenomenal surfaces of the world. Insofar as this permeation is the product of real dynamic and historical relations among individuals in the family, the workplace or the community, the everyday world of objects can be said to realize or express the life-process of the individual and the community. When, however, these meanings do not arise directly from the social interactions of individuals, but are super-imposed upon the familiar objects and scenes of their everyday lives, these same objects are alienated from subjects; they grow increasingly opaque to those whose life-process they no longer express. The objects of everyday life are thereby increasingly swallowed up by the fetish-objects that make up the world of commodities and men and women come to respond to them in daily life in a dependent and authoritarian–submissive way.

The mythologies and romantic values disseminated via the silver screen enter into the very textures of everyday life, of everyday attitudes, postures, conversation and social relationships. They serve not simply as a repository of meanings or 'signifieds' assimilated from mass cultural goods but as a model for making, for 'signifying'. The construction of reality comes to be less and less distinguishable from the construction of ideology; as a consequence, it can no longer provide a source of genuine experience from which to critique the ideology that it has itself become. A critical consciousness demands the independence of reality and ideology no matter how closely they interact. What Adorno calls the 'pseudo-realism' of film undermines that indepen-dence, assimilating the former to the latter.

The point can be illustrated by reference to Adorno's discussion of an early Aldrich episode written for a TV drama series and entitled *Dante's Inferno* (Adorno 1998: 59–71). From the very opening moments, he argues, the audience is in little doubt about what is to happen. The layout of the nightclub, tables, bar and furniture and the appearance of the characters – the man drinking at the bar; a woman, heavily made up, seated, legs crossed, on a bar stool – informs the audience that some real violence and murder is going to take place. The woman is probably not going to be the murderer but is very likely the victim whose fate will be some kind of retribution for her 'fast' life-style. The whole piece is put together as a recognizable and standardized schema (actually Aldrich went on later to become a highly rated exponent of film noir). Adorno's concern is not, however, with the fact that we draw on stereotypes in order to interpret situations. He accepts, as do psychologists generally, that stereotyping is an important aspect of information processing and essential at some level. The key issue concerns the way in which stereotypes are held. When they are simply initial con-figurations that are open to modification in the light of experience they are valid. However, when they are rigidly imposed on a content and are not open to being changed in response to that content then they become part of the pathology that Adorno labels authoritarianism (1998: 62).

In reflecting on the Aldrich piece, Adorno is claiming that the cliché-forms of typical television dramas are rigid and standardized and not open to change. They are literally closed structures with all their effects carefully calculated and predetermined. In a deeper sense, however, Adorno is also arguing that this closure is brought from mass cultural goods into everyday life where the assimilation of these standardized schemas effectively reduces ordinary human relations to cliché-forms and stereotypes. In order for a schema to change, the subject must be able to hold it up to the light of real experience and find it inadequate. This is not possible for the subject who has no recourse to anything outside the schemas and ideologies that envelop everyday life. Change in both art and life emerges from the dialectical tension between the two spheres. Experience is genuine experience only when this tension is maintained and it is only genuine experience that can expose the falsity of the claims of current schemas. When this tension dissolves and the forms of mass culture are sublated in the constitutive praxis of everyday life, then the new cannot be experienced as such; we meet with the hardened casing of a reality mired in cliché-forms; a reality that is condemned simply to repeat itself.

From the point of view of method and analysis, Adorno's radio papers are in a category of their own. They all centre on the single topic of radio's presentation of serious music to mass audiences. Adorno is an expert on music and he is able to use his philosophy of music and his musicology to argue that radio degrades serious music, transmuting it into the form of 'cultural goods' produced by the culture industry. When looking at television or film or the variety theatre, however, his stance must necessarily be different. He makes a degree of compromise, at least at the level of the verbal nod, with the objectives of a research process that he despised and rejected, in the paper 'How to Look at Television' (Adorno 1991d: 136–54). He begins by claiming that the kind of critical deconstructive work he proposes to do will provide a means of not only improving programmes but of sensitizing the public at large to some of the deleterious effects of televised material. 'Yet our approach is practical. The findings should be so close to the material, should rest on such a solid foundation of experience, that they can be translated into precise recommendations and be made convincingly clear to large audiences' (1991d: 136). Readers of the paper may well find it difficult to see how any such translation into 'precise recommendations' can even occur let alone how such recommendations could have any part to play in Adorno's project.

In the television studies his data is largely made up of the typical drama productions of the day shown on American television. He is not concerned to show, however, that the typical television drama is a debasement of some model of drama taken from serious theatre. In fact the concept of what constitutes 'good' drama hardly plays any part here (certainly not explicitly), whereas the concept of what constitutes good music is central to the radio papers where the structural aspect or 'form' of good music and its degradation is an issue. In the television papers, Adorno's principle focus is the *content* of the drama. He seeks to disclose the 'messages' that are conveyed to mass audiences through the content of the dramas and to argue that these provide a distorted view of reality, reinforcing the false values, childishness and dependency of audiences in a manner characteristic of the culture industry generally.

Notwithstanding the focus on the content of dramas, the plot detail and so forth, Adorno does rely on a formal model as his critical lever and comparator. That model is not provided by drama as such but by depth psychology, specifically psychoanalysis, as this bears on Adorno's concept of an autonomous adult individual. It is this model that he sees travestied and degraded in the television dramas and his deconstruction of these dramas consists largely in seeking to show how this is done. The 'form' of television dramas manifests the standardization, repetitiveness and self-sameness that Adorno holds to be characteristic of all products of the culture industry. As such, television tends to produce 'automatized' responses in its audiences and to weaken the power of the individual to resist. Adorno turns not to classical drama as his model here, either, but to the example of the early 'bourgeois' novels. The bourgeois novel form allows for the continuous introduction of new material and characters – sub-plots, digressions, etc. – that have not been prepared for in advance and seem to pop up as though from nowhere and take up the thread. The readers did not know what would happen next. Indeed, anything might happen next. By contrast, the TV drama is a closed and predictable affair in which nothing genuinely surprising can really occur. 'Every spectator of a television mystery knows with absolute certainty how it is going to end. Tension is but superficially maintained and is unlikely to have a serious effect any more' (Adorno 1991d: 138). This inevitability ensures that the spectator feels on safe ground all the time and has only to be minimally activated with respect to the material. The desire for safety and security reflects, in turn, the change from a free competitive society (an earlier entrepreneurial capitalism) to a virtually closed society dominated by the fear of not belonging or not being included.

The dialectic of inner–outer plays a key role in Adorno's critiques of modern culture. This is particularly true of the television papers. In the time of the classic nineteenth-century bourgeois novel, the element of an 'innerness' shaped by Protestant values was very much a feature of middle-class consciousness. There was a clear fit between the ideology of moral decency, obligation and duty, etc., which underpinned the construction of character in the early novels, and the ideology of the classes that read them. Adorno claims that this is no longer the case in the age of television.

Certainly the ideology survives in modern television dramas. There is still a set of underlying assumptions about decency, moral responsibility, sexual modesty, etc., but this value formation no longer has any basis in the real-life conditions of the classes that subscribe to it. When this happens, such values cease to constitute an autonomous agency, an internal gyroscope, and become, instead, an externalized and authoritarian set of prescriptions. Thus commodified, they enter the realm of fetish-objects. A woman's sexual restraint in the time of the early novels was bound up with the tense conflict between sexual desire and Christian ideals. It survives (distorted argues Adorno) in the message of numerous television dramas of the 1950s that 'getting married' is the only prize worth having for a woman and that only 'nice' girls get married. What may have had its origins in a dialectical process involving an inner conflict of genuine values has now become transmuted into values of a different sort, property values, in which the 'virtue' of a woman, like her clothes, make-up and facial features, adds to or subtracts from her 'exchange value'. The element of inwardness and inner conflict is gone. The cry of the classical heroine, who had succumbed to the seducer's advances, that she had been 'undone' and 'betrayed' meant far more, inwardly, than that her value on the marriage market had been lowered, although it no doubt included that.

Adorno's point here is that in the age of other-directed men and women the conditions of life that formerly demanded a dynamic and historically constituted innerness have weakened greatly among the middle classes, and with that weakening there has been a continuous decline in those intellectual practices requiring sustained concentration, 'indwelling', erudition, critical thinking. In the modern world the management of information comes to displace the creation of meaning. In Adorno's view, the new intelligentsia does not equate to the old 'cultured classes'. Both it and the masses of consumers who are now being offered cultural goods that were formerly inaccessible to them are a product of these new social conditions. They cling to the romanticism of traditional bourgeois values that no longer have any relevance for their real-life conditions. Adorno has used similar arguments in connection with music. The late Romantic composers reflect just such a degradation of the classical tradition for Adorno. Because the life-world conditions for which that tradition in music was created have now been superseded by very different conditions, music written in that form now lacks truth-value. It is therefore easily assimilated, along with all other alienated and commodified forms, to the culture industry.

If it is the case that the romantic ideology of traditional middle-class values survives in modern television dramas in cliché-form, it is also the case that the modern television drama mimics the multi-layered character of the traditional narrative. In order for the classical bourgeois novel to reach the inmost levels of experience, its meanings had to be disseminated at many levels at once. In the television drama, Adorno argues, this multi-layering of meaning is simulated without the innerness that was characteristic of an earlier time. The meaning of multi-layered thus undergoes important changes. In the end it comes down to a distinction between the manifest 'message' of the dramas and their latent 'message'. Adorno's deconstructive content analyses are aimed at disclosing the latent message that is hidden beneath the surface and which he claims serves to reinforce the powerlessness and dependency of the mass television audience. This latent message is carried in the content of the drama and at every level in the format of television programmes, the mode of address, the reduced and simplistic plot-forms, stereotypes and so forth.

Situation comedy

Adorno's deconstruction of television programmes while often perceptive and insightful, is neither particularly sophisticated nor refined as method. The manifest level of meaning equates roughly to a surface reading of intentions and events, what the programme makers intend to convey to the audience about the characters and situations and events. In a situation comedy about a young teacher who is attractive, witty, good-natured and with no money, engaged in constant skirmishes with an insensitive and boorish school principal, the characters portrayed, the comic situations that trade on the central character's need for money and a good meal and her witty, inventive and often unsuccessful strategies for satisfying her needs, together make up the manifest level of meaning (Adorno 1991d: 143–4). At a latent level, Adorno argues, such comedies convey messages that disarm resistance and reinforce exploitative social relations and regressive social attitudes. The depiction of the teacher as both witty, charming and attractive and as an abused person in what are degrading situations that the audience laughs at, achieves a compromise between the hostility and contempt for intellectuals that Adorno sensed in American society and what might be called a cringing respect for culture. The audience is suppose to identify with the teacher and not, of course, the caricature of an autocratic principal. The hidden message, according to Adorno, is that no matter what exploitation you undergo, or what indignities are inflicted upon you by those in authority, they will have no dominion over you if you are as witty, charming, resourceful, inventive and as free from resentment as is this young teacher.

Adorno also identifies another character that appears in both comedy and serious drama, namely the 'bitch heroine'. Her principle characteristic is that she is manipulative and cruel but is depicted as somehow desirable; and her rude and aggressive behaviour towards her father or lover has no real consequences for her but serves as a sign of objective judgement for the audience. One of Adorno's examples deals with a serious drama in which the 'cute girl' is a criminal. Adorno argues that after her obvious appeal in the very first scene, the viewer is not to be disappointed. Sentenced to a long term of imprisonment, she is pardoned and is set to marry her victim (Adorno 1998: 63). She has, after all, remained sexually pure. Such a figure reinforces both the notion of woman as a desirable property and the social acceptance of parasitic behaviour. Adorno interprets this in Freudian terms. Just as modern consumer capitalism produces dependency, so the combination of dependency and aggression involved in the exploitative relations of the bitch-heroine draws acceptance and even approval. It is dependency and aggression which together make up what Freud termed *orality.*

Another figure that Adorno claimed was widespread in television comedy and drama was the stereotype figure of the artist as an effeminate and abnormal weakling, unsuited to meet life's challenges and a somewhat ridiculous figure, introverted and sexually ambivalent. The figure is taken up into popular culture's glorification of the virile man, the man of action, where it supplies the contrast structure of the despised intellectual. This denigration of the intellectual was something Adorno saw as deep in the culture industry. It was matched only by the latter's servile and sancti-monious reverence for the reputations of great artists and intellectuals.

Such ideological manipulation of the audiences cannot be attributed to the wicked intentions of programme-makers: 'The sickness lies not in wicked individuals but in the system' (Adorno 1991d: 64). As a result, even drama that is serious in intent is undermined. Adorno provides the example of a script in which a famous and successful young actress is cured of her narcissism and learns for the first time to love. The instrument of her salvation is a young (and this time a sympathetically portrayed intellectual) dramatist. He writes a drama in which she plays the main role. Her con-frontation with the role is supposed to produce all the tensions and conflict resolutions that are needed to move her from her more malicious self to the ultimately more noble impulses which the audience and her dramatist know to be a latent presence. This is a common reversal of psychoanalytic insight that occurs in many dramas. Freud made the socially acceptable side of human nature visible on the outside of the person and claimed that the darker side with its primeval instincts – the id – was both hidden from view and unconscious. The heroine, here, and in many other dramas, wears her id on her sleeve and allows us to discover the sweetness of disposition that she is hiding behind it. Adorno points out that modern mass cultural drama is parasitic on Freudian and even Marxian insights, distorting them in the process so that they are as bereft of truth-value as they are pretentious in their claims to account for real human behaviour. Truly objective conditions and problems are given a private and personal causation that trivializes them and renders the solutions proffered wholly implausible.

Modern mass culture takes its leave of the 'traditional middle-class procliv-ities for inwardness, ambivalence and internal conflicts', the stuff of classic bourgeois literature. Middle-class requirements bound up with internalization, such as concentration, intellectual effort and erudition, are continuously and everywhere slackened and diminished. However, society still retains intact the ontology with which that inwardness was associated, the moral code, the code of decency. This code ends up superimposed on a mentality quite different from it, one that lacks the inwardness that would make sense of it; the code appears, therefore, in a fetishized and authoritarian guise. There is no longer a balance between ideology and actual life conditions. Modern popular culture retains and disseminates the ideology of an earlier society that is completely disjunctive with the lives people actually live. Its manifest message may be one of Puritan values but its latent message reflects the overwhelming pressure to conformity in an increasingly authoritarian and hierarchical society. The mentality reinforced by the majority of television shows is marked by gullibility, intellectual passivity and smugness; all attitudes which Adorno believes to be encouraged by totalitarian creeds and which may be conveyed even when the manifest content of a show is anti-totalitarian.

Adorno's attitude towards film was ambivalent and some of his most interesting remarks on media are to be found both in his criticism of the realist tendency of film and in his later insights into the potential of film to become serious art. 'Transparencies on Film' offers some intriguing and insightful reflections that point to more positive possibilities and conclusions concerning mass media and its evolution than were present in the original analysis of the culture industry (Adorno 1991e: 154–61).

Film, after all, can resist and overcome its characteristic false immediacy and pseudo-realism. In the first reflection, Adorno acknowledges that cinema is not always the polished Hollywood model of the culture industry. The latter always exploits to the full the technological means available. Not all films are made by the Hollywood machine, however. Some are low-budget movies that convey the rough and accidental character of life. If this merely indicated that they were made by poor relations and suffered a deficit as a consequence, they would be inconsequential. Adorno argues, however, that in their stark, unglossed immediacy they hold out the possibility of something serious and good. The technically polished standard of the typical Hollywood movie betokens its utter standardization, its planned, predigested and already integrated character. Authentic life, which is always open, and which continues without the certainty of what is going to happen next, has been drained from the product. Film productions in which this technical closure is foregone, films which are often made on a shoe-string budget and which surrender to the possibilities of the uncontrolled and the accidental, hold out the hope of a liberating transformation of mass culture. 'In them the flaws of a pretty girl's complexion become the corrective to the immaculate face of the professional star' (Adorno 1991e: 154).

The move Adorno makes here is an interesting one. While he opposes a realism (pseudo-realism) in which art slavishly copies the objective construction of the world – the elements of the status quo – he embraces the ideal of a naturalism that records the sensuous stream in which the subject is conscious of the world. The objects that are out there are already the product of construction and are caught in a web of pre-digested meanings. The very solidity of objects arises from the rigidity of the frameworks and schemas in which the sensuous responses of the subject are embedded. We see objects not in terms of the immediate sense impressions that are there for us in encounters with them but in terms of our constructed experience, of what is not present, of the already-made. The whole development of modernist art was towards a disembedding of objects from their pre-established contexts, even a disintegration of objects, in order to generate sensuous elements sufficiently plastic as to be amenable to a sensuous construction of the world on the side of the subject. In a sense, one might see this move in art as a movement from object-cliché to subject-realization. It is impossible to understand modernist art without observing what it was in the process of destroying and the necessity for this destruction as a basis for the reconstitution of art on the side of the subject. The pre-digested images of a Hollywood pseudo-realism are faces and objects that have been transformed by the rigid schemata of the market-tested commodity. When Adorno praises the 'amateurish', rough-and-ready, uncontrolled appearance of some low-budget movies he is approving the disembedding of objects and faces from the standardized schemata that come with the polished technique of film. The realism to which he points is a naturalism, a sensuous subjectivity that is, nevertheless, utterly objective – the subjective rendered objectively. If this is all there is to the matter, Adorno might have embraced the Impressionist artists who also sought to liberate the object through recording the truth of sense impressions at an instant – ignoring the moments on either side. However, while Adorno approved the disembedding of the elements of sensuous response from a false construction – that is, their deconstruction – he did not accept that as the goal of art but as a means for achieving a renewed constructive plasticity. Adorno's embrace of this recovery of the subjective substratum of experience was never an embrace of a radical subjectivism of the kind that led to the development of phenomenology, which he opposed. Reality had to be re-made on the side of the subject. From being a closed and already constructed world imposed upon the subject it would then become an open and dynamically constituted world, which emanated from the subject in interactions with each other, a fully social subject.

The second reflection concerns the narrative aspect of film dialogue. The focus here is a film of Musil's novel *Young Torless* by the German director Schlöndorff, in which large chunks of dialogue from the novel itself were substituted for the lines of the scriptwriters. Adorno points out that even when dialogue is used in the novel, the spoken word is not directly spoken but is rather distanced by the act of narration – perhaps even by the typography – and thereby abstracted from the physical presence of living persons. Thus the fictional characters of the novel never really resemble their empirical counterparts. But this distance is abolished by film. To the extent that a film seeks to be realistic, the semblance of immediacy (false immediacy, pseudo-realism) cannot be avoided. The solution of inserting prose from narrative fiction will not work because it sounds pompous and unreal. The film must therefore find other means to establish immediacy. Adorno suggests that improvisation, which systematically surrenders itself to unguided chance, might be the best alternative. (It is curious to note here the hostility that he elsewhere shows to the universally acknowledged examples of jazz musicians improvising.) Certainly there are examples of film-makers in recent years that have moved in this direction.

In the key third reflection, the mimetic possibilities of film are redirected from the task of copying the world in its facticity towards the modelling of the subjective mode of experience. It is this that opens up the possibilities of film to become genuinely artistic. Adorno invokes the notion of a subjective experience that consists in an interior monologue of images – in response to experiences of nature – which he likens to writing that 'moves before our eyes while fixed in its discrete signs'. Such inward image-writing, he argues, is to film what the visible world is to painting or the acoustic world to music. He insists that irrespective of the technological origins of the cinema, the aesthetics of film will do better to base itself on this subjective mode. As the objective recreation of this type of experience, film may become art. This is a neat manoeuver in which Adorno contemplates a reversal of orientation for film. He had criticized it for its slavish duplication of the objective, 'what is out there'. He now redeems it with the realization of its possibilities for duplicating the subjective, 'what is in here'. And in one of those subtle turns in critical theory of which he is a master, he comments, 'The technological medium par excellence is thus intimately related to the beauty of nature' (1991d: 156).

Yet another irony is exploited in considering the positive possibilities of film. It concerns the effects produced upon the audience in reception. The audience sometimes responds in ways that conflict with what is intended in the manipulations of the culture industry. There are always other ways of using the material on offer that an audience can seize upon. In its attempts to manipulate the masses the ideology of the culture industry becomes as internally antagonistic and contradictory as the society it seeks to control. It thus contains the antidote to its own lie.

The realistic nature of film means that it does not permit of absolute construction: its elements, no matter how abstract, always retain something representational; they are never purely aesthetic values. Adorno never ceased to oppose the realist simulation of immediacy in film art. 'Tending to rein-force, affirmatively, the phenomenal surface of society, realism dismisses any attempt to penetrate that surface as a romantic endeavor' (Adorno 1991e: 157). Film must seek a way of resolving that dilemma by finding a suitable procedure. Adorno suggests that the obvious answer is 'montage', which does not interfere with things but rather arranges them in a constellation akin to writing (note the different view of montage taken here from that taken elsewhere with respect to Brechtian technique). Also, he suggests, the most promising potential for film lies in interaction with other media such as music. Not surprisingly, therefore, Adorno took a keen interest in film music.

Film music

As Graham McCann says in his 'new introduction' to *Composing for the Films: Suggestions and Conclusions*, the collaboration between Adorno and Eisler linked two of the most significant aesthetic traditions in twentieth-century Marxism: Brechtian artistic practice and critical theory, with all the dissonances clearly present (Adorno and Eisler 1994). The book sought to achieve a balance between Adorno's critique of standardized musical structures that had informed all his attacks on popular music and Eisler's Brechtian commitment to overcoming these standardized techniques through making their mechanisms visible, that is, through a version of Brechtian alienation technique. The critique of the culture industry appears here in prototype in the analysis of the deficiencies of commercial film music. The contradiction that the authors point up is that between the pretense of the movie to offer realism and the technological and manufactured character of film-making. Music was simply called in aid of the illusion. As for film music itself, it had never had any real autonomy. It subordinated itself entirely to meeting the requirements of a text outside of itself and thereby became, in Adorno's terms, 'use-music'.

In the concluding chapter of the book the opening pages disclose something of the experience of attempting to resist the anti-artistic practice of the Hollywood studios. Adorno had never composed music for films but Eisler certainly had and the authors note the inevitability of the breakdown of attempts at reform 'because of the disproportion between the hypertrophied power of a system rationalized to the point of absurdity, and any possible individual initiative' (Adorno and Eisler 1994: 115). Some respond by surrendering to the power of the culture industry and make a virtue of absolute conformity to the mass-market criterion of truth. Others claim to be rebels and oppose the system but end up producing essentially similar products to those who are absorbed by it. The authors refuse to put their faith in any notion of piecemeal or gradual reform but insist upon strenuous efforts to achieve an unofficial tradition of genuine art, making the point that when subject matter that is unworthy in itself is actually approached in an objective manner an element of truth is introduced that asserts itself against the existing limitations. No film music, however, can be better than what it accompanies:

Good music accompanying hackneyed or idiotic action and meaning-less chatter becomes bad and meaningless . . . In claiming to be something that is compatible with the picture, it [music] loses all right to function as purely musical expression. In a conventional film, conventional essentially spurious music can occasionally be 'truer' than genuine music, because the former at least does not degrade truth into an element of spuriousness.

(Adorno and Eisler 1994: 117)

Technique and spirit are linked by the authors in their analysis. To subject cinema music to objective requirements, as determined by the composer, is to represent the public's 'objective' interests as against its 'manipulated' interests. The distinction recalls the classical Marxist distinction between true and false consciousness, true and false interests. Knowing, however, the difference between the two is not easy and certainly not knowable in advance as it were. In each individual case one has to determine, on the basis of the function and nature of the music, to what extent it actually fits its mission or to what extent its humanity is used only to mask the inhuman. Applying a version of the principle of non-identity, the authors suggest that the music should not over-eagerly identify with the event on screen but should be able to assert its distance from it and thus accentuate its meaning.

The authors oppose the idea of music as mere duplication of pictures, as the attempt to decrease the distance between picture and spectator by creating moods. Rather, film music should stress the mediated and alienated elements in the photographed action, thereby preventing confusion between reality and reproduction, a confusion that is made more prevalent by film technology. 'A proper dramaturgy, the unfolding of a general meaning, would sharply distinguish between picture, words and music and for that very reason relate them meaningfully to each other' (Adorno and Eisler 1994: 122). The achievement of surface accuracy in film as when an effort is made to get all the historical details of a period piece right is deplorable enough, argue the authors, when the film itself is a travesty of political and social realities. However, in the case of film music, not even this surface accuracy, 'the art of make-up' is achieved since ready-made snatches of composed music are literally stolen from anywhere and used to accompany wholly unsuitable and incompatible actions.

Adorno and Eisler argue that a film composer should not write a note that overlooks the social–technological prerequisite of the motion picture, namely its nature as mass production. No such music should seek to have the same character of uniqueness that is desirable in music intended for live perfor-mance. 'The aim is to write music that abandons itself to the uniqueness of its concrete occasion and at the same time it should take care not to seek its fulfillment in the triumph of intruding upon this uniqueness' (1994: xx).

Film music, they argue, must never take itself seriously, always maintaining a tongue-in-cheek relationship to its object, an awareness of its own technical determination that can serve to distance it from its object. Film music does not attract the listening attention of concert music; its effect is almost subliminal; it must be sensible and yet slip by the listener, understood in parenthesis, as it were. Good cinema music, therefore, must achieve everything that it does achieve on the surface, its whole structure must be instantly disclosed; it must not become lost in itself. The more that film music adds the lacking depth dimension to the picture, the less it must itself develop in depth. All this implies a striving to make everything completely sensuous, in contrast to musical transcendence and inwardness. In a radio interview, many years ago, the lyricist Oscar Hammerstein discussed the difference between writing song lyrics for a musical as compared with writing poetry. Lyrics for a musical, he said, have to deliver up their idea immediately in the moment they are heard. The listener is not able to go back on the action to ponder and unravel the meaning or to search for the idea beneath the surface.

10

WOODY ALLEN'S
CULTURE INDUSTRY

At the heart of Adorno's critique of popular culture is his insistence on linking truth-value in culture to a particular mode of response in the face of what he and others perceive as the crisis of modernity. The alienation that divides subject from object can only be overcome, according to this view, by preserving the dynamic and expressive connection between the two. The identity of individual and society was central to bourgeois ideology in the early nineteenth century. The expressive link between 'subject and object', 'individual and society', was presupposed and reflected in the very structuration of art works – the structuration of a Balzac novel or a Beethoven symphony. The advent of monopoly capitalism had shattered the illusion that this positive link was real, that the individual could truly see her life reflected in the larger social reality. The resulting alienation provoked the reactions of what we now call the modernist avant-garde.

Modernism can be said to have embraced a number of strategies in response to alienation in the modern world and it developed a variety of aesthetic techniques that are now widely used even in popular culture. Adorno is often thought of as a champion of modernism but he really championed one particular modernist strategy in responding to the crisis of alienation: the strategy of making the alienation of the subject do the work of linking subject and object by using non-identity with an oppressive world as a vehicle for expressing the life-process damaged by it. Thus while Adorno criticized any art that sought to perpetuate the illusion that individual and society were reconcilable or reconciled under modern conditions, he also refused to give up the 'ideal' of identity. It was the pursuit of this ideal that disclosed the suffering of the individual in the totally administered society and it did so by keeping subject and object (negatively) yoked together. Adorno rejects any aesthetic response that does not seek to preserve this link, that abandons it in the hope of recovering sensibility as its own object.

Presence

The culture industry, from Adorno's point of view, is both a manifestation of the alienation of individual and society and a means of denying it. The

151

sensuous life of the subject gets reduced to the sensuous effects that can be worked upon him. The construction of these effects is determined by considerations of market and profit. The sensuous effects themselves are subject-alien in the sense that they are not expressive of the subject's life-process. We can describe the production of effects, here, using two terms that Adorno used often, namely 'construction' and 'mimesis'. I will theorize them in my own way but my reasoning, while different from Adorno's, is at least resonant with his perspective so far as these two concepts are concerned.

The most obvious way to look at a sequence of actions is in terms of means–end relations. We can make sense of what someone does if we know what s/he is aiming to achieve, the result s/he is seeking to bring about. The actions of a car salesman can be understood in terms of the exigencies of overcoming the sales resistance in a customer and making a sale. The means–end schema is central to sociological thinking about action. Nevertheless it is not sufficient in order to describe adequately the action process. The same sequence of action can also be referred to its 'intrinsic' or sensuous logic. The car salesman manifests a demeanour in the situation, a sensuous presence. We might describe it as energetic, tense, aggressive, warm, etc. That presence is very much what he is acting from; it is a 'readiness', a capacity that accompanies his actions. Whether the individual is a car salesman, an airline hostess or a diplomat, s/he has to produce not only the sequence of actions necessary to bring off the sought-after result but also the sensibility and agency (presence) – the capacity – in and through which these actions are performed. Aesthetic work is therefore essential to everyday life and to the most ordinary daily acts (Witkin 1990). The sophisticated form it takes in the development of art works and cultural goods ought not to be allowed to obscure this fact.

Construction

If we think of a sequence of acts on its own, purely in terms of its extrinsic logic, the component acts can be described as 'subject-alien'. They are ordered through a process that is best described as *construction*. The mode of rational-technical manufacture that governs the micro-division of labour provides an obvious example of this. Tasks are broken down into elementary units that are alienated from any kind of creative or expressive subjectivity. These units are then subject to a complex process of construction that is 'mechanical' rather than 'organic'. To the extent that the presence of the subject in the situation is purely an adaptation to the extrinsic demands of the situation, then this presence, too, can be seen in the same way. The sensuous elements of which it is constituted are first rendered subject-alien and the required presence is then mechanically constructed from these alienated elements. The proverbial airline hostess's smile might be thought of in this way. The cultivation of the appearance of pleasantness and warmth need not be a genuine expression. It can be constructed not merely as a mask but as a 'tension structure', from sensuous elements that are alienated from the subject. The airline hostess's smile may not be at war with her disposition towards the customer; it may come easily to her. Nevertheless, it may be a constructed smile for all that, a crafting of effects. The subject-alien character of the elements is not lessened because they accord with what the subject wants or desires.

The construction of action that can successfully master the object is action that has 'copied' its resistances into its inner structure. This process extends to the construction of presence inasmuch as this same set of resistances is copied into the incipient readiness to act and not just into the actions themselves. Construction, in the sense in which it used here. is closely identified with 'copying'. Thus the making of a sale or the serving of a customer or any other set of actions oriented to the bringing about of some end, effect or result can also be seen as anticipating – copying or encoding – the 'resistant surfaces' of the object to be engaged; a process that extends to the construction of the presence of the actor in the situation. Adorno's claims concerning the culture industry and the products of mass culture would bring it within the realm of 'constructed presence and action' as theorized here. The question to be considered is whether or not Adorno is justified in treating all or even most of popular culture in this manner.

Mimesis

Another term which plays an even more central role in Adorno's work is 'mimesis'. The term has been central to a great deal of theorizing about art and culture. Auerbach's famous critical study of Western literature is titled *Mimesis*. Even where different words are used it is frequently the case that the concept is being invoked. Susan Langer speaks of 'semblance' and the artist as undertanding feeling because 'he makes its likeness' (Langer 1953). The introduction of the term 'mimesis' in the *Dialectic of Enlightenment* is not accompanied by a definition and there is no doubt that the widespread use of the term argues for a greater degree of theoretical clarity. Adorno and Horkheimer associate mimesis with the kind of sympathetic imitation of natural forces that occurs among so-called 'primitives' – shaman rituals and so forth. Confronted by the force of nature, primitive man sought to become like nature – imitated nature – to gain some degree of control over his world.

Adorno is really asking two things of the concept: that mimesis should involve the notion of an activity that copies the object and at the same time that this copying should be seen as an act of self-surrender – as a subject's moulding of itself to its object – 'snuggling up' to it. These two aspects belong, respectively, to two different levels of operation. A primitive sympathy might describe an undifferentiating awareness in which the subject has the sense of its objects as present in its own activity in respect of them, as if, in and through the free exercise of that activity, these objects 'come into existence', thereby conferring upon the subject a sense of 'being the cause' of this coming into existence of its objects; of possessing mastery, not over its objects but as one with them and with the environment.

'Making a copy', however, is a focussed and deliberate act. The link between the two levels of operation is via expression. Although mimesis, like construction, involves an idea of the 'copy', I want to distinguish in a way that Adorno does not, between mimesis as the 'expressive' formation of semblance and the 'constructed' copy. The copy is constructed on the outside from the standpoint of the object and, as I have theorized it, makes use of elements that have been rendered subject-alien for its material. Mimesis originates in a 'primitive sympathy' of a sensuous kind between subject and object – the presence of the object in the activity of the subject. It is through *expressing* this identity, through forming its 'semblance', that the subject realizes *objectively*, and in the same form, both a semblance of subject–object identity and its own relational distance from that idenity; that is, its non-identity. Expression, unlike construction, works only with subject-centred elements as its material for forming a semblance. Mimesis is the reflexive intelligence of sensuous intra-action, the subject's *sensing* of its own sensing through the *formation of its semblance*. The expressive formation of semblance thus gives rise to the realization of subject–object differentiation in and through the realization of subject–object identity. The 'copy', in the case of mimesis, reflects the subject's real condition in respect of its objects.

Mimesis is as much a universal feature of ordinary everyday life and relations in the world as it is of art. It becomes a focus of special attention in the case of modern art because of the very disjunction of subject and object that is registered in the concept of alienation. In the paintings of Cezanne, as well as those of Manet, one can see, in progress as it were, that withdrawal from the historical dimension of action, complete with its individuals possessed of inner lives and interacting with other individuals in the construction of a larger social whole. Dialectical relations were draining from the works of these artists as was the sense of an inner world of feeling that is expressed in outer forms. We cannot truthfully look on Cezanne's portrait of his gardener and claim that we are seeing in his outer form an expression and reflection of his inner feelings – something that Alberti had proclaimed as an ideal of art in his famous fifteenth-century treatise *On Painting* (Alberti 1966). Modernist art systematically undermined that ideal. This shutting down both of depth and historicity in the work of art – the dialectic of 'inner' and 'outer' – was associated with a deliberate attention to sensuous and aesthetic qualities torn from the objects and relations in which they had once been embedded. As pictures became flat the purely 'aesthetic' aspect of painting was brought to the fore. The logic of object relations receded and modernist art ceased to reflect it. On the other hand, the ordering of aesthetic values in the work of art increasingly reflected the demands of a constitutive sensuous process – the formation of a 'sensibility' and an 'agency' – from the range and variety of subject–object relations that make up elements of the intra-subjective or intra-actional life. Modern art ceased to be an integral unity that was both 'object-reflexive' and 'subject-reflexive'; it became increasingly centred on the subject-reflexive. In other words, the link between the subject and the object world that Adorno insisted on preserving through a negative dialectics was relinquished by many modern artists. For them, the breaking of that link became in itself a strategy of liberation just as Adorno sought liberation through the opposing strategy of maintaining (negatively) that link.

Popular culture

Adorno's critique of popular culture brings it within the sphere of what I have labelled 'construction'. His claim is that it is a manufactured culture, the market-tested construction of predictable and calculated effects. The sensations, emotions and responses it arouses in its receivers may be desired or sought by them but they remain subject-alien for all that. They are triggered by the appropriate formulaic stimuli but they are not material that the subject forms in expressing or realizing a life-process. It is easy enough to agree with Adorno that a great deal of commercialized culture may have this character of being a constructed and subject-alien culture in the above sense. However, the blanket invocation of the market and of profits does not decide the issue of whether cultural works are subject-alien or not. Critics of Adorno have always found it hard to credit the lumping together of work of such vastly varying quality within a monolithic indictment of all popular culture. The culture industry does not consist of one market but of many and the same consumer may buy in different markets. There has always been popular culture that does not fall into the category of the mechanically constructed article, popular culture that is genuinely expressive. Insofar as such culture is genuinely expressive, it is the work of mimesis rather than construction. I am aware that Adorno theorizes these terms differently and links them in a way that my own theorizing avoids.

That Adorno is not able to make this exception may be associated with his concern to critique all art that does not seek to conserve the link between subject and object and especially art which seeks liberation through breaking the link and abolishing alienation in the psyche without changing anything in the world. In this respect he is set against many developments in so-called serious art as well as popular art. The counter-claim that can be made, however, is that it is precisely through the breaking of that link that the sensibility of the subject, freed of its 'guilty' associations with the object, can be exercised and developed. The reformation of the sensibility of the subject must of itself impact upon the world which ultimately depends upon it, even at the level of material and economic life.

Readiness

In front of Rembrandt's famous painting, the *Night Watch*, in the Rijksmuseum in Amsterdam, I have often been struck by the sense of anticipation, the tense 'aliveness' of the moment in which something is about to happen. The painting captures that high-energy moment that is preparatory to action – the readiness the instant before. This readiness is integral to the relations and interactions among the participants in the scene, to the narrative truth of the painting, which is a portrait of a militia. But it is important to distinguish analytically between the presence the subjects manifest in the situation and the actions and interactions in which they are involved. Aesthetically, this presence seems to be central to Rembrandt's painting. All is concentrated in the busy moment before the captain, with arm outstretched, at the head of his company, begins to march. However, if the company had actually begun to march, the line of our attention would still be drawn along that moment-to-moment wave of readiness that is there the instant *before* every step.

In Rembrandt's painting, the 'readiness' of the instant before is integral to the process of action – the narrative action – that is its outcome, its realization. Mentally, we can complete the action, the march in which this readiness is realized. But this integral identity and continuity cannot be taken for granted. The readiness of the subject (his or her presence) in the situation may not translate smoothly into action. The actions demanded of the subject in the situation may be in conflict with those that might express the subject, thereby preventing the subject from becoming what s/he is. In other words the intra-actional formation of sensibility and agency – that is, of the incipient readiness to be and to act – may be alienated from the world and therefore incapable of filling out the subject's actions as their spiritual core. The crisis of modernity represented just such a dislocation – a fissure – between the formation of subjectivity and the construction of presence. It is the argument of the theorists of alienation that the condition of the subject – its state of being – finds no ready means of expression in a world that is dominated by a rational-technical instrumentality. Evidence for this can be found in the narcissism and heightened anxiety of modern subjects (Lasch 1979). Adorno pointed continuously to an increased dependency behaviour, a resort to the 'irrational' in modern culture, de-individuation and the loss of personal responsibility and direction. However, the same exclusive focus on intra-actional process can be seen to have its own utopian possibilities. Freed from their 'guilty' ties to an outer reality, the elements of sensibility are subject to a process of 'reformation'. Such a reforming of sensibility holds out the prospect of a changed relationship to objects and with it a transformation of possibilities in an outer reality as well.

In Goffman's sociology the subject is engaged in an anxious and harried attempt to manage presence and impressions under conditions where everything threatens to fall apart. The insecurity of the Goffmanian self is marked.

Nothing can be taken for granted. The modern self is multiple, divided; its forms are 'evanescent' in the sense in which Baudelaire attributed that characteristic to modernity. The dependence upon the peer group to provide consensual validation of one's being as a subject means that all one's efforts are open to continuous appraisal by others. The ontological insecurity of the subject that is built into this process becomes the motivating force for the entire performance.

The anxiety surrounding the subject's formation of presence typically results in coping strategies for holding anxiety at tolerable levels. In some cases this may lead to an avoidance of social contacts and that may help the individual to sustain his or her self-concept through not exposing it to disconfirmation. More usually a similar result is attained by careful selection of interpersonal contacts; those that are more likely to provide mutual support for participating individuals and to offer a safe means of comparison with others that is useful and which leads to manageable efforts at self-improvement. This latter response to the threat of anxiety suggests a close cultivation of interpersonal and solidary relations, relations of intimacy. Whether such relations are with friends, family members or sexual partners, they work for the individual when they are mutually supportive and allow for the 'safe' exposure of personal vulnerability. Interpersonal relations of this kind have as their material the 'making of presence'. As relations that are oriented to the production of what is an intra-actional process, they are essentially *ensemble* relations among peers. Collectively, the members of the ensemble lay down a pattern on which, as individuals, they improvise, in a way that is analogous to the improvisatory work of a group of jazz musicians. In this way the presence formed by the individual in the action situation is a particular figuration of a shared presence, a social being, that belongs, collectively, to the 'ensemble' in which he or she participates.

The 'Woody' figure

I know if I listen intently to a piece of jazz or watch a 'good' movie, that there is something unrecognized and unacknowledged in Adorno's perspective. I get the same feeling when I watch a Woody Allen movie. It makes little sense to see Allen's movies in terms of any kind of developmental, historical or dialectical process whether positive or negative. They are not about action and its effects in the world. The Woody figure exhibits many of the characteristics of an alienated consciousness that Adorno attributed to modern mass culture. In an Allen movie, however, alienation gets 'normalized'. It becomes the defining condition of a resourceful and inventive praxis, one aimed at successfully bringing off what Adorno derided as a hallmark of modern pseudo-culture, the practice of selfhood without a self. The Woody figure attends principally to the subject, to the problematics of 'presence'. His film-life is kind of 'running commentary' on events and relations viewed from the intra-actional standpoint of making presence. He engages reflexively in the task, shrewdly and ironically self-aware throughout.

In the movies in which he appears, Woody usually draws on the resources a small support group, a solidary ensemble through which a shared sensibility can be secured. Sociality, here, is oriented to the (re)formation of sensibility and agency and not to the repair of the rupture between subject and object. It is as though the world is not the product of social relations but merely provides an occasion for them. Alienation becomes the prerequisite of an ordinariness made innocent and perhaps, as utopia surfaces, 'enchanted'.

The culture industry itself has played a key role as topic in certain of Woody Allen's films. *Radio Days* and *The Purple Rose of Cairo* recall the golden age of radio and of cinema that Adorno was writing about. Allen's filmic constructions of alienation resist being subsumed by Adorno's model of the culture industry. Nevertheless, it is interesting to set Allen's explorations of popular culture beside Adorno's, not only because of the contrast in treatment but also because of certain similarities or shared insights between the two perspectives concerning the formal construction of popular culture. The comparison seems strange at first because the language which is used to discuss the experience of the modern subject and his or her relationship to mass culture – alienation, ego weakness and dependency, etc. – is one that may sit comfortably with a Marxist philosopher such as Adorno, but it may actually serve to occlude what is fresh and meaningful in the work of a creative film-maker like Woody Allen.

Notwithstanding, I would argue that there is some real point to exploring the Woody Allen movies discussed below in the light of their particular treatment of mass culture. Alienation, ego weakness, dependency, etc., are terms that are in fact very appropriate to a discussion of his movies, so long as we remember that the artist's intentions are quite different from that of the Marxist critic and this difference is clearly reflected in their respective treatments of the culture industry and particularly the inflection that each gives to the human condition in modern society. Allen's vision, no less than that of Adorno, acknowledges all the characteristics of the condition of alienation in the modern world but from a perspective that no longer recognizes alienation.

Life imitates art

Allen's movies are instances of ensemble playing centred on problematic solidary relations. His movies remind me of jazz, with which, in any case, he has a personal affinity. In a number of movies, and especially those discussed below, Allen dissolves the boundary between the world of everyday solidary social relations and the world of popular culture and the mass media. He sets up a continuous passage between the two, infusing everyday life with cultural material and shared sensibility drawn from popular culture. Life's imitation of art plays a big part with him in the particular response he makes to modernity. In *Play It Again Sam*, the Humphrey Bogart character of the film *Casablanca* appears in Woody's apartment seated on a settee and offering him advice on how to relate to and make love to a woman. The material of art works transforms the ordinary everyday experience of objects and events with which they are associated. We respond in a changed way to a world that has been changed by art works. Adorno deplored what he saw as the contamination of ordinary objects, places and items of culture by their simulation in movies. However, it is just this feature that is the most powerful and radical aspect of the new art, its capacity to develop and reform the 'sensibility' of the subject and by that means to transform the relationship of the subject to the world. Insofar as everyday life draws on references and models provided by the culture industry, that process might be given, contra Adorno, a positive rather than a negative inflection. The voices, gestures, faces, songs and clichés that make up the stream of popular culture, provide resources that mediate, sustain and even nourish immediacy. They provide material – language – for making 'presence' – sensibility and agency – in ordinary life and not just in popular culture. To the extent that they do so, art's imitation of life is overtaken by life's imitation of art. Such a positive view is heresy, of course, in the context of Adorno's philosophy. The valorization of the alienated consciousness of everyday life could serve only as an apology for the culture industry. A fusion of ordinary life and the products of the culture industry was, Adorno believed, a capitulation to the barbarism of the existing state of affairs.

Life in an Allen movie does not so much imitate art as *quote* from it. Quotation preserves the distance between art and life, remains conscious of the difference. Moreover, quoting from popular culture in pursuit of real-world relations does not leave the 'quoted' world unaffected. There is a sense in which popular culture – and the relationship of individuals to popular culture – is continuously changed and developed by the life-process that quotes it in using it. Adorno himself saw that works of art enter into an outer history and are changed over time through reception and so forth. The model I am developing here uses the same point to argue against his treatment of popular culture as a one-way manipulation of the psyches of individuals.

Radio Days

There is a positive warmth and affection in Allen's film for the people and times in which radio was so prominent a feature of daily life. It is a warmth that stands in sharp contrast to Adorno's more or less unremittingly negative perspective. *Radio Days* is not only shrewdly observed but demonstrates an underlying grasp of the human condition in the modern age that bears comparison with that of Adorno. There is no real plot to the film, which is a collection of vignettes of the lives of a small group of family members from

Brooklyn, New York, in the 1940s. Each vignette is more or less complete in itself and it hardly matters where one ends and another begins.

The thread that runs through this kaleidoscopic montage of reminiscence is radio. Radio is the backdrop to everything that happens and each scene develops different aspects of the relationship with radio and recalls different programmes of the day. The radio is always switched on. It is seamlessly and sensuously interpolated with everyday life. The old radio with its valves and large speaker was an item of furniture. It appears in Allen's film as something that is as familiar to the members of a household as any room or familiar object could be. Radio is attended to but with the distractive awareness with which Benjamin claimed that one appreciates a building that one lives in and knows very well. There is seldom more than one person in front of the radio giving it their full attention. Family members bustle around doing chores and for most of the time the radio is simply on in the background. Nevertheless, its presence, in Allen's film, is all-pervasive. Family life and personal relationships are all mediated by the endless stream of information, advertising, items of human interest, news items, sports items, adventure series for children, drama, quiz programmes, gossip and so forth.

Radio provides material for conversation and interaction and music for marking mood and occasion. Radio music also runs throughout the film as a backdrop to everything that happens. This is the era of the big bands. The pieces selected whether sentimental ballads or novelty numbers or dances are all chosen for their mood-setting possibilities. They accompany the action and encapsulate its mood – leitmotifs of their time. In one scene, young Woody's cousin Ruthie appears in the living room dressed as a flamenco dancer complete with towelled headgear decorated with a bunch of grapes and cavorting around like a parody of a Latin diva to the sound of Carmen Miranda issuing from the box in front of her. Allen reveals the power of the medium not only to commodify music and presentation but to commodify the listener too, who, through identification and imitation, becomes, in the process, a fetish-object to herself. Even here, however, radio still demands something in the way of imagination from its listeners that, for the most part, is not required by television, which does the viewer's imagining for him.

In Allen's retrospective, the characters are not portrayed as authors of their destiny or as personally responsible for what they do. His characters engage with chance and luck and supra-natural forces. All the features that Adorno labels ego-weakness, dependency behaviour, superstition and stereotypy are there in abundance. If Allen had not so arranged it that fate smiles on his characters, they would not have the inner resources to solve their problems. The common denominator here is that in an alienated relationship to the world the individual lacks a spiritual centre in that world, a centre of moral responsibility. Again, Adorno and Allen perceive similar facts but in radically different ways and with equally opposed interpretations.

The reliance on luck and fortune is a major theme binding together the elements of Allen's film. Not only are there the ubiquitous quiz programmes but also they intervene in ordinary life as paths to fate. The aunt takes her family to a quiz show and ends up taking off the prize. Two burglars are in the process of robbing a house when the phone rings and a radio quiz show host announces that their telephone number has been selected from the directory and if they can identify the titles of three popular songs they will have won a house full of goods and appliances. Such is the power of the medium that the burglar pauses in his task of robbery and at once sets to, earnestly, to answer the questions correctly; with a little difficulty and hesitation he identifies all three songs. The next day the bewildered couple returns from holiday to find their house has been burgled and there is a pantechnicon outside ready to unload a houseful of appliances and goods.

Dependency behaviour, a lack of personal responsibility, those Adornoan marks of a commodified existence, are present too in the behaviour of the young Woody character. His fantasy relationship to Biff Baxter, the 'masked avenger', is central to his life. When he needs money to purchase a secret code ring, he steals from the collection box in which he has been collecting money for Palestine. He is not responsible for the crime; the masked avenger told him to do it. When he appears before the rabbi with his parents and the rabbi confronts him with the moral depths to which he has sunk, he solemnly replies, in imitation of the masked avenger, 'You speak truth my fine and noble friend'.

Among the many programmes of the period that Allen draws upon is that of the couple who attend society functions and first nights and then broadcast the next morning – as a conversation over breakfast – an intimate and gossipy account of the whole occasion. They do so for listeners who, themselves, will never be invited to such venues and, in the normal course of events, would never be selected by those who do attend them to hear an account about what went on. Commodified by radio, however, all such events can be 'vicariously experienced' by anyone, regardless of social class. A genuine understanding of a world apart from one's own would require that the individual be able to supply from his or her own experience the very elements and relations that make it a world in the first place. Exposure to another's world without being able to supply this is a mark of an alienated existence, of a consciousness that binds itself to 'the worthless outside' – that is, the commodity. What has been communicated has an authoritarian hold on its audiences. It is the material of fetish consciousness. Allen's touch is always affectionate and he appears to have no inclination to theorize about alienation, commodification or fetishization or to judge those who indulge them. His observations on life are, for all that, utterly relevant to the kinds of problems raised by those who do.

Acquiring identities in this sense is made easy by commodification. The individual is offered any number of ready-made identities. They are all flat and one-dimensional, however, and partake of all the characteristics of the commodity form. To be someone is much more than to appropriate the outside of the person. The fascination with impersonation has become ever more widespread. There are actors who impersonate their characters and even themselves as their own characters. Impersonation is itself a form of commodification. It alienates the animated appearance of a character from the life-world that animates it, conferring the power, not of 'being like' but of 'seeming like', upon the thief of appearance. In *Play It Again Sam*, Allen tackles love with the help of the screen persona of Humphrey Bogart, more precisely the screen persona of Humphrey Bogart in *Casablanca*. In *Everyone Says I Love You* there is a scene towards the end where Allen and his former wife pursue their relationship at a fancy dress party, both of them in the persona of Groucho Marx. Impersonation and quotation become prerequisites of the reformation of sensibility. Allen is a past master at the business of witty reference and the crafted use of cliché. His 'quoting' and 'sourcing' from other films – e.g. Bergman's *Smiles of a Summer's Night* or Fellini's *Amacord* – is key to his method. One unnamed reviewer on the web has said of *A Midsummer Night's Sex Comedy* that it 'also riffs off Shakespeare, classical paintings and the earliest incarnations of film-making among other inspirations. His characters, like those played by Jose Ferrer and Tony Roberts, not only seem like Bergman characters, they also resemble the actors who played in his films. Woody's character is also a combination of characters from other pieces, Bottom from Shakespeare, among others.' But quotation is not simulation. *Radio Days* is not *Amacord* and *A Midsummer Night's Sex Comedy* is not *Smiles of a Summer Night*. Allen's treatment of *Radio Days* is not simply nostalgic; nostalgia is its subject-matter. Allen uses the memorizing work of the subject as the work of utopia. The past is not remembered as it really was but in this retrospective nostalgia, the present is perfected through remembering.

Whether taking part in quiz programmes or engaging directly with Orson Welles's *Invasion from Mars* broadcast that successfully simulated a newscast, radio listeners were living and engaging with radio as an integral part of their 'habitus'. While radio can provoke thought and active engagement it is at its most typical best when it delivers its idea in the moment of utterance, when it does not ask of its listeners that they ponder the meaning. The quality for which Adorno 'disliked' radio, namely that of being commodity, pure surface, is the quality necessary to make a good song lyric as distinct from a poem. It is also the quality necessary to liberate language and gesture from its historical precipitates, to make it anew and to reform sensibility. It is the quality I see as central to Allen's positive treatment of modernity

The characters in Allen's film, for the most part, take radio listening for granted. Only once is it directly commented upon when the Jewish mother in the film accuses her son of wasting his time listening to radio all day instead of applying himself to his education and to getting on in life. He retorts that she and his dad are always listening to radio. In a response that might almost be used to parody Adorno, she replies, 'that's different, our lives are ruined already'. Always and ever radio appears to orchestrate life for its listeners, even to script it. In Allen's film it is an all-powerful source of affect-laden experience, of mood-making, of communitas. It bridges worlds that are normally held apart. There is the touching scene in the movie where the entire family, and all other families like it, break off from every activity to stay glued to the radio broadcast of the desperate attempts to save a little girl trapped in a well. The power of radio to draw people together and even to deepen the sense of family and community is made clear and heightened with the cut to Diane Keaton singing plaintively, *You'd Be So Nice to Come Home To.*

All the characters that make up the movie's ensemble have something of the Woody-style about them. By the movie's ensemble, here I mean the group of communicating characters as presented to us and not the actors' methods of working. Standardization becomes a necessary feature of this type of ensemble work, the laying down of the basic pattern of sensibility that is differentially figured in the different characters. This type of ensemble playing demands a heightened interpersonal sensitivity. The problems addressed, those encountered in the formation of a sensibility under modern alienating conditions, are experienced through the medium of anxiety. Anxiety and the continuing need to discover new sources of interpersonal validation is the *énergétique* that drives the ensemble work in Woody Allen's movies as it increasingly does in life outside movies.

The Purple Rose of Cairo

The figure of the lonely individual – usually a woman – who, in the days before television, spent hours in the cinema watching her favourite movies again and again, represents a more or less classical instance of alienation. How many people went several times to the cinema to see the film *Sound of Music* in the 1960s? I remember reading of a woman in Birmingham who had attended a performance of that film every single day for two years. The cinema gave her a free pass in recognition of the fact. I recall, too, as a young sociologist, discussing that particular movie with one or two elderly people that I knew; they were admirers and had themselves seen it several times. It seemed that they identified with the world portrayed in the movie (which at the time I saw only as an annoying cliché-ridden fiction) as representing values that they believed in and which they felt had been lost in the post-war period.

Woody Allen's film *The Purple Rose of Cairo* plays with the interface between film cliché and everyday reality. It deals with the 'escapist' cinema of the Depression years in America – the very years in which Adorno formed his understanding of cinema. From the outset, the film sets up a contrast between the seedy drabness of New Jersey at the time of the Depression and the glamorous world of the movies. The central character, Cecilia (played by Mia Farrow), is a tired and worn-down housewife, married to a drunken, philandering oaf who mistreats and humiliates her. She is also movie-obsessed and spends all her spare time at the cinema. She has an encyclopaedic knowledge of actors, their films, their marriages and divorces, not to mention whole passages of dialogue from the movies she has seen. Cecilia has attached herself with real desperation to the cultural goods on offer. No longer able to cope with the real world and its horrors, she lives only in and through the movies. None of the passion, knowledge and focus she is able to bring to bear is given to struggling with her conditions and life; all is expended on a fantasy world. Hers is a classic instance of alienation.

Allen is truly inventive in exploring different levels of experience and in forcing a confrontation between them. His probing of the condition of alienation goes much further than a straightforward confrontation between the real-world life of the central character and the fantasy world of the movie she is watching for the fifth time. The breaching of the boundary between life and art is given a special twist by Allen who has the hero in the movie (Tom Baxter) step out of the film to enter into relationship with the movie-obsessed heroine in the darkened auditorium. In this way the character in the movie is drawn into a direct encounter with the very world that Cecilia has been trying to escape. In a further twist, Allen splits reality yet again. He sets off the actor, Gil Shepherd, who plays the part of Tom in the movie, against his own character. Gil becomes Tom's rival for Cecilia's affections, competing with his own character. Allen thus plays off two levels of unreality – actor and character – against a third, the escapism of a woman who has lost the will to live in the world as it is.

The film explores, aesthetically, a number of contradictions that are central to Adorno's treatment of movies and cultural goods generally. It brings into direct confrontation the ideological material manifest in the actual content of movies – the heroes with their middle-class decency, their moral code and their freedom from the marks of toil, care and distress – with the drab and seedy world of downtrodden Depression America. Allan does not seek to make a political point but, with an artist's eye, to depict a truth that a political individual would certainly recognize. The film that is the focus of Cecilia's attention in this movie – the film within Allen's film – is about a group of socialites on a vacation in Egypt who return to their penthouse world bringing with them a young archaeologist (Tom Baxter) whom they have met out there and who has an affair with a nightclub singer. Cecilia already knows the movie backwards and can recite every line of dialogue. When the character of Tom Baxter, the young archaeologist, addresses her directly from the film, declares his feelings for her and steps down from the film to join her in the auditorium, the rest of the cast are stopped in their tracks. Unable to leave the plot, they sit around in the penthouse, dismayed and confused, waiting for him to return. Allen points his device for playing off film and reality in both directions; exploring the effects of a character stepping out of the film not only upon the world he enters but the world he leaves.

Tom is fitted out with the cultural values of a typical Hollywood cinema hero, obedient to the rules of that code of bourgeois decency that Adorno identified as the soft core – a defunct and sentimental romanticism – of every glossy Hollywood movie. Allen's device brings the code into direct confrontation with the society that supposedly subscribes to it. What is made clear throughout, and with real humour as well as pathos, is not simply that reality is not like films but that people are conscious of this difference between art and life; they experience it as a loss, the sense of which they find reassuring or comforting as though it was proof of their ultimate human value. This again is similar to Adorno's analysis of the idolization of film stars referred to above.

Tom has no sense of the 'disciplines' of hard work or the privations of Depression America. He knows nothing about vice or about prostitutes and is incapable of being anything other than the thoroughly decent hero that the screenwriters have ordained. When he finds himself, unknowingly, in a brothel, his gallant attitudes and chivalrous conduct towards the women astonishes them; his romantic innocence touches them *as if they were at the movies.* They fall for him and even offer to provide freely to him what they normally offer only for money. In another scene, Cecilia's husband, finding her with Tom, attacks him, kneeing him viciously in the groin. Tom is simply amazed at the commission of an act that violated the Hayes code. As a film character, Tom also has difficulty in coping with the idea of religion and with the concept of God. It is a puzzle that he dimly associates with the mystery of the great screenwriter above. There is a double-sidedness to the portrayal of Tom. He is at once an example of fresh romantic innocence that the world approves at an ideological level; on the other hand he is a continuous reminder of the childishness of movies, of the stunted consciousness manifest in the plots and ideological material. Adorno, too, pointed repeatedly to this institutionalized childishness. It was a problem for him (perhaps not for Allen).

At this point, Allen introduces his second major device. The actor who plays Tom Baxter, Gil Shepherd, is threatened with the ruin of his career as a result of all the Tom Baxters who are stepping down from the screen in cinemas across the country. Economic issues are to the fore here. This mingling of film and reality turns out to be very bad for business. Gil Shepherd decides to go to the town where all the trouble began. He meets Cecilia and strikes up a romance with her. Tom is desperate to compete with him and the only way he can do this is by taking Cecilia into the film to share the weekend in Manhattan promised by his socialite friends – the other characters in the movie. However, when Gil, Tom's actor, appeals to her from the auditorium, she hesitates and then abandons Tom to join the more 'substantial' Gil, leaving the *Purple Rose of Cairo* to continue from the point where it was interrupted. Cecilia's exchange is something of an Aesopian bargain. She is immediately abandoned by Gil, who returns to Hollywood to resume his career. In the final scene she is at the cinema once more and the camera shows her sad eyes lost in the dream world of Ginger Rogers and Fred Astaire, dancing together.

Some critics believed that Allen had produced a tragedy. Others merely berated him for making a drab unhappy film with a sad ending. He himself commented wryly that the original ending had been sad but that he had relented by providing his heroine with the consolation of that last scene, that is, the further 'shot' of movie fantasy. Reading the negative critics especially, it is clear that it is Allen's aesthetic attitude towards his subject-matter that is on trial. It is an aesthetic attitude that stands in sharp contrast to Adorno's. A palpable nostalgia inheres in his 'memoirs' of radio and of film. Life's relationship to and imitation of art is a theme Allen continuously explores in his films. Allen's characters always appear to be living the pop-psychology of film clichés and mass cultural stereotypes as though mass culture somehow holds open the possibility of re-enchanting a life that has become drab and disenchanted. Conflicts are ironed out with seamless sentimental resolutions. Harmful thoughts are banished as is real anger, antagonism or wickedness.

The world of the blockbuster musical with its lush orchestration, its soppy sentiment, romantic songs and polished singing is recalled in Woody Allen's 1995 film *Everyone Says I Love You*. There is one notable difference. The actors are not professional singers and all but one of them sings using their own voices. In this way the full gloss and hugeness of the Hollywood musical background and visual settings are made to support the textured ordinariness of a vocal production, gestural repertoire and dance movements that are life-sized, exuberant, but whose charm lies in their contrast with their supporting structure. The film is not simply a musical but a self-aware exploration of the genre together with its utopian possibilities. Bursting into song at key moments may be ludicrous but doing so provides a way for enchantment to find its continuation in the modern world. And the songs here are chosen from the 'hits' and 'standards' of the past. The device, again, sets up a passage between fantasy and reality that estranges both, holding them at a distance.

Getting things done in the world, interacting with others in the pursuit of goals and projects, bringing off successful actions, plays very little part in Allen's movies. There appears to be a suspension of a dialectics, of inter-actional relations, in which subject and object, self and other change each other, mediate each other. His characters come together more as an ensemble of sensibilities. Sensibilities are intra-actional or intra-subjective. They have a shared aspect to them; they develop in and through a 'communion'. The different characters in an Allen movie all talk a little like him. Relations among the sensibilities contributing to this communion are essentially sympathetic, non-antagonistic. They lay down an affinal texture, a common chord of sensibility that is the ground of all subsequent figuring of difference. And in that figuring of difference the impression is created of a kind of naturalism, of an improvisatory process.

Utopia surfaces

Adorno's vision is utopian. Utopia, for him, is not to be approached through any kind of positive vision or to have its likeness painted. It is to be glimpsed only in the revelation of what it is not. Critical thought, relentlessly pursued, is Adorno's *via negativa*. He rejected any attempt to overcome the alienated condition of the world within the work of art by conjuring images of some supposedly non-alienated folkish condition. Whether it was Wagner or Stravinsky, Adorno set himself against magical transformation, intoxication and phantasmagoria, all of which left the condition of the real world untouched. The task of art was to objectively register the alienating forces of modern society in and through the resistance (non-identity) of a subjectivity mutilated by it. Serious art for Adorno was a record of suffering – consciously resisting, not passively weeping.

Nevertheless, Adorno and Horkheimer maintained their contacts throughout their exile with fellow intellectuals who worked at the heart of the culture industry in Hollywood. They were 'closer' to that world than were the mass audiences who consumed its products. They were also aware that there was a utopian aspect to the culture industry. In a recent article on 'the émigré critics', Saverio Giovacchini takes up this point about the utopian element, citing a letter from Horkheimer to Lowenthal written in 1942:

> Unlike Dwight Macdonald and many US intellectuals, some of the members of the Frankfurt School were intrigued by the Utopian dimension inherent in popular culture and, specifically, by its emphasis on mass consumption. 'We cannot blame people that they are more interested in the sphere of privacy and consumption rather than production,' Max Horkheimer wrote to Leo Lowenthal in 1942, 'this trait contains a Utopian element; in Utopia production does not play a decisive part. It is the land of milk and honey.'
>
> (Giovacchini 1998)

Adorno, himself, recognizes this utopian aspect of the culture industry: the shop-girl's attachment to her screen idol, he argues, is the recognition both of a 'utopian' happiness and of the impossibility that it could ever be hers. However, Adorno's critical rejection of the culture industry and all its works was in no way slackened by this recognition of the utopian aspect of the culture industry. Any such utopia or consumer's paradise was easily unmasked by the Marxist model of commodity fetishism and the Freudian mechanism of wish fulfilment. Moreover, the conjuring of a false or illusory utopia that contrasts with the reality it cannot replace is not productive of truth or of progressive action. The subject who surrenders to the dream world of the movie does not discover there either the will or the means for changing her world; she is drawn into a false utopia as a means of escaping from the world.

Woody Allen's vision is also utopian but in a contrasting sense. If Adorno's utopia is an escape from surface – transforming presence into suspense – Woody Allen's is a movement in the opposite direction, an escape from depth – transforming suspense into presence. He draws attention to the surface, to the 'picture plane' of relationships. If life and relationships are a mess and can never really be fixed, the business of doing relating has, of itself, a utopian quality to it. Relationships may be ultimately antagonistic in a highly competitive world but in Allen's films the need of individuals to give and receive emotional support and intimacy is made central to a 'going on' of life. His characters tend to be likeable and vulnerable. It is rare to meet with anyone truly unsympathetic. This feeds the critical view that he is merely sentimental. No less a critic than Pauline Kael described Allen as 'an old-timey movie pasha of the lump-in-the-throat school of movie-making'. However, if the sentimental lays claim to a phony depth, Allen's characters have nothing to do with that or with its pretensions. They exist only on and for the surface. He takes away from them any serious content or intent and depicts them in the quality of their presence and in their gestures, expressions and relating. The irony lies in the fact that it is here in the most visible surface features of presence that coherence, continuity and depth is to be found.

If the father and mother in the New York Jewish family of *Radio Days* are always arguing and quarrelsome, we are offered the affectionate view of quarreling that has no real point to it and no real intent to harm. It is not that Allen cuts away the causal substructure of relationships altogether, leaving only the surface gesture. The underlying reality is often allowed to appear but only through transforming itself into surface. Thus in *Mighty Aphrodite*, Allen seeks out the natural mother of his adopted son and discovers she is a 'hooker' who performs in pornographic movies. She sweetly recounts in graphic matter-of-fact detail what would conventionally be seen as degrading sexual activities involving multiple partners. Here, the construction of the cliché of the 'dumb blonde' is used to recover an innocence. Kafka and Mahler both used 'language', in their different ways, against the intention of the reality conveyed through it. Kafka's cool prose made the totalitarian terror conveyed by it all the starker. Allen uses a contrast between expressive means and reality in a way that neutralizes horror, discovering innocence in the immediacy and presence of his characters. Allen's habit of excising the harm from harmful acts leaves him with his utopia, with innocence. But it also makes 'language' innocent again and opens a path to a renewal of expression.

The more cluttered is life with the demands of instrumentality, the harder it is to squeeze spontaneity or 'presence' from its fractured surfaces. In the darkened auditorium of the cinema, audiences were brought visually up close to their movie idols – to Gregory Peck or Ava Gardner or Humphrey Bogart – standing thirty feet high; to Alan Ladd 'doing looking' or to Ginger Rogers 'doing kissing'. The sensuously charged 'surfaces' of the movie flood the audience with *presence*, with that moment-to-moment wave of 'presence' carried in the ambient surface of the action. It is a truth that may be more or less independent of the truth-value of the movie's plot, its narrative and historical construction.

Adorno's modernism was not one that was prepared to abandon the subject's responsibility for the object world. The impossibility of the subject expressing its life-process in the world in a positive sense resulted in the effort to do so negatively. This is essentially the solution proffered by Adorno's 'negative dialectics'. In that way subject and object are held together through acknowledging the rupture between them, through making the subject's resistance – its refusal to fill out such a world – into the content of art works. However, while Adorno fiercely defended exponents of his version of modernism, he was equally fierce in his condemnation of those modern artist whose work I would characterize as abstracting the process of self-formation – the formation of presence – in order to work on it and to reform it, liberated from its ties to the object.

It is not difficult to credit Adorno's viewpoint concerning the triviality and inauthenticity of much of what passes for popular culture. It is more important, however, to consider the criterion of truth-value operating in popular culture such as the Hollywood film and to ask whether there are films, made in what to him would be a 'feature-rich, structure-poor' format, that possess truth-value and whether we can formulate criteria that are relevant to determining its presence or absence. In the movies of Woody Allen that I have discussed above, the draining of dialectical process at the level of inter-action is replaced by a development of the intra-actional structuration of art works that can also be described as 'structure-rich' in a sense that is not acknowledged by Adorno's perspective.

In Woody Allen's treatment, the sentimental cliché-forms, the imitation of which some would berate as a descent into childishness, become a new natural language for a life worn inside-out, a neurotic life in which inter-personal relations are centred on the resolution of intra-personal conflicts. Allen's screen character appears to many to be self-involved to the point of indulgence. While his wit is ironizing, its ironies do not point to an inner or deeper layer of reality but are all bound up with the world of foregrounded events, with ordinariness, with the world in which everyone's life goes on, continues, like music. This resort to the intra-personal brings with it its own renunciation of a 'grown-up life' of exploitation and antagonism. It is possible to see such a renunciation as merely sentimental and childish. Perhaps, instead, we should see it as contributing to the development of a discourse that is more modern than Adorno's.

11

WALKING A CRITICAL
LINE HOME

Adorno claimed that 'loneliness' was the inner law of the modernist works that he admired, those of the Schoenberg school, with which he identified, or the plays of Samuel Beckett. The oppressive isolation of the individual in the modern world, the sense of spiritual bleakness and the decay of community made up the reality he saw inscribed in the inner cells of modernist art. To the masses, these art works may have appeared incomprehensible. To Adorno, what mattered most was not so much that we understand art but that art understands us. Artistic 'languages' are sensuous; they model 'experience' *in perceptua*. To be true, however, the model must be equal to the facts of social life. Art can also weave illusions, fulfil dreams or wishes or provide means of escape from reality by disguising or distorting it. In Adorno's analysis, popular culture always finds itself on the wrong side of the dividing line between truth and lies. In this final chapter I will continue the process of putting this thesis under a degree of critical pressure. At the outset, my analysis, though differently constructed (and without some of Adorno's more important theoretical commitments), runs parallel to his. Notwithstanding, our two paths diverge; what is offered does not constitute a proper critique but, rather, a continuation of a critical line that I began 'walking' in the last chapter of *Adorno on Music*.

Adorno claimed that serious art and popular art are two torn halves of an integral reality that does not add up. As a 'thought experiment', I will choose two examples, one of serious and one of popular art, respectively, and confront Adorno with them – to ask him why they do not add up. The two artists selected were more or less contemporary with Adorno and they have both been widely held to exemplify, through their respective arts and perhaps for different audiences, the 'loneliness' that he declared to be central to the modernism he embraced. Of the two I have chosen, one is a major American painter and the other a popular vocalist.

When I look at Edward Hopper's paintings, especially the painting *Nighthawk*, they seem movingly to capture the sense of isolation and loneliness that Adorno claimed was the truth at the heart of the modern city.

Nighthawk depicts a diner. One can well imagine it as an appropriate setting for the singer Frank Sinatra – hat pushed back, cigarette in his hand, the Sinatra of the album *The Wee Small Hours*. I am tempted to see a connection between the two. But in my thought experiment I want to ask whether Adorno would have acknowledged such a connection if he had been asked (I actually have no idea whether he ever thought about or discussed either of these individuals and can only guess that he might have responded in the way suggested below). 'Loneliness' is probably the most frequently uttered 'descriptive' of Hopper's paintings, and Sinatra, in his way, was a great vocal artist with a gift for modelling feelings and none more effectively than the feeling of loneliness. Sinatra's singing of 'Mood Indigo' or 'The Wee Small Hours' conveys an intimate experience of losing in love that belongs to nothing so much as the city and the night. In my thought experiment – which takes the form of a piece of script-writing for Adorno's intellectual persona – he is not persuaded. The line of argument, I imagine, might run something like this.

> Loneliness certainly describes the feeling that Sinatra conveys on that album. However, it is not clear that the word actually serves as a good descriptor for Hopper's paintings despite its widespread use. Sinatra discourses in reflective mood on his feelings, his moods, his relationships, his sense of being abandoned, of being sad and so forth. In short he communicates or *performs* (subjective) feelings of loneliness. I don't get any sense of subjective feelings of loneliness from a Hopper painting. If I, like countless others, am inclined to apply the term 'loneliness' to a Hopper painting, it is to describe the alienation that is built into the very architecture of his depictions. We don't know what the individuals in the diner feel in *Nighthawk*. The painting as a whole constructs a state of being that can be felt in the light, the night and the linear structure. There is an impression of transience, of passage in Hopper's paintings, intimately connected with the city and with modernity. Movement is arrested in a stilled or frozen moment in what may be a place of transit, a hotel room, a lobby, a bar, a diner, railway yard, house or shore. Even where nature looms large in his paintings it is still a kind of 'second nature' imbued with the anxiety and foreboding that is at the heart of the metropolis There is something monumental in these works, their forms 'petrified' and silent. The distance between people is unbridgeable; the fragility and isolation of the figures is more solid and tangible than the figures themselves. Each site in a Hopper painting is a kind of limbo, stilled and hermetically sealed. None of these places are 'home'. Home requires connectives, a 'body' to be at home in. In Hopper's paintings the connectives between places – between people, between what is here and what is there,

what is inside and what is outside, what is nature and what is human – have been broken. We are confronted with our human condition as subjects in the modern metropolis. We see the isolating fragility of the subject, the menace of otherness. It is as though we have access, through Hopper's paintings, to loneliness, not as feelings subjects have about themselves but as the subject's state of being in the modern world.

To perceive the loneliness of the human condition at the heart of a play by Beckett or a story by Kafka is not a matter of communicating the feelings of those involved. We can see and feel the brokenness of life, its emptiness and isolation without concerning ourselves with what feelings the subjects themselves may claim to have or seek to communicate. It is the subjective process itself that is objectively modelled in such works. I have made this point clearly in my account of Schoenberg's *Erwartung*. The loneliness and desperation of a woman searching for her lover who comes across his corpse in the dead of night is inscribed in the very cells of the music. However, what is conveyed – objectively and in case-study fashion – are what I have called the genuine emotions of the unconscious, the convulsive 'shocks' and 'crystalline standstill' undergone by the subject – experience I have described as 'intra-subjective'. I distinguish this sharply from the situation in which the objective of art is to communicate the subjective feelings the individual consciously has in respect of his or her experience – feelings of happiness, sadness, loneliness or whatever. Thus, modernist art was often deeply expressive and affective yet it appeared to many to be cold and intellectual because the masses were oriented to a model of art as the communication of subjective feelings.

It is the culture industry and mass art that has exploited subjective feelings and has kept in play a defunct romanticism. It has produced many works in which the expression of loneliness is central, the so-called 'blues' for example and, of course, the singing of Frank Sinatra on that album. People love to listen to all this music that sighs and moans; it makes them feel good. Perhaps they hear the sentiments expressed as sincere. Certainly a good vocalist, with good phrasing – and Sinatra has that – will be able to produce 'soulfulness' and sincerity for you – as you would expect of a fine actor. That does not make the sentiments expressed true. I have always believed that feelings expressed in this sensuous way, in modern works of art, are a form of consolation, of acquiescence and of false consciousness, through which the subject affects reconciliation to the world and to its condition of social dependency. The subject who weeps for consolation in this vale of tears has no resistance to offer, can do nothing to ready the spirit to summon better times. The true force of modernity silences the expression of subjective feeling; it kills it through refusing its inscription. This is why I once referred to Tchaikovky's music as 'despondency with hit tunes' and said of jazz, that 'everything in it seeks to announce something soulful'. The spiritual consolation afforded to the subject by such art is the enemy of truth. And that is why I will not equate or even connect the art of Sinatra, singing about his loneliness, with the paintings of Hopper; paintings that comprehend the alienating condition of modernity. I might connect Hopper, more reasonably, to Kafka or to Beckett.

The intelligence of feeling and expressivist theories of art

It is difficult to write seriously about art and the aesthetic without recognizing the proximity of art to the sensuous life, to the subject, to subjectivity, emotion and affect. However, models of art as the expression of feeling (Langer 1953; Reid 1969; Dewey 1934) are most certainly controversial and frequently attract criticism. Adorno was not the only thinker to set himself against an expressivist theory of art that reduced art to the expression or communication of subjective feelings. In his book *Objective Knowledge*, Karl Popper, the philosopher of science, explicitly attacks what he calls expressivist theories of art. Art, for him, is something more objective and elevated than the expression of an artist's feelings. Beethoven was avowedly an expressivist. Popper distances himself from what he calls Beehoven's 'method'. Even the personal life of Beethoven and all his personal feelings are of no importance to Popper, and if his music is great it must be because it has a more elevated content than the detritus of his personal life. Many other critics of so-called expressivist theories would no doubt agree. Actually, many so-called expressivist theorists of art would also have little difficulty agreeing with the specific point being made here. Popper's critique sets up a straw man in that it does not represent the claims of expressivist theories of art but a caricature of them. On the other hand, even sophisticated expressivist theorists – Adorno is no exception – have not distinguished clearly among the elements of the affective life nor have they developed a framework adequate to analysing the role of the aesthetic in the development of intelligence and understanding and in the social formation generally. Such a task is difficult because modernity itself has fostered a model of cognitive and social functioning, including the functioning of affect and emotion, that impedes the development of a theory of art that would do justice both to the sensuous and the social. Little more will be done here than to focus on a single distinction that I hold to be important – that between 'emotion' and 'feeling'.

In my first attempt at theorizing the aesthetic in connection with the creative arts in education (Witkin 1974), I made three related decisions at the outset: (1) to identify myself with the close connection established between art and affect (the so-called expressivist model); (2) to identify art specifically with feeling rather than with emotion; and, following from this, (3) to see feeling as a mode of intelligence – as a reflexive process – and to see art as exercising this intelligence – the intelligence of feeling (Witkin 1974). Moreover, aesthetic perception and the intelligence of feeling are not restricted to art and certainly not to what are called works of art. The intelligence of feeling belongs as much to ordinary everyday life that may know little or nothing of art works.

Emotion as subject-reactive

The emotions and sensations that are undergone by the subject – what Dewey called 'undergoings' (Dewey 1934) – are not simply impacts passively absorbed by the subject. They impinge upon an organized system of affective response, a *sensibility*. The subject as a whole – that is, the subject as an organized an organizing sensibility – actively responds to incoming stimulation. What is experienced, what is undergone, is a result of the interaction between this sensibility and the impinging stimulus. It is the response the subject makes to the impinging stimulus that determines its character as emotion or feeling. When the subject's response is *reactive*, the resulting experience can be labelled 'emotion'. When faced with a threatening situation, for example, the subject is afraid and prepares for flight (in whatever order we choose to place these events). His attention is directed entirely upon the object or situation in respect of which he must act. The subject has no interest in his own response, in his fear. He is not concerned to reflect upon it or to gain insight into it, nor to assimilate it through the development of his sensibility. His emotion is a reaction to the situation and motivates him for flight. Whenever the subject responds reactively (subject-reactive response) to an impinging stimulus we can speak of that response as emotion.

Feeling as subject-reflexive

On the other hand, there are situations in which the subject's interest is not in the objects or situations that impinge so much as in the sensations undergone, in affective experience itself. Instead of responding reactively to an objective situation, the individual responds reflexively to a subjective state of affairs. This subject-reflexive response whereby the individual assimilates the sensations undergone to his/her developing sensibility is what I mean by *feeling*. Feeling is a reflexive and intelligent act, the subject's perceptual response to its own sensing. It is in and through feeling that the individual assimilates the sensations and emotions undergone to the (intrasubjective or intra-actional) process that is constitutive of the subject, of its 'sensibility' and its 'agency', of its orientation in the world. The self-development of the subject is realized in and through the response that the subject makes to its own sensing. If subject-reactive behaviour is purposeful and directed to the accomplishment of action in the object world, subject-reflexive response is, in the Kantian sense, purposefully purposeless. It is a form of 'knowing' (subject-knowing as distinct from object-knowing). Such knowing is 'perceptual' – the subjective process is modelled *in perceptua*.

Subjective feeling and objective feeling

Within the domain of subject-reflexive action (feeling) we can distinguish between two levels of abstraction. Feeling can be formed as an 'interpretation' of the experience undergone; this gives rise to what are normally called the feelings that the subject has in respect of its objects or of itself. We might describe this as *subjective feeling*. The subject's feeling can also be formed as a response to itself – as the 'sensibility' that is in the process of experiencing, of undergoing. The constitutive relations of subjectivity themselves then become the object of feeling. We can describe the latter as *objective feeling*. Feeling in both cases is reflexive and involves a perceptual distancing of the subject from its own experiencing. In the first case the subject distances itself (perceptually) from the affects it has undergone; in the second, it distances itself from itself as the very sensibility (intra-subjective process) that is in the process of undergoing. The factors that determine truth-value at the level of 'objective feeling' cannot be used to determine truth-value or the lack of it at the level of 'subjective feeling'. Adorno's critique of popular culture is dimissive of the claims of what I am calling subjective feeling, denying its claim to truth-value. In my view, this conclusion is questionable. It ignores the fact that aesthetic discourse is an important part of the configuration of everyday life and relations (Witkin 1990, 1995; DeNora 2000) and that the truth-value of what is accomplished there can only be decided there in terms of the particulars of the dynamic interchanges constituting the situation.

Sensibility as readiness

A sensibility is best thought of as a sensuous readiness (a presence) and a preparedness for action (agency). It is a product of the totality of the subject-object relations that are the elements of the intra-actional process. The sensibility of the subject always extends beyond the constraints and conditions of any specific action situation and this secures a distancing of the subject from the action situation. Nevertheless the specific presence that the subject brings to the action situation is a response to the demands of that situation. In any given situation, a subset of the subject's sensibility – a range of sensuous values – will be drawn into the formation of a 'sensible presence' and an 'agency' that answers to the situation – the presence with which the individual tackles the life-world demands of being a nurse, a teacher, a miner, lover, parent and so forth. This range of sensuous values – this *sensuous figure* – becomes the very building block of a 'sensible presence'. Thus the different sensuous values that are drawn into an intra-actional formation together form a sensuous unit that is the basic constitutive element of that sensible presence, the brick from which it is built (in *Adorno on Music*, I went so far as to use Schoenberg's twelve-tone methodology as a metaphor for this process). This basic unity is 'figured', 'ornamented' and 'featured' in the process of answering to the specific characteristics of action situations but its composite foundation remains unaltered throughout.

The formation of a sensible presence and an agency (that is, of a readiness) as I have theorized it here, is responsive to action situations from the outset. The subject's selection of sensuous values that goes into the basic unit of presence is responsive to the action situation and the subsequent figuration of that presence is the product of a dynamic interchange between subject and situation. While the presence formed by the subject in response to the action situation may be integral with the construction of action, that need not be so, as I have argued in Chapter 10. When a social presence reflects the sensibility of the subject, it possesses truth-value. By contrast, when a social presence is formed that does not reflect the sensibility of the subject, it becomes a rigid schema that lacks truth-value, is inauthentic. The expression of subjective feeling in popular art can posses truth-value just surely as it can be inauthentic. There may be countless instances of vocalists whose art lacks truth-value in the sense outlined here. Equally, I maintain, the best examples of the popular art of Adorno's time in America, for example, that of vocalists like Ella Fitzgerald and Frank Sinatra or jazz musicians like Louis Armstrong or Duke Ellington, ring with 'presence' that is true to the times – the sound-track of its age. Adorno's blanket dismissal of popular culture on the grounds that it does not meet the inappropriate test of reflecting the alienation of the institutional order of late capitalism makes no distinction between works of higher or lower quality. He elects to see the difference as merely technical; to acknowledge that there are differences in talent and skill but to insist that the greater the talent the worse the deception and the greater ability to mask the lack of truth.

The Enlightenment ideal of identity

Modern society, in Adorno's analysis, has all but destroyed this mediating process at the level of part–whole relations and at the level of relations between individuals too (part–part relations). This extinguishing of the two levels of mediation destroys temporality and historicity and with it the power of the individual to express or realize a life-process. It leaves the individual dependent upon external forces, upon psychic manipulation. Adorno's efforts to place the 'ideal' of reconciliation as a mediating element

176

in social relations is not without contradictions. He insists on the spontaneous building of relations from the ground up, from particulars, from the interacting subjects themselves. For a mediation by the larger social process to be genuine it would have to be brought out of the direct spontaneous relations between the participants, drawing on the particulars of the situation and materials at hand. The key problem for me concerns the role attributed to *ideology* and its relationship to everyday experience. It is the exigencies of coping with a range of life-world experience that embraces history, suffering and mortality, which ensures that the larger mediating process is immanent in social relations and not ideology. Ideology functions to give this (immanent) mediation process an objective and transcendental form. The vital spontaneity and autonomy of the subjects interacting is only preserved, however, to the extent that the mediation process arises from their immediate social relations. When ideological forms no longer truthfully interpret the mediation process on the ground they fall away or become instruments of reaction. However, the introjection or internalization of a 'mediator', whether in the guise of the ego-ideals of parents or the Enlightenment or God can only operate to subvert the autonomy and spontaneity of the actors whose relationship to each other comes to be mediated by the relationship of each to the mediator.

While Adorno explicitly criticizes any attempt to set up an ideology as a transcendental mediator that can make positive sense of the human condition in the modern world, he nevertheless does argue that the Enlightenment as ideology can make sense of the world, in the negative sense by providing the utopian light in which reality's deficit appears as suffering. In his paper on 'The Theory of Pseudo-Culture' (1959), Adorno insists that even when Culture proper has failed to meet the needs of the times we must still hold on to it because our only hope is to develop the critique of pseudo-culture and, for that, Culture with a capital 'C' is necessary. However, this is the result of an authoritarian move, the installation of the mediator within the personality of the subject. It is not a mediation that grows spontaneously from relations between subjects on the ground drawing on the particulars at hand. Social relations become 'triangulated'.

In his study of the modern novel, Rene Girard identified triangulation in human relations as a 'metaphysical sickness' in the modern consciousness (Girard 1976). Girard claims that from its beginnings in the eighteenth century, the novel was marked by a structural condition in which the desire of the hero for his 'object' was transcendentally mediated. Don Quixote's desires and relations are all mediated by his relationship to and imitation of, the chivalric hero from mediaeval romances, the knight Amadis. All Quixote's relationships in the world are tainted by it. They lack substance and reality because desire is not immediate and direct between subject and object but is the product of an imitative process, that is, of desiring what one's mediator desires.

It might be argued that Quixote's 'errors' were simply the result of a positive and therefore false mediation that confounded reality with its utopian ideal; by reversing the sign and realizing a negative identity between subject–object relations in the world and subject–object relations in the mediating ideal, Quixote's relationship to Dulcinea and to the world would be perceived in its distance from – its non-identity with – the mediating ideal. It would, therefore, have truth-value. But if this point is made in order to exempt Adorno's reliance on the 'mediator' from the charge of 'metaphysical sickness', it will not do that. It is the insistence on holding on to what Adorno calls the truth-moment of ideology that is the problem here. The imitation of the mediator is at the heart of the construction of the subject's relationship to its objects – whether positive or negative. In Girard's sense this weakens and erodes the autonomy and spontaneity of the subject in relations with others. The introjection of the Culture of the Enlightenment may have replaced the imitation of Christ in Adorno's discovery of the falseness of the world but the process would appear to be just as triangular in Girard's sense. Of course, it can be argued that Adorno's concern with the ideology of Enlightenment merely reflects something that is universally characteristic of social existence in all societies. I believe that the anthropologist Victor Turner understood this when he chose to counterpose the spirit of *communitas* to the conventional rule-governed social order and, adapting Martin Buber's concept of the I–Thou relationship, to insist on the universal recurrence of a liminal state defined by direct and open social relations (relations that can be conceived of as having escaped triangulation) on the interstices of conventional society. Not for nothing, his book *The Ritual Process* was subtitled *Structure and Anti-Structure* (Turner 1969).

Adorno's rejection of what he saw as the standardized or rigid schemata of popular art reflects his pre-occupation with a dialectical model that had been superseded in both 'high' and 'low' art in the twentieth century. Insofar as it survived, it did so in precisely he sense in which he theorized it – as a negative dialectics – and then only for a minority of highly significant artists who took that particular turn. It was the undoing of the temporality of the art work, its retraction to the present and its refusal to construct in the moments on either side, that was key to recovering the intra-subjective. Truth-value is sought at the level of the formation of sensibility – of the intra-subjective process, that is. When Picasso and Braque dissolved the unitary object into multiple perspectives and partial viewpoints, they recovered the constitutive power of the intra-subjective process, which gathers all the discrete moments in which the object is encountered ('moments' which are lost in the unitary construction of the object that experience makes from them). Perceptual values released from their obligations to the logic of the object-world were freed to perform intra-subjective work, to engage in the reformation of sensibilities. The driving tendency of modern art was towards the intra-subjective and this *reformation of sensibility*.

Jazz and the culture industry

Adorno's critique of jazz reinforces the classical sociological understanding of modernity as a system for the instrumental management of object relations. The emotional or sensuous life of the modern subject is seen as an impoverished reflex of this modernity, a kind of distractive and self-indulgent sensationism. The culture industries are then theorized as designing their products to appeal to this sensationism, to configure the desociated body of the subject in order to render it docile and susceptible to totalitarian organization. Modernity, in the classical sociological canon, constructs the metropolis as a vast system of object relations in which individuals appear as objects even to themselves. Means–end relations predominate. As Simmel argued, in his famous essay 'The Metropolis and Mental Life', life in the city follows the circulation of money and not the flow of the seasons (Simmel 1951). Simmel could see, too, that there was an emotional reaction among city dwellers to a life that reduced each individual to the status of a cog in a machine; in response, he argued there was an exaggerated cultivation of idiosyncratic and assertive personal styles, a cult of personality and emotional expression.

While emphasis is often placed upon the shallow and trivializing aspect of the affective and sensuous life of the city – and Adorno certainly aligns himself with that view – such an emphasis occludes the positive role that the configuration of affect, and its infusion into the leisure spaces of city life, can be said to play in resisting the totalitarian instrumentalism of modernity. As Berendt, Hobsbawm, and numerous writers on jazz have pointed out, the amazingly direct appeal to the emotions (in my terms, the word 'feeling' would be substituted for 'emotion' here) is key to the jazz experience (Berendt 1992; Hobsbawm 1989). It is no doubt key to popular music generally. Adorno himself notes that the *espressivo* of jazz is to announce something soulful. But it is this very *espressivo*, its colour and its affective charge, that is expunged from the normal praxis of social production in the metropolis.

The working day, in the technical and administrative apparatus, puts a premium upon rational, objective and dispassionate social relations – upon the abstraction of the head from the body (Witkin 1990, 1995). The emotions that surface in the blues and in jazz celebrate a life that is suppressed and mutilated by modernity, and jazz has as much claim to being considered a medium of resistance as does the art of the high priests of modernism. The principal difference is that this suppressed life, the life of the body rather than the life of the mind, has a space in which it can be lived, namely the space of the interpersonal, the domestic and the leisured world. Its dynamic is not that of a negative dialectics aimed at the totalitarian collective, but of a sensuous and charged affectivity, lived and celebrated on the margins of rational-technical modernity, configured in relation to it and always rubbing up against its grain. As I have argued elsewhere, however (Witkin 1997), the construction, by sociologists, of this distinction between the instrumental and the socio-emotional aspects of social relations has been, in itself, part of the process through which the instrumental order acknowledges the socio-emotional as its excluded 'other', embracing it by seeking to assimilate it to the instrumental order, that is, by treating it in terms of the rational satisfaction of *egoistic* needs for which the instrumental order can provide (Witkin 1997).

The development of the culture industry is an inherent aspect of such provision. Its aesthetic commodification of the sensuous aspect of social relations desociates the latter to the level of the egoistic needs of the individual. However, it is necessary to distinguish here between autonomous culture creation, which is characteristic of social relatedness at the most everyday level, and the culture industry, which works through a relentless process of commodification. Typically, the latter has processed cultural invention that originated beyond the compass of its design initiative. It has never been the case that the culture industry is synonymous with all aesthetic creation that does not belong within the category of so-called serious art (Adorno used the term so widely that it even embraced a large part of that). The culture industry's capacity to process and commodify aesthetic material, to manufacture the marketable item, feeds upon aesthetic process, upon aesthetic praxis and aesthetic choices that it does not invent. Without culture creation on its margins, the culture industry would lack the raw material it needs. The most interesting questions may not be those that result from contrasting the standardized products of the culture industry with the so-called serious works of art but those that explore the aesthetic choices made in the construction of everyday life.

Jazz is not simply synonymous with popular music, as Adorno would have it. For most of its history, jazz has stood in a close symbiosis with popular music but it has, nevertheless, remained distinct. This symbiosis is the key to developing an analysis of the workings of the culture industry that can serve as a critique of Adorno's treatment. Although Hobsbawm and Adorno differ greatly in their view of jazz, they are actually remarkably close concerning their characterization of popular culture:

> so long as variety merely means another unit of standardized production – another young man with gleaming teeth (probably reconditioned by his backer and agent as a preliminary investment in stardom), virtually indistinguishable from his predecessor, another processed loan from the full bag of hillbilly melodies and the like – no problem arises. The real difficulty occurs when the public wants something really different. Here the pop industry is helpless. At this point jazz enters it.
>
> (Hobsbawm 1989: 164)

180

Hobsbawm sees the popular music industry as necessarily parasitic upon raw material that is not of its making. Its business is to process available material and it remains ultimately dependent upon autonomous cultural creation genuinely expressive of a life-world. Because popular culture is governed only by the principle of saleability, it is, paradoxically, completely unprejudiced and willing to embrace more or less any development whatsoever. Jazz overlaps and interpenetrates with pop music. As Hobsbawm puts it, '[jazz] lives within it as water lilies live in ponds and stagnant streams' (1989: 167). Although Hobsbawm acknowledges that jazz can sometimes become pop music and be indistinguishable from it, that is not usually the case. He suggests that jazz resists this fate because even when jazz musicians are minded to become pop musicians, they are often not very good at it and, in any case, many actively choose not to 'sell out'. Unlike Adorno, however, Hobsbawm insists on the distinctiveness of ways of working and of producing in both jazz and pop music and provides an account of these differences at an institutional level in his observations on the music industry and the jazz business.

Hobsbawm is not alone, of course, in pointing to the dependence of the culture industry upon a process of cultural creation that stands outside the design initiative of the ring of commodification. Hall and Jefferson (1976), in their theorizing of British youth culture of the 1960s and 1970s, rejected the notion that these styles were the creation of commercial entrepreneurs. On the contrary, youth styles such as 'skinheads' and 'punks' developed as authentic responses to social conditions that were class related. Once these styles had crystallized, however, the entrepreneurs of the culture industry pounced upon them, 'defusing and diffusing' them (Hebdidge 1979) in order to make them saleable to a mass audience. From this point of view, the marketing of the Beatles as a pop group can be seen to have run the gamut of youth culture styles originating in the British class structure, although none of them was actually invented (as distinct from developed and exploited) by the culture industry. The Beatles, in their early Hamburg days, presented a leather-jacketed image that was closely associated with the 'hard' image of the lower working-class 'rocker'. Following their discovery by Brian Epstein the group achieved world fame, presenting a carefully defused version of a transitional working-class 'mod' culture. The later Beatles developed an equally defused version of a middle-class 'hippie' culture. The culture industry that commodifies such developments but does not create them, may, nevertheless, seek to manufacture 'copies' (the Monkees) by abstracting the formula. Sooner or later, however, the possibilities of the invention are exhausted and the culture industry must return to the sources of authentic aesthetic creation that lie beyond the compass of its design initiative. It is necessary, however, to drive this argument concerning the distinction between culture creation and cultural exploitation beyond the point of merely establishing their distinctiveness. Although genuine source materials that derive from the needs of real social groups and realize social processes are actually transformed by the culture industry in its production and marketing of them as commodities, the different aesthetic codes through which local social groups strike their attitudes, configure their experiences, are conserved in these commodities, albeit in abstracted and defused form.

Thus, the very activity of the culture industry in exploiting and commodifying this aesthetic creation serves, in the process, to transmit new symbolic resources to a mass audience – new means of expression that would otherwise be accessible only to the social groups in which they originated. Paradoxically, therefore, commercialization and commodification serve to universalize the aesthetic codes that configure experience for specific social groups. From this point of view, the culture industry may actually enrich the aesthetic resources and the range of expressive possibilities available to individuals and social groups in everyday life and thus helps to stimulate cultural invention that it then goes on to commodify. If this admittedly conjectural view is correct, it suggests that the greater the degree of commodification, the greater is the degree of opportunity for genuine aesthetic creation to occur on the margins of that process. The polished banalities of the culture industry may also be dynamically reconfigured in aesthetic practices of everyday life. There is a need for genuine empirical research concerning actual aesthetic practices in everyday life and their relationship to the culture industry as a counterweight to an almost theological level of assertion from critical theorists. Is it possible that the draining of dialectical process from works of art and popular culture that Adorno abhorred may actually be a prerequisite for the development of an aestheticizing praxis in everyday life (DeNora 2000)?

Every grief and every excitement presupposes a presence, a relatedness among individuals from which it derives its unique character and qualities. The precondition of all authentic sentiment and affect, therefore, is the social being or social presence engendered by relatedness. It is this social being which is configured in the feelings experienced by the individuals who are parties to that relatedness. In an earlier work I referred to such relations as *subject-reflexive* (Witkin 1974). In the pure subject-reflexive relationship, the identities of the parties are reflexively 'improvised' in and through relatedness itself. Identities are not things that the parties bring to the relationship; they are modes of being they live out of it. I want to suggest that subject-reflexive relations can best be thought of as 'I–Thou' relations. As already noted, Victor Turner borrowed this term from Martin Buber and used it as the basis of his concept of *communitas* – a 'being present to one another' – which can be said to constitute social being (Buber 1987; Turner 1969). The term 'I–Thou' captures a key aspect of this type of relationship, namely its fluid undifferentiation in terms of parts or elements, its variegated and unitary character. I–Thou relations are not you-and-me relations, nor are they 'we' relations. They have nothing to do with homogeneity in the sense that an expressive crowd is sometimes made up of individuals who appear to be moved by one idea. The I–Thou relationship is the medium through which individuals can express themselves, can become what they are. In the course of such a relationship, the presence of the parties undergoes a progressive figuration, it becomes 'featured'. The process can be likened to that in which a sculptor, carving from a single block, brings out of it the different features of a face, each feature being a figuration of the whole that emerges in an affinity with all the other features. The I–Thou relationship has no career and no development; it is present-centred, delivering its affective charge from moment to moment and knows none of the cumulative suspense that dialectical process has made central to post-Renaissance art (Witkin 1998). In all such figurational processes, subjects share a presence or 'community' and live out of it a realization of personal being. Like the best jazz, the living out of it is 'improvised'.

The emotional heat of the personal and interpersonal life may be self-referential but it is, nevertheless, developed in relationship with and in response to the institutional order; it may even issue in or be directed as a howl of complaint against that order, but it remains, to a greater or lesser degree, outside the control of wider administrative structures. It is here, I would argue, that jazz and the popular arts have their home. Jazz helps to articulate the affectively charged but disparate elements of the interpersonal life and it contributes to a discourse of values through which the interpersonal is socially configured. The culture industry, which draws upon jazz as a major raw material, effectively transmits its aesthetic codes, making them universally available as resources in the configuration of sensuous experience.

Popular art and the intra-personal

The more that the art work became centred on the formation of sensibility as subjective feeling, the more did the dialectical movement of expressive action (as in life-world projects, for example) drain from the art work – and with it the temporalizing moment – embedding itself in the praxis of ordinary life. The work of art itself became a constitutive sensuous machinery (Witkin 1995). Finding an attunement among different subjects through a juxtaposition of sensibilities at an intra-subjective level is key to the social construction of agency. By agency, I mean the incipient readiness or capacity for action of a given sort and not action itself. Once this shift in the level of abstraction from expression to sensibility and from action to agency is acknowledged, the techniques of modernism in both 'high' and 'low' art – all of which lead to that draining of dialectical relations from the text, which Adorno abhorred – can be seen to provide a link between the two torn halves of that integral freedom. The deepening division between high and low art reflects the progressive withdrawal of high art from the realm of subjective feeling and its communication and expression. By contrast, the popular arts made the intimate and the interpersonal the focus of their attention. It was inherent in the very intensification of this division of labour between the two levels of intra-actional process, that of objective and subjective feeling, respectively, that a complex interplay developed between them from which what was drawn apart was brought together again.

The culture industry had a major part to play in this. The accomplishments of serious art are diffused (if also defused) in mass culture over time. Familiarity with the 'codes' of art is necessary in order to be able to make or read aesthetic praxis. Mass culture and the culture industry have a significant part to play in making those codes more widely available. It may once have been the case that unless you had heard the music of concert hall ensembles you would never have been able to acquire the necessary experience to enable you to make sense of the music of composers like Bach. Bach's cantata widely known as the 'Air on a G-String', is familiar to everyone in England who has ever seen the TV commercial for Hamlet cigars. Some classical music lovers are appalled by that treatment, regarding the whole performance as a degraded travesty. If degraded it is, it remains the case that those who hear it grow more familiar with the code governing its construction. Images from the arts continuously fall prey to the voracious appetite of publicity, marketing and advertising; everywhere, as John Berger saw (1972), the codes of old masters are recycled through the medium of advertising, film and television. The reworking of these codes in mass cultural forms is precisely what defuses and diffuses them, loosening them from their moorings in a specific class habitus and making them widely available for reappropriation, reworking and recontextualization. My point of view might be considered to extend Benjamin's argument in his famous essay on 'The Work of Art in an Age of Mechanical Reproduction' (Benjamin 1992). The emphasis is placed here upon the semiotic abstraction, reconfiguration and transmission of the aesthetic codes that govern the construction of works of art.

The products of serious art enter, indirectly, into every aspect of modern design; they are refracted, via the culture industry, in the praxis of everyday life. Television, radio and film have plundered the modernist music repertoire for many of the effects that they deploy in constructing presentations and in composing theme music, just as modern classical composers from the time of Mahler have drawn freely on so-called vulgar music. In so doing, what originated at the level of objective feeling is brought into play at the level of subjective feeling and vice-versa. Moreover, so-called popular art continuously develops toward high art in its more avant-garde forms. Thus, the label 'jazz', once applied to any dance band music, now encompasses avant-garde music such as that of Ornette Coleman, Miles Davis, or John Coltrane; moreover, from within the jazz idiom, these composers have developed their own explorations of the possibilities afforded by atonal composition. In terms of the outline model developed here, what belongs to the level of subjective feeling in 'low' art is recycled, used as a resource at the level of objective feeling in 'high' art. The oft-trumpeted claim that postmodernity involves a progressive collapse of the distinction between high and low art might conceivably be validated at the end of a long process of mediation of the kind referred to above. Both the works of so-called 'serious' artists and those of culture industry professionals can be seen in terms of their mutual mediations. However, the direction in which this development points may be toward the growing possibilities available to individuals in everyday life to deploy aesthetic resources and to make aesthetic choices. Perhaps this process should be seen as one of strengthening an exiled subjectivity, reassembling it, as it were, and ultimately as making possible the reconquest of the praxis of everyday life that Peter Burger assigned, as a failed project, to the artistic avant-gardes (Burger 1984). In my model such a project would have no chance of success without the work of the culture industry.

Is Adorno still relevant?

The question of Adorno's relevance is quite distinct from the question of whether he will ultimately be proved right or wrong or what other points of view concerning modernity and the culture industry should be considered. I am personally sceptical about many of Adorno's judgements but am conscious of the extent to which the critical line I walk remains critically dependent not only upon Adorno's thinking but upon the entire tradition in which it participated. Any critique of his work must ultimately confront the problem of discovering a ground for genuine sociality and moral responsibility in a late capitalist society. His relevance for a sociology of art and more widely for a sociology of culture is something I have never personally doubted.

For one thing, Adorno has done more than any modern thinker to place the arts, both 'serious' and 'popular' at the very centre of a theory of modernity. This was achieved in the face of intellectual developments that moved in the opposite direction and which were themselves part of the problem that Adorno addressed. The very development of thinking in both academic psychology and sociology throughout the twentieth century reflected the triumph of instrumental reasoning and science; the arts were relegated to a back room, receiving relatively little attention. Adorno changed all that because, in his hands, the arts became important and consequential, vitally linked to the major questions that Max Weber (after Goethe) claimed that science could not even address, How shall we live? What shall we do next? In the process of developing his critical theory, Adorno provided a way of thinking about the homologous relationship between art and social life that will continue to influence the sociology of the arts long after the specific generalizations he made in relation to the popular music of the mid-twentieth century have been superseded.

But have those conclusions been superseded, even now? Critical theorists of a later generation have not yet set them down. Hullot-Kentnor in the 1990s analysed the Beatles' song 'I Feel Fine' in order to demonstrate that it had all the classic characteristics that Adorno originally identified with the degraded model of popular music, the same threadbare schema that was unchanging in response to its elements, that was superimposed upon them, the dissonances that do not escape from the tonal harmony which sanctions them and so forth. Hullot-Kentnor's paper (1991) seems to me to be precisely the kind of paper that Adorno would not have produced. It is a 'replication' of Adorno, a 'repeat performance' that is concerned to support his conclusions. What is needed now, as then, is theorizing that is truly in a reflexive relationship to new and changed times.

In his reply to Hullot-Kentnor, Volpacchio (1991) dismisses what he sees as a failed attempt to deploy the aesthetic dimension as a critique of popular music in the hope of pointing to the possibilities of an emancipatory music. All such aesthetic criteria are irrelevant now, according to Volpacchio. The commodification of culture is now so technologically advanced that it functions independently of the aesthetic dimension that Kentnor is seeking to recover. Volpacchio's conclusion is 'that since it is impossible for music to resist commodification, rather than abolish music as art we should abolish political and social evaluations of music'. But if such a conclusion was intended to demolish Adorno's analysis by declaring it to be irrelevant it would only have succeeded in proving the very opposite since Adorno's analysis itself pointed to Volpacchio's conclusion, not as something to be accepted but as something coming and as something to be resisted with all one's might.

It is to be hoped that sociologists and cultural theorists will develop a much needed interest in the aesthetic dimension and will consider afresh its social and political implications. They need not be bound to 'replicate' Adorno or to seek the aesthetic dimension in the same place as he did. An area that needs to be studied more closely is the involvement of ordinary people in aesthetic making in everyday life (DeNora 2000; Witkin 1990). To take but one example, the same changes that have made totally manu-factured music have been accompanied by others that have put awesome technical resources in many an adolescent's bedroom, not only powerful computers but also the technical resources of a mini-recording studio, not to mention movie cameras and so forth. While these changes might still be in their earliest stages they point to a growing involvement in (even a pressure on) ordinary people actively using technology themselves in 'making' and 're-making'. As Volpacchio points out, with the advent of digital technology and audio processors, it is not only possible to produce the tonal and dynamic ranges of performing groups in one's own home, but also the exact acoustics of pubs, concert halls, sports arenas, etc. 'With the proper mixing equipment, one can become the concert sound man in one's own home and edit, mix and modify the "performance" on the recording to suit one's taste.' We may ask whether what is marketed in the future will simply be aesthetic raw materials: whether ordinary social life will come to embrace the idea of significant aesthetic work by each individual as his or her own artist in the praxis of everyday life. If that argument has anything in it, then political and social evaluations of music – and, therefore, Theodor Adorno – will, *pace* Volpacchio, continue to be relevant.

REFERENCES

Adorno, T. (1941) 'The Radio Symphony', in P. Lazarsfeld and F. N. Stanton (eds) *Radio Research: The Popular Music Industry*, New York: Arno.

Adorno, T. (1945) 'A Social Critique of Radio Music', *Kenyon Review* 7 (2): 208–17.

Adorno, T. (1973) *Negative Dialectics*, London: Routledge and Kegan Paul.

Adorno, T. (1978) 'On the Social Situation of Music', *Telos* 35: 129–65.

Adorno, T. (1980) *The Philosophy of Modern Music*, New York: Seabury Press.

Adorno, T. (1983) *Prisms*, Cambridge, Mass: MIT Press.

Adorno, T. (1989) 'Uber Jazz [On Jazz]', *Discourse* 12 (1).

Adorno, T. (1990) 'On Popular Music', in S. Frith and A. Godwin (eds) *On Record, Rock Pop and the Written Word*, London: Routledge.

Adorno, T. (1991a) 'On the Fetish Character in Music and the Regression of Listening', in J. Bernstein (ed.) *The Culture Industry*, London: Routledge.

Adorno, T. (1991b) *In Search of Wagner*, London: Verso.

Adorno, T. (1991c) 'Culture Industry Reconsidered', in J. Bernstein (ed.) *The Culture Industry*, London: Routledge.

Adorno, T. (1991d) 'How to Look at Television', in J. Bernstein (ed.) *The Culture Industry*, London: Routledge.

Adorno, T. (1991e) 'Transparencies on Film', in J. Bernstein (ed.) *The Culture Industry*, London: Routledge.

Adorno, T. (1992) *Quasi Una Fantasia*, London: Verso.

Adorno, T. (1993[1959]) 'Theory of Pseudo-Culture', *Telos* 95: 15–39.

Adorno, T. (1994a) *Stars Down to Earth and Other Essays on the Irrational in Culture*, ed. Stephen Crook, London: Routledge.

Adorno, T. (1994b) 'Analytical Study of the NBC Music Appreciation Hour', *Musical Quarterly* 78 (2): 325–77.

Adorno, T. (1996) 'Chaplin Times Two', *Yale Journal of Criticism* 9 (1): 57–61.

Adorno, T. (1998) *Critical Models: Interventions and Catchwords*, New York: Columbia University Press.

Adorno, T. and Eisler, H. (1994) *Composing for the Films*, London: Athlone.

Adorno, T. and Horkheimer, M. (1979) *Dialectic of Enlightenment*, London: Verso.

Adorno, T. and Horkheimer, M. (1991) 'The Schema of Mass Culture', in J. Bernstein (ed.) *The Culture Industry*, London: Routledge.

Adorno, T. *et. al.* (1980) *Aesthetics and Politics*, London: Verso.

Adorno, T. *et. al.* (1982) *The Authoritarian Personality*, NewYork/London: Norton.

Alberti, L.B. (1966) *On Painting*, London: Yale University Press.

Baxandall, M. (1988) *Painting and Experience in Fifteenth Century Italy: A Primer in the Social History of Pictorial Style,* Oxford: Oxford University Press.

Becker, H. (1963) *Outsiders: Studies in the Sociology of Deviance,* Glencoe, IL: Free Press.

Becker, H. (1982) *Art Worlds,* Berkeley, CA: University of California Press.

Benjamin, W. (1992) 'The Work of Art in an Age of Mechanical Reproduction', in *Illuminations,* London: Fontana, pp. 211–44.

Berendt, J. (1992) *The Jazz Book: From Ragtime to Fusion and Beyond,* New York: Lawrence Hill Books.

Berger, J. (1972) *Ways of Seeing,* London: BBC/Penguin.

Bernstein, J.M. (1993) *The Fate of Art,* Cambridge: Polity Press.

Bourdieu, P. (1984) *Distinction: A Social Critique of the Judgement of Taste,* London: Routledge.

Bronfenbrenner, U. (1960) 'Freudian Theories of Identification and their Derivatives' *Child Development* 31: 15–40.

Brown, R. (1965) *Social Psychology,* New York: Free Press.

Buber, M. (1987) *I and Thou,* Edinburgh: T. & T. Clark.

Buck-Morss, S. (1977) *The Origin of Negative Dialectics,* Brighton: Harvester Press.

Burger, P. (1984) *Theory of the Avant-Garde,* Manchester: University of Manchester Press.

DeNora, T. (2000) *Music in Everyday Life,* Cambridge: Cambridge University Press.

Dewey, J. (1934) *Art as Experience,* Chicago: Minton, Balch and Co.

Eco, U. (1985) *Reflections on the Name of the Rose,* London: Secker and Warburg.

Festinger, L. (1954) 'A Theory of Social Comparison Processes', *Human Relations* 7: 117–40.

Giovacchini, S. (1998) 'The Land of Milk and Honey: Anti-Nazi Refugees in Hollywood', *Historical Journal of Film, Radio and Television,* August.

Girard, R. (1976) *Deceit, Desire and the Novel: Self and Others in Literary Structure,* Baltimore: Johns Hopkins University Press.

Gorer, G. (1948) *The Americans: A Case Study in National Character,* London: Cresset.

Gorer, G. and Rickman, J. (1949) *The People of Great Russia: A Psychological Study,* London: Cresset.

Greenberg, C. (1992) 'Avant-Garde and Kitsch', reprinted in C. Harrison and P. Wood (eds) *Art in Theory 1900–1990,* Oxford: Blackwell.

Hall, S. and Jefferson, T. (1976) *Resistance Through Rituals: Youth Subcultures in Post-War Britain,* London: Hutchinson.

Hebdidge, D. (1979) *Subculture: The Meaning of Style,* London: Methuen.

Hobsbawm, E. (1989) *The Jazz Scene,* New York: Pantheon Books.

Hohendahl, P. (1992) 'The Displaced Intellectual? Adorno's American Years Revisited', *New German Critique* 56: 76–100.

Hullot-Kentor, R. (1991) 'The Impossibility of Music: Adorno, Popular and Other Music', *Telos* 87: 97–117.

Huyssen, A. (1983) 'Adorno in Reverse: From Hollywood to Richard Wagner', *New German Critique* 29: 16–43.

Jay, M. (1973) *The Dialectical Imagination: A History of the Frankfurt School and the Institute of Social Research 1923–1950,* London: Heinemann.

Jay, M. (1984) *Adorno,* London: Fontana.

Kluckhohn, C. and Murray, H.A. (1953) *Personality in Nature, Society, and Culture* (2nd edition), London: Cape.

Langer, S. (1953) *Feeling and Form: A Theory of Art Developed from Philosophy in a New Key*, London: Routledge and Kegan Paul.

Lasch, C. (1979) *The Culture of Narcissism: American Life in an Age of Diminishing Expectations*, New York: Norton.

Lukács, G. (1971) *History and Class Consciousness*, London: Merlin Press.

Marx, K. (1986) *Karl Marx: A Reader*, Cambridge: Cambridge University Press.

Paddison, M. (1993) *Adorno's Aesthetics of Music*, Cambridge: Cambridge University Press.

Polanyi, M. and Prosch, H. (1975) *Meaning*, Chicago/London: University of Chicago Press.

Popper, K. (1972) *Objective Knowledge,* Oxford: Clarendon Press.

Reid, L. (1969) *Meaning in the Arts*, London: George Allen and Unwin.

Riesman, D. (1961) *The Lonely Crowd*, Newhaven/London: Yale University Press.

Rokeach, M. (1960) *The Open and Closed Mind*, New York: Basic Books.

Rose, G. (1978) *The Melancholy Science: An Introduction to the Thought of Adorno*, New York: Columbia University Press.

Schachter, S. and Singer, J. (1962) 'Cognitive Social and Physiologial Determinants of Emotional State', *Psychological Review* 69: 379–99.

Seargeant, W. (1959) *Jazz: Hot and Hybrid*, New York: Jazz Book Club.

Simmel, G. (1951) 'The Metropolis and Mental Life', in K. Wolff (ed.) *The Sociology of George Simmel*, Glencoe, IL: Free Press.

Subotnik, R. (1990) *Developing Variations: Style and Ideology in Western Music*, Minneapolis: University of Minnesota Press.

Subotnik, R. (1996) *Deconstructive Variations: Music and Reason in Western Society*, Minneapolis: University of Minnesota Press.

Taylor, F. (1947) *Scientific Management*, London: Harper and Row.

Turner, V. (1969) *The Ritual Process: Structure and Anti-Structure*, London: Routledge and Kegan Paul.

Volpacchio, F. (1991) 'The Unhappy Marriage of Music and Emancipation', *Telos* 87: 118–23.

Wagner, R. (1993) *The Art Work of the Future and Other Works*, Lincoln, NE: University of Nebraska Press.

Wagner, R. (1995) *Opera and Drama,* Lincoln, NE: University of Nebraska Press.

Witkin, R. (1974) *The Intelligence of Feeling*, London: Heinemann Educational Books.

Witkin, R. (1990) 'The Aesthetic Imperitive of a Rational-Technical Machinery: A Study of Organizational Control Through the Design of Artifacts', in P. Gagliardi (ed.) *Symbols and Artifacts: Views of the Corporate Landscape*, Berlin: Walter De Gruyter.

Witkin, R. (1995) *Art and Social Structure*, Cambridge: Polity Press.

Witkin, R. (1997) 'Constructing a Sociology for an Icon of Aesthetic Modernity: Olympia Revisited', *Sociological Theory* 15(2): 101–25.

Witkin, R. (1998) *Adorno on Music*, The International Library of Sociology, London: Routledge.

Witkin, R. (2000) 'Why Did Adorno Hate Jazz', *Sociological Theory* 18 (1): 145–70.

INDEX